THEN,
THEY WERE TWELVE

THEN,
THEY WERE TWELVE

The Women of
Washington's Embassy Row

MARILYN SÉPHOCLE

Foreword by Ambassador Andrew Young

PRAEGER

Westport, Connecticut
London

Library of Congress Cataloging-in-Publication Data

Séphocle, Marilyn, 1961–
    Then, they were twelve : the women of Washington's Embassy Row /
    Marilyn Séphocle ;   foreword by Ambassador Andrew Young.
        p.   cm.
    Includes bibliographical references and index.
    ISBN 0–275–96833–2 (alk. paper)
    1. Women ambassadors—United States—Interviews.   2. World politics—
1989– 3. United States—Foreign relations—1989–   I. Title.
D1071.S46   2000
327.2'082'09753—dc21   99–054741

British Library Cataloguing in Publication Data is available.

Library of Congress Catalog Card Number: 99–054741
ISBN: 0–275–96833–2

First published in 2000

Praeger Publishers, 88 Post Road West, Westport, CT 06881
An imprint of Greenwood Publishing Group, Inc.
www.praeger.com

Printed in the United States of America

The paper used in this book complies with the
Permanent Paper Standard issued by the National
Information Standards Organization (Z39.48–1984).

10 9 8 7 6 5 4 3 2 1

CONTENTS

FOREWORD

Achieving success in the diplomatic world has been a long and arduous path for women. Lack of equal access, equal rights, equal protection under the law and equal representation in decision making institutions have prevented women in many countries from rising to the top jobs in general. Diplomacy is no exception. Diplomacy is probably one of those bastions of male dominance where breaking the proverbial glass ceiling is the toughest. In the United States the history of the appointment of women to diplomatic posts almost mirrors that of minorities. It was not until 1949 that the first woman ambassador, Eugenie Anderson was appointed career ambassador. It was not until 1953 that the next woman, Francis Willis, was appointed ambassador. They were by far the exception.

The classical picture of an embassy is that of an institution headed by a man in a chauffeur-driven limousine flanked by his perfect wife who arranges tea parties and receptions while he discusses world events in cigar smoke–filled parlors. Today that picture is slowly but steadily changing. Women all over the world are legitimately no longer satisfied with handling flower arrangements and the social calendar of embassies. They are now entering the diplomatic corps and some even manage to attain the top diplomatic post of ambassador. For the first time, they are in the double digits in Washington! And Africa is leading the way: half of the women ambassadors posted in Washington are currently from Africa! The percentage of women from the international diplomatic corps posted in Washington is still abysmally low (12 out of 172). And the U.S. State Department only counts 22.8 percent women in the foreign service, with African American women representing only 2.4 percent. Though these figures show an improvement over the last three decades, they are still hardly commensurate with those of the general population!

Observing these trends, Marilyn Séphocle took the initiative to organize the first-ever academic Annual Women Ambassadors Conference held for the first time on the campus of Howard University, an event which has obtained rave reviews from First Lady Hillary Rodham Clinton, Secretary of State Madeleine Albright, the *Washington Post*, the *Washington Times* and other national and international media. *Then, They Were Twelve: The Women of Washington's Embassy Row* draws its inspiration from the Women Ambassadors Conference. The number "twelve" in the title refers to the largest delegation of women ambassadors posted in Washington until the year 2000.

Then, They Were Twelve is a historical account of these female envoys who are changing the international diplomacy scene by adding to it their own dynamics, methodologies and perceptions. Countries represented in Washington by a woman at the turn of the millennium include Bulgaria, the Democratic Republic of Congo, Costa Rica, Cyprus, Ecuador, El Salvador, Lesotho, Liberia, Luxembourg, Macedonia, Pakistan, Saint Lucia, Singapore, South Africa, Trinidad and Tobago, Swaziland, Uganda and most recently Bolivia. Most of them are featured in this book. The majority of the women ambassadors share two common factors. They come from countries that are either facing a difficult crisis or recovering from it. They are also academically and professionally well prepared for their mandate. Their presence in Washington is certainly a testimony to the new but growing phenomenon in our male-dominated world: increased confidence in the skills women have to offer. In other words men are growing up.

The author of *Then, They Were Twelve* had the delicate task of handling interviews that are not based on reminiscences but rather on current accounts. In doing so she has managed to retain the candid aspect of the interviews while remaining careful not to jeopardize delicate on-going negotiations between the host country and the embassies. That in itself is quite a diplomatic feat. Each chapter offers the reader a snapshot of the ambassador's country, cultural attitudes towards women's rights, candid insights about the ambassador's life, her career path, the hurdles she has had to overcome, her conduct of foreign policy. her passions and her outlook on the world.

The ultimate effeect on the reader is a new appreciation for the diplomatic career. Whether tackling the wars in Congo or Kosovo, the aftermath of the wars on Cyprus, El Salvador and Liberia, post-apartheid in South Africa and issues of armament in Pakistan, this volume enlightens the average reader about the lives of diplomats and is sure to be an inspiration for both female and male students of international affairs, women's studies, current events and history.

Andrew Young

Ambassador Andrew Young, Chairman of GoodWorks International, has had a distinguished career in business and public service. He has served as Ambassador to the United Nations, as a member of the United States Congress, Mayor of Atlanta and Chairman of the Southern Africa Enterprise Development Fund. He serves on several boards, participates in many philanthropic activities and has long championed the cause of women in the United States and around the world.

ACKNOWLEDGMENTS

Finally the most awaited and pleasant moment, when I get the chance to thank the entire support team behind *Then, They Were Twelve*, has come! A bookish and less glittery version of an Oscar ceremony acceptance speech but a most sincere one.

First, I would like to thank my mother for years of unwavering, infallible support and positive reinforcement. At age 12 when I expressed the desire to participate in the activities of the only feminist organization on the island of Martinique, my mother—who had already joined the organization—embraced the idea and encouraged me. Thus I became the youngest addition in the "Femmes Avenir" meetings. Backed by my late father, a hardworking, distinguished man and devoted father—one of the rare men on the island who as early as the 1960s was skilled in the art of diaper changing and house chores—my mother made our home a wonderful intellectual hub. In that environment, in the eyes of both parents, "feminism" was not a mere concept or "ism" but rather a normal part of life that molded my siblings and me into the new college-bound generation. So when I announced in 1996 that I was writing a book on women ambassadors my wonderful mother jubilantly embraced the idea—not as a foray into "feminism," but as a normal and logical part of my life. She encouraged me every step along the way and for that I am very grateful.

I owe just as many thanks to my sister, Monique, a brilliant woman whose courage in the face of adversity and whose inner strength often fuels my own fortitude. A civil engineer by trade, she finds herself in a situation similar to that of the women ambassadors introduced in this book: a competent woman in a profession dominated by men. In our discussions about the book there was never a dull moment. Her frank, constructive and encouraging comments were a most valuable part of the project. In the process she always managed to boost my confidence when I needed it the most and provided the much needed lifeline of optimism when I was reaching a dead end. She is simply and truly a remarkable human being!

I owe an intellectual debt to the editor of this work, Juliette Bethea. Once I got used to her initial approach, that of boot camp–like critique, I learned to appreciate her bright and provocative intellect. Pretty soon this avid art collector and book aficionado was trimming redundancies not only in my text but also in my diet, constantly reinforcing the importance of eating right to think right. A cleaner text and better eating habits are due to her influence. She also taught me a little secret I am sharing only with the readers of this book: gazing at the moon and strolling in the zoo can awaken the inspiration buds of those who are writing. Her experience in the literary world, her political savvy and her flexible schedule made a big difference in the production of the book.

I extend very warm thanks to my brother Marcel and his wife Dalila. While changing the diapers of my nephew, precious little Andrew, they patiently listened to my reading of various chapters. As a political scientist and a true internationalist, Marcel offered sound advice. Dalila encouragingly pictured the book on the shelves. My cousins, Catherine and Herman Hewitt were just as supportive. During the hot summer of 1999 I ran away from my overheated Washington row house and took refuge for a few days in their lovely and cool suburban home in Maryland in order to write. By nurturing me they vicariously nurtured the book. I will never forget their puzzled and sympathetic looks once when I told them that gazing at their lawn was inspirational.

My aunt Amélie Mothie, an extraordinary woman, a symbol of woman's strength and independence, a nurse and Vietnam veteran who joined the Peace Corps at age 66, also inspired me. Upon her return from the Peace Corps she congratulated me on my endeavor. So did my uncle, Victor Boclé, who thoroughly read the first drafts of the book. Receiving the stamp of approval of one of my role models, the great poet and playwright Aimé Césaire, in the form of his marked enthusiasm, was most precious.

I would like to express my gratitude to Ms. Anna Hawkins of the State Department who always helped me keep abreast of developments among the women of the Washington-based diplomatic corps, as did Ms. Yamile Salas of the embassy of Costa Rica.

Thanks to all the people at Greenwood/Praeger who helped produce and promote the book, particularly Dr. James Sabin who believed in the project since its inception and Ms. Rebecca Ardwin, the production editor who was my constant contact with the publishing house. Her prompt, diligent and mostly sympathetic e-mails helped facilitate the process. They allowed me to appreciate electronic communication. I now spell e-mails: Efficient Means for Ardwin and I to link on the subject (of the book).

I certainly should not forget to thank Janis Kearney, Robert Richol and James Kennedy who kindly read the book and offered constructive and insightful comments. My gratitude also goes to Dr. Edwin Nichols, a true mentor to many and a gracious host whose elegant gatherings at his home provided a venue for the ambassadors to meet in the multilateral sense. My gratitude also extends to Dr. Audra K. Grant, and to Dr. Carolyn Jefferson-Jenkins, one of the most distinguished national presidents the League of Women Voters has ever known. Their coffee hour discussions and meetings constituted a healthy and supportive environment for the project. Among journalists, Anne Orleans of *The Washington Diplomat*, Nora Boustani of the *Washington Post*, Marcelle Chery of "Au Salon de Marcelle" and James Morrison of the *Washington Times*, should be acknowledged for keeping the discussions on the endeavors of the women ambassadors current in the media, thus providing more material for this book.

Last, but certainly not least, my most special thanks to the ambassadors who have contributed to this book and who have made this four-year journey in the diplomatic world inspirational through their interviews, caloric by their wonderful receptions and insightful thanks to the information provided about their countries. They have opened their embassies and residences to me in the most generous and gracious way. In so doing they demonstrate that they adhere to the principle that "what is not recorded is not remembered." They are also aware of the fact that public hunger for change in the condition of women is not something that can be fomented but rather something that is born out of necessity. This book is born out of that very necessity; the ambassadors interviewed have all contributed to do justice to the project, as did Mrs. Alice Pickering's very engaging discussions on the life of the residence. I also thank the very cooperative staff of the embassies, particularly, Ms. Veda Simpson of the embassy of Liberia, Mr. Rifat Husain of the embassy of Pakistan, Mr. Ong of the embassy of Singapore, Ms. Monica Gross of the embassy of Ecuador, Ms. Julia Velkoska of the embassy of Macedonia, and Mr. Andreas Kakouris of the embassy of Cyprus.

I take the opportunity given by these acknowledgment lines to thank all those who showed their support for the Women Ambassadors Program I organize annually. The book in turn draws its inspiration from the conference, a part of the program. Let me share with you a letter written by Secretary Albright on the occasion of the Fifth Annual Women Ambassadors Conference held at Howard University in March 2000:

Your Excellencies and Distinguished Guests:

Thank you for inviting me to take part in this momentous event, the first Conference of Women Ambassadors to Washington. It is very significant that this event is taking place on the campus of Howard University, and I commend Dr. Marilyn Séphocle, Founding Director of the Women Ambassadors Program for honoring these Ambassadors. The Howard University Women Ambassadors Conference, now in its fifth year, brings together the spheres of academia and diplomacy.

As First Lady Hillary Rodham Clinton stated during her speech delivered at the university's commencement on May 9, 1998, this program is indeed "one more example of Howard being at the forefront—and pushing the boundaries."

Of the 172 international ambassadors stationed in Washington, 10 are women. These women of state demonstrate a unique approach to diplomacy, and as one of the largest delegations of women ambassadors ever to be posted in Washington at the same time, they are indeed pioneers. I commend their commitment and that of their American counterparts to inform and mentor our students.

I applaud student participation in the annual essay contest about the role of women and the importance of foreign languages in diplomacy, two of my favorite topics. This component of the annual conference certainly contributes to making foreign affairs less foreign to Americans.

Let me congratulate Howard University President, Dr. H. Patrick Swygert, and the Ralph Bunche Center for bringing about such a fine program.

Sincerely,

Madeleine K. Albright.

Finally I thank all those whose name I might have omitted and who have contributed to this book in one form or the other.

INTRODUCTION

My curiosity was piqued when I found out that there were ten. So, I invited them to address the students at Howard University. They all came. The *Washington Post* describes the event the following way: "For those keeping track, the number of female ambassadors here is the highest ever, ten out of 172. McKnight, 58, is their doyenne, and all say they work twice as hard as their men to 'arrive.' [They] gathered at Howard University on Tuesday invited by professor Marilyn Séphocle, and enthralled students with their experiences and their wisdom. 'Diplomacy is like banking: it is about building up a deposit of goodwill to use when necessary, communication, consensus building and a good grasp of detail,' said Singapore's Ambassador Heng Chee Chan [*sic*], diminutive steel lily of the diplomatic corps. 'I fought intensely and felt passionately. I was never in the forefront of feminist groups. I am a feminist by being.' ... This year she negotiated the purchase of up to seventy-seven Boeing 777 aircraft from the United States at $12 billion. ... Pakistani Ambassador Maleeha Lodhi, speaking recently about the number of female envoys, joked that 'we are getting into the double digits. Soon we will go up to half, but the real measure of progress will come in a few years when there will be six or eight men on this podium telling us how it feels to be a male diplomat.' "

On that day I was asked, "What prompted you to initiate and organize the Women Ambassadors Program?" The short answer is that I am not a feminist by choice but by birth. There is a longer explanation, however. I worked as a public information assistant at the United Nations headquarters in New York in the 1980s. Whenever I walked in the chamber of the General Assembly, the largest body of diplomats in the world, I was always struck by the sea of male suits dominating the scene. Rarely would one spot a woman. Later, as an educator preparing young minds for leadership, that UN scene left an indelible mark in my mind. Clearly it became the equivalent of prohibiting more than half of my class to participate in an assignment! The world in many instances, certainly in diplomacy, is operating at less than half of its brain capacity. How ironic it is to exclude women from a field that requires the very qualities that even the most chauvinist of men recognize in women and which form the basis for stereotypes directed at women. Aptitude for dialogue, a sense of civility, non-agressive attitudes, the ability to compromise and a reluctance to use force are all qualities necessary in diplomacy. They are also qualities often associated with women. In a recent article in *Foreign Affairs* magazine, Francis Fujiyama traces feminine "diplomatic qualities" in the gender-based socialization of chimpanzees. I will certainly not go that far! Women have acquired these so-called "diplomatic qualities" through millenniums of gender-based socialization. Thus the near absence of women on the diplomatic scene is a glaring paradox. At the beginning of the year 2000 out of 190 foreign ministers there are only twelve women. The rare women figures in diplomacy are noticed. Secretary of State Madeleine Albright or Bulgarian Minister of Foreign Affairs Nadhezda Mikhailova stand out.

Mikhailova was born in 1962. On a trip to Washington Secretary of State Madeleine Albright gave Minister Mikhailova a photo they took with the Minister of Foreign Affairs of Sweden—a rare snapshot of three women foreign ministers strolling together. "We have a small group of women foreign ministers. We have to support each other every place we can," says Madeleine Albright. The next time they meet, during the Spring of 1999 at the Sheraton Hotel in Sofia for a press conference, the number of issues on the plate has mushroomed to include the demilitarization of the Kosovo Liberation Army (KLA) and public order in Kosovo, the role of Bulgaria on issues concerning southeastern Europe, the Stability Pact, the U.S. Congress approval of $25 million in economic support for Bulgaria, and of course the North Atlantic Treaty Organization (NATO). Meanwhile, in the capital of the free world at the Bulgarian embassy a woman is also at the helm. Quite a feat for a country where the word "feminism" does not necessarily have the best connotation.

The General Assembly of the United Nations is not unique in its failure of embrace of women. Mr. James Wolfensohn, president of the World Bank, desirous of increasing women's participation in his organization invited a panel of experts including CEOs of companies, to address the subject and provide some direction to the feminization of Bank. But at the end of the session, when a Caribbean woman with multiple degrees and impressive credentials brandishes her c.v. (curriculum vitae) to one of the CEOs, weeks go by with no response, not even an acknowledgment. In large international, national, public and private organizations will women continue to be the first victims of the immovable bureaucracy? In the United Nations system, the appointment of two highly competent women—Mrs. Sadako Ogata as high commissioner for refugees and Mrs. Mary Robinson as human rights commissioner—are certainly milestones on the international scene. However, women are still the absentees of what the western media would consider the "important" summits. All the G summits— the G7, the G8, the G15 summit—show the reality for what it is: The world is ruled by men. Among the 190 heads of state, one would be hard pressed to count on the fingers of one hand the number of women presidents of nations. At the end of the twentieth century, Panama, Ireland, Liberia and Finland are among the rare nations that choose to place a woman in the highest office. Similarly women ambassadors in what is considered by many as the highest diplomatic post—Washington—are few and far between. So, when their number reached the double digit of ten in 1996, there was cause for celebration. The following year they were twelve, the highest number in the last four years of the millennium.

Africa is by far the continent that trusted women the most in handling bilateral relations with the United States. Half of the women of the Washington diplomatic corps are African. At the dawn of the new millennium these extraordinary emissaries represent the Democratic Republic of Congo, Liberia, Lesotho, South Africa, Swaziland and Uganda. For Liberia, sending a woman to an important diplomatic post is certainly not a novelty. In the 1960s Mrs. Angie Brooks-Randolph was not only the representative of Liberia to the United Nations, she was also the president of the UN's General Assembly. Looking at history one discovers that African women have always played a crucial role in international affairs. In 1623 Nzinga, queen of Ndongo (currently known as Angola), in an effort to strengthen her power and fight against the slave trade, engaged in negotiations with the Dutch to create an alliance against the Portuguese. She often sent women as envoys to discuss the terms of the alliance with the

Dutch. In Europe female relatives of monarchs acted as envoys. Henriette-Anne, Duchess of Orleans, acted as Louis XIV's envoy when she negotiated the secret treaties between France and England in 1670.

Today the female component of the Washington diplomatic corps is overwhelmingly African. In major organizations, black women have made a noticeable difference. One recalls the visionary Dame Nita of Barbados whose comments on human rights used to take the General Assembly of the United Nations by storm. The fine political strategist, Mary McLeod Bethune, the founder of the National Council of Negro Women, ensured that her organization in spite of the obstacles thrown in its path be present at the founding of the United Nations in San Francisco in 1945. She also urged the United Nations to appoint black women in key committees. In 1950 Edith Sampson became the first African American woman member of the U.S. delegation to the United Nations. Her main battle in the General Assembly was regarding the rights of prisoners of war. Marian Anderson, the famous African American contralto also became a voice in the General Assembly dealing with cultural and humanitarian issues. Patricia Roberts Harris, cabinet member and ambassador to Luxembourg, had a distinguished career. She rose before the Assembly to talk about the prejudices women face in the work place. Coretta Scott King's work in the General Assembly was the culmination of many years of collaboration with Ambassador Andrew Young. In general what made the contributions of women of the African Diaspora valuable was often their commitment to be the voice of the "wretched of the earth."

In the initial and subsequent well attended events organized in honor of women ambassadors at Howard University, many came to hear firsthand about the experiences of these women in diplomacy and about the diplomatic relations between their region and the United States. In countries that are for the most part male-dominated, they have risen to the top through education, perseverance and hard work. It was not an easy road. These women are currently reshaping diplomacy, giving it their touch, adding to it a dynamic combination of grace, intelligence and a certain intuition coupled with strength of character. Their appointments are a significant victory for women around the world but this is not the end of a struggle for asserting women's rights on the planet. The reality is such that the ratio is still not in favor of women. There are currently twelve women ambassadors out of the 172 ambassadors posted in Washington, D.C. Women represent more than 50 percent of the human population of the globe. There is still a long way to go!

Perhaps the ratio of women representing their countries in Washington is a reflection of women's participation in the decision making aspect of political life around the globe. Women's participation in decision making is in turn a function of the fact that most countries granted women the right to vote only between the 1920s and the 1960s. In the world classification data compiled by the Inter-Parliamentary Union (IPU), 179 countries are classified by descending order according to the percentage of women elected to their lower or single house. The results are quite telling! Sweden ranks first, with women making up forty-two percent of their lower House or Congress. Germany has put a premium on a form of affirmative action or quota system for women and reaches an honorable seventh place with 30.9 percent women in the Bundestag. The People's Republic of China ranks seventeenth with 21.8 percent women in a house of 2,979 members. In the late 1990s France made a bold move by appointing women to half of its cabinet posts. Too good to be true—days later, in a testosterone-charged reshuffling of the cabinet by the same prime minister who had appointed them, the majority of the women cabinet members were sent back home. This lack of confidence in women's ability to lead is reflected in the election results, where French women make up only 10.9 percent of the "députés" in the national assembly, placing France fifty-fourth in the chart, right below Trinidad and Tobago. The sole superpower does not fare much better. In the United States, at the beginning of the year 2000, only 13.3 percent of the members of Congress are women, thus ranking the United States fortieth in the chart, along with Jamaica, San Marino and Saint Kitts and Nevis. In the constitutional monarchy of Kuwait women are simply not eligible and do not have the right to vote. For Cheikh Jaber al Ahmad al Sabah this is unconstitutional. As of end of July 1999 the all-male parliament had not passed the legislation allowing women to vote, leaving the Cheikh and his militant wife with an uphill battle. In the same region in Qatar, however, women do vote and are eligible and steady progress toward their advancement has taken place, while in Saudi Arabia questions of voting rights and eligibility are simply not on the table. It has been made clear that women should not try to compete with men. That attitude is reflected even in the countries that boast of their democracy. This brings to mind a quote often uttered by Rev. Jesse Jackson regarding the desegregation of baseball in the United States: "We did not know how good baseball was until everybody could play." The same principle ought to apply to democracy. We do not know how good democracy is until women and "minorities" participate fully and in representative numbers at the decision making level.

With regard to representation in Washington, it is very significant that developing countries, particularly Africa, are leading the way. Bulgaria, Costa Rica, Congo, Cyprus, Ecuador, El Salvador, Lesotho, Macedonia, Pakistan, Liberia, Luxembourg, Saint Lucia, Singapore, South Africa, Swaziland, Uganda and Trinidad, and Tobago are the countries that have chosen to send a woman to handle bilateral and sometimes multilateral relations in the world's most demanding and prestigious post. Their presence in Washington today is a measure of how far women have come and of the degree to which education has opened doors for women. The women ambassadors in Washington generally have one solid common denominator—a strong educational background. Not the coattail of a husband or a father, not incredible wealth, but rather education, talent and strength of character. Their very presence crushes age-old myths about the limitations and frailties of women.

The countries they represent have certain similarities. They are usually countries recovering from a crisis or in the midst of a crisis. Cyprus, Macedonia, Liberia, South Africa, Lesotho and El Salvador are recovering from a crisis, Congo and Ecuador are facing very difficult times. The women ambassadors come, therefore, from countries that necessitate very sharp diplomatic skills in order to make the difference. Perhaps their presence is signaling a new era, that of trust in the competence of women at the highest levels in the most difficult situations. The purpose of this book is to provide some insight into understanding the path of these women in diplomacy in breaking this "glass ceiling" and to provide motivation to other women and girls in achieving similar quests.

AMBASSADOR FAIDA MITIFU OF THE DEMOCRATIC REPUBLIC OF CONGO

"People made fire and cooked food with their bed frames and their chairs. They had no electricity and no water." Ambassador Mitifu is firmly holding a chair rest vividly conveying the horrors of the war. "Many wanted to kill the rebels responsible for the chaos and in some cases they did, setting them on fire," she says, her otherwise serene face contorted with pain. "The nonsense has to stop. We have to build our nation," she continues. Amidst the visits of ministers, calls breaking the silence of the nights with frantic news of the horrors of the war in the Democratic Republic of Congo, the instructions of President Kabila at three in the morning and comforting Embassy officials on the death of loved ones, Ambassador Faida Mitifu hardly finds time to sleep. Adapting to her schedule I met the ambassador at midnight in her simple apartment in northwest Washington. Her youngest son, 12-year-old Alex, is quite aware of the situation in his country but tunes out watching cartoons. Brought up in the United States he hardly knows the motherland. Nevertheless he cannot figure out why there is so little television coverage of the war in his homeland which is inhabited by 43 million people and geographically is seventy-seven times larger than Belgium and one quarter the size of the United States. There is a saturation of television coverage on the war in Kosovo, a country of 1.6 million inhabitants and geographically a third of the size of Belgium. Alex thinks about this often. The media is not always logical.

"Fighting Mobutu in the underground was extremely hard. So Kabila did hire some willing Rwandan soldiers in prominent positions in his army. After helping Kabila they turned against him, playing favorites among the soldiers, paying some well and starving others. Of course the starving soldiers rebelled against Kabila. Why did the Rwandan soldiers do all this?—to be in control and to plunder our country after having devastated theirs! The population turned against the Rwandan soldiers and rebels. So Kabila created a camp to shield them from the wrath of the population. Guess what? He is accused of running concentration camps!" Thus, the Ambassador explains the war in her country. Even at this late hour, she is impeccably dressed in a red suit. A very long day awaits her tomorrow. Well, it is already tomorrow. For the professor turned war time diplomat there is not such a thing as a twenty-four-hour day. There are tense moments and intense negotiations. One cannot help thinking how much of a change her new post means in her life. Until then she led a quiet academic life teaching African and Francophone literature. Leopold Senghor, Aimé Césaire, Chinua Achebe, Aminata Sow Fall, Maryse Condé were among the names that peopled the thoughts of this thorough intellectual with tremendous inner strength. Today the register of names she uses bears other overtones.

Her embassy immediately reminds one of the war ravaging her country. The ambassador brings dignity to her office, but the beautifully constructed turn-of-the-century building in the heart of Dupont Circle has chipping paint and appears desolate. Inside the embassy, a large portrait of President Laurent Desiré Kabila looms in an ornate golden frame.

A large wooden map of the country behind an unwonted plexiglas counter is there to remind visitors of the immensity of the long lost kingdom of Kongo, a powerful nation ruled in the fifteenth century from its prestigious capital of Mbanza. The kingdom was prosperous until the sixteenth century when it started trading slaves for beads with the Portuguese, depleting its population. In the nineteenth century further depletion of resources occurred when King Leopold II of Belgium decided to claim Congo as his personal property. Belgian rule in Congo was so ruthless that British Consul Roger Casement publicly denounced the atrocities. Until the late 1950s Belgians settled on large estates and collected ivory, forest products, gold and diamonds.

At independence on June 30, 1960, power struggles marked the country's history and culminated in the assassination of the much-loved Congolese hero Patrice Lumumba. Lumumba had hoped to unify the country, redistribute its wealth and bring prosperity. Also victim of the crisis was United Nations Secretary General, Dag Hammarskjöld, whose plane crashed on the way to Congo. One of Lumumba's major concerns was the rich province of Katanga whose secessionist rebels were backed by European business interests.

The year 1965 marked the beginning of the three-decade reign of Joseph Désiré Mobutu known for corruption and inequities. Statistics speak volumes. In a country of 43 million inhabitants, 5,000 people earned half of the population's total wages. Mobutu was known for his extravagances and his lavish lifestyle. In 1971, out of concern for his legacy, he introduced a policy of "authenticity," an effort to return the country to its Africanity. The name Congo became Zaire and Christian names were discarded for a return to African names. President Joseph Désiré Mobutu became Mobutu Sese Seko. At Congolese embassies around the world men replaced their European suits and ties with more traditional African garments.

On another occasion I met with Ambassador Mitifu to talk about the man who succeeded in unseating Mobutu Sese Seko, the war, and the people of the Democratic Republic of Congo. While waiting for the ambassador I am greeted by her assistant, Mrs. Tshabala, who is quite a conversationalist. Mrs. Tshabala immediately invites me to visit Congo when the war is over. Her favorite topic was parent-child relationships. She deplored what she perceived as the lack of respect which children exhibit in the United States and Europe and advocated a traditional African style firm grip on the new generation. Her animated discourse was interrupted by an announcement that the ambassador had arrived.

MLS: What is the challenge in representing a country at war?

Ambassador Mitifu: Congo has been through thirty-two years of dictatorship. During that time we have had ups and downs. Between 1990 and

1997 the country went through a long transitional period which led to a dead end despite the national conference preparing the Congo for changes in the future. We were unable to get rid of the dictatorship. With this new government people were very hopeful. I arrived to Washington on July 30, 1998, and the war started two days later on August second. Washington was a new place for me. I lived in the United States before. I lived down south in the state of Georgia where I was teaching at Columbus State University. The political world of Washington and the political intrigues of Washington were new to me. I was very enthusiastic and ready to learn, hoping that I would start under normal conditions and have time to learn and figure things out. But I found myself in the midst of a war. The biggest challenge was to try to erase the torn image of Congo in Washington and the negative image of the President I was representing in Washington. Our President has been preparing for this work for a long time. It is always easy to plant something but it is always difficult to uproot, to demine. I was taking care of the image of the country through the image of its president. I was battling on several fronts—on one hand trying to clean up the image of the country and its President, on the other hand trying to do everything I can to contribute to put an end to this absurd crisis. For the Congolese people this is really an absurd war! It was not very easy at the beginning. It is still not easy. I did everything I could. Imagine someone who was supposed to do what we call in French "l'état des lieux," which is essentially report back to the President and return to the host country to start heading the embassy. I came back with no time to do the "état des lieux" and I had to battle my way through Congress, to contact anyone I could, anyone that had influence in Washington to help me in my task.

MLS: Talking to some Congolese one gets the feeling that there is no clear enemy in this war. How would you characterize the conflict?

Mitifu: I hate to use the word "enemy" because I have been used for many years to calling Rwandans my sisters and brothers. But this was truly an invasion. There is no doubt about it. When two foreign armies cross the border to come in another country and then to try to cover up the invasion by an apparent civil war by using or manipulating some people who originate from the invaded country, it is truly a war, an ugly war. The armies of Uganda and Rwanda invaded my country. At first they denied the invasion. On September 15, 1998, we had a hearing in the United States Congress. The Congressman chairing the session asked the Rwandan ambassador whether there were Rwandan forces in Congo. The Rwandan ambassador denied the invasion at that point. However, a month later the Rwandans and Ugandans acknowledged publicly that they had invaded Congo from the beginning. It was truly an invasion. I am not denying that we had our own political internal problems. These internal issues cannot be solved through arms. Our internal problems could have been solved through a national debate. It was truly an invasion. No doubt about it.

At the present both countries do not deny that their armies have invaded my country. They have used the fact that there were rebels from their countries who were hiding in the Congo territory. Problems can be worked out through governments. My government organized a solidarity conference in April 1998 to implement strategies to tackle these types of problems and to establish peace in the Great Lakes region. The presidents of Uganda and of Rwanda both attended that conference. Problems cannot be solved by invasion.

MLS: My next question might appear rather naive but I cannot resist asking it. Does the fact that the ambassador of Uganda is also a woman facilitate the negotiations?

Mitifu: As far as my colleague from Uganda is concerned, we have had several contacts. She is not my enemy as a person. I am not her enemy as a person. I have always advocated women's involvement in politics. I am proud to have colleagues that are women. I am proud of her and of what she has accomplished in her career. She does her job and I do mine. I do not consider her as my enemy. We are two African sisters who are working hard doing their jobs.

These are countries at war. We do greet each other when we meet. We are very civil with one another. I do not have any issue with her as a person. I can hope that she does not have any problem with me as a person. So we talk when we meet. We meet during conferences, during debates. Everyone does her job.

One of the main motives behind the war is the plundering of natural resources, particularly in the eastern part of the country in the Kivu province. There are statistics out there that prove it. You have countries such as Rwanda, Uganda, and Burundi that are exporting more than fifteen times more gold than Congo even though they do not have gold mines. Those countries are also exporting diamonds even though they do not have diamonds. The diamonds are coming from the eastern part of Congo. They have been digging illegally in our country. Recently they have even accused one another of plundering Congolese resources. They are exporting our timber as well. It is very clear that there are leaders in Rwanda and Uganda who have put themselves in very compromising situations. People close to the president of Uganda have been actively involved in the plundering of Congolese resources. The other motive behind the war is the desire to retain that part of the country. The Congo is a very large country and extremely rich in natural resources.

MLS: What is the most challenging aspect of your role in Washington?

Mitifu: It is not a challenge to convince American lawmakers and the American public of the fact that Congo is a very big country, extremely rich in natural resources and with great potential. That's a fact. I would like to project the image of not just Congo but of an Africa ready to be a partner of the United States. The partnership issue is very important. We should not simply pay lip service to the concept of partnership. Partnership should be put into action. Africa should not be perceived as a continent that is just there, sitting there and waiting to receive aid. I am telling Americans that Africa has something to offer. The partnership between Africa and the United States should be an exchange. Has it been a challenge to convince Americans of a possible partnership? Of course! It is a great challenge to convince people to invest in your country, to exchange with you experiences when your country is at war. It is very difficult. Business people must feel safe to travel to your country and invest there. Similarly for lawmakers and State Department officials, it is difficult to work with a country at war. It is a situation of instability. My challenge is to prove to them that the government I am working for is the government that will lead the country to stability. It is a constant challenge.

MLS: You have said that you want to place emphasis on trade rather than aid in a partnership with the United States. Concretely what would be the ideal partnership between your country and the United States?

Mitifu: In every case when you have a country that is coming from as far such as Congo—Congo has been mismanaged for thirty-two years—it is difficult, especially for such a big country, to get back on its feet. The international community that has supported the government that was there for thirty-two years, I could hope that they can feel at least responsible for what the country has gone through and give some kind of aid, perhaps only the initial phase—a jump-start to the country, so that the country can get back on its feet and start producing. That is the way the partnership should be established. It is very difficult for a country like Congo to merge into this concept of globalization. How can you compete with countries that are at least 100 years ahead of you? So the countries that are 100 years ahead should give Congo a jump-start.

MLS: In order to do that they must have full confidence in Congo's current leader. Why should the international community think that President Kabila is going to do a far better job than his predecessor?

Mitifu: The international community should trust the people. The United States is a democratic country. Democracy means "power of the people." The United States should trust the people of Congo. If the people of Congo are ready to give a chance to Mr. Kabila so that he can prove what he is able to do, then the international community should do the same. Mr. Kabila has not been given a chance. President Kabila arrived in Kinshasa only in May of 1997.

MLS [interrupting]: But that was not through elections . . .

Mitifu: That was not through elections but you have to remember that the international community was generally enthusiastic about him because it was the only way. . . . They have tried to go through that long democratic transitional period with Mobutu and Mobutu would not go away. The only language that Mobutu could understand was the language of force. He was given a chance of ten years of transitional period.

MLS: Who is President Kabila?

Mitifu: I had not been back home for more than ten years when I went back home in June of last year. My biggest satisfaction at the time was to notice how people were for the first time hopeful, people whom I met there on the streets of Kinshasa where I had the opportunity to talk to as many people as I could from different backgrounds. I had to talk to these people first to make sure what I came there for was really what I wanted to do. For the first time the Congolese people were hopeful despite the fact that President Kabila from day one did not receive any outside assistance. The country was literally autonomous, functioning under very difficult conditions with makeshift means but you could see changes. You could see changes and people loved it. Little things. You would travel to the airport and no one would bother you and ask you for money in order to get through. There were no military soldiers arresting people on the streets or asking people for money. There was order. There was an effort to repair roads. There was a willingness to crack down on corruption. For the first time there were members of the government being jailed for corruption which never occurred before. There were positive steps and people love it. And this was only one year later. You have to be realistic. You cannot ask someone to fix in one year a country that has been destroyed in thirty-two years.

MLS: Who is actually the President and how did he appoint you?

Mitifu: The president actually is a man who has been fighting Mobutu's dictatorship for thirty-two years. We had many people who started with him, who started before him. Some of them were eliminated physically. Others had been corrupted by former President Mobutu. President Kabila does not fall into any of these categories. He is a man who had an ideal for his country. He has a degree in philosophy, but has spent most of his time fighting Mobutu in the "maquis." That is where he spent most of his time. He is a man with determination. No one ever gets the stamp of approval of everybody but his people liked what they saw in him at the time. The "civilized" world which promotes democracy should take into consideration what the people want. The people liked what they were seeing and were ready to give him four, five years and see what he would do. The people had more realistic expectations.

MLS: Will he do like President Museveni of Uganda, hold elections to legitimize his power to his own people and to the international community?

Mitifu: You know, . . . we had a plan. We were scheduled to have a constituent assembly by August 15. All the applications were in. When I left my country in July, they were working through the applications. We had already a commission that was working on the draft of a new constitution. I call it a draft because this constitution was to be submitted to the Constituent Assembly. This draft was to be submitted to different groups of people from different backgrounds, to different political parties, and to the civil society. Everybody had a chance to look into this draft and make their own amendments and those amendments were to be included in the draft of the constitution. That draft of the constitution was to be submitted to a referendum. Then we could have organized elections. This president came with a commitment to democratize the country. Even during a time when the country is at war, he initiated a national debate. Whatever the result of the national debate, hopefully, those results will guide our country for many years to come. The commitment was there. The commitment is still there. This was not a joke. And it still is not a joke. Despite the war the constitution has been distributed to everybody. Even at the embassy here, we have announced it and asked our Congolese brothers and sisters to look at it, write to us and amend it. We did the same thing at the embassy as we did in country. The commitment to democracy is still there. I am referring here to real democracy, not the kind where leaders finance political parties to give the impression that there are different political parties and that there have been real elections.

   I have been living here in the United States, but while here I had been very active in a Congolese organization which was called the All National American Conference on Zaire (ANACOZA) during Mobutu's time when the country was still called Zaire. Today we changed the name to ANACCO. I was active in that organization. Of course there were very few women. As you know, traditionally, politics and political militancy were taboo among women in my country. I was involved and active in that organization. This organization supported and welcomed the 1997 revolution. My appointment might have originated in my militancy in that organization. I did not apply for the position as such. I was happy teaching at Columbus State University in Georgia. One day as I was coming from the classroom I got the phone call. It was my husband. "You just got a phone call from Kinshasa.

Apparently, President Kabila would like to see you," he said. Of course I thought it was a joke. My husband spent about twenty minutes trying to convince me that it was not a joke. I had to return the call. It was true. I was indeed asked to come to Kinshasa as soon as possible. So I told my chair and dean at the university about the unraveling event. I was granted the permission to go and serve my country. When I arrived in Congo, I met with President Kabila for the first time. I used to hear about President Kabila, this person who lived in the "maquis" and had almost a caricatural image of this person. When I finally met with him, we talked for more than an hour. He told me about his dream for the country. A country with such huge potential should have highways. The children should not go to bed hungry and should get a good education. They should have access to computers and get back to their three meals a day. The workers should have better work ethics and be paid on a regular basis. Of course the task was huge. There was a big challenge to overcome. But everything he was talking about were things I had been fighting for within that organization. That is why it was not difficult for me to accept his offer to represent the country in Washington. The rest is history.

MLS: In the international community when people hear of a leader marching to the capital and seizing power without elections, it conjures up images of dictatorship. You have been in this post for less than a year. Reading the newspapers, it seems that the image of President Kabila is not as problematic now as a few months ago. You have been successful in changing his image. What is the extent of that success?

Mitifu: Thank you for that, by the way. I have been doing everything I could through conferences, through interviews, through contacts. My aim was to humanize this president who has been caricatured by the media. My task has been to counterattack all the lies that have been spread about him and about the Congolese people. It has been to denounce the great injustice that has been perpetrated against the Congolese people. The Congolese people found themselves the victims of an attack and later on were demonized and linked to killings. At the beginning it was like bumping my head against the wall. But it was worth it to keep talking about it. In the end, it has been proven that there was a great deal of truth in what I was saying. In the very beginning we denounced the plundering of natural resources and finally, through statistics, people came to the realization this was true. Uganda and Rwanda have a problem in their countries, that of the rebels. The international community has come to realize that those problems from those countries cannot be solved by invading another country. It is not up to Congo to solve the problems of Rwanda and Uganda. If there are rebels in those countries, it means that there is also a problem in those countries and that a solution should be found internally in those countries, the same way solutions should be found internally in my country in order to reach peace.

MLS: What is the average situation like for the average Congolese?

Mitifu: The situation right now is very difficult as for all countries at war. We have many displaced people. People are coming from the east running away from the invaders and their cronies. There are many people living in the rural areas who have been running away from the rural areas towards the urban areas because they feel safer in the urban areas. Most of the mass killings of populations of women and children take place in the Kivu province and other rural areas. People in the rural areas are unsafe. As you know, 98 percent of people in the rural area practice agriculture. They are the ones who feed the country. So you can imagine the problems we have in terms of food shortage, in trying to accommodate displaced persons in a huge country. In addition, we have refugees from our next door neighbor, Congo Brazzaville. We have refugees from our next door neighbor, Angola. We have our own Congolese people seeking refuge in other countries that border Congo. We have refugees in Tanzania. We have refugees in Uganda. We have refugees in the Central African Republic. Things are not easy. We have a shortage of everything. The little money the country is able to produce is diverted to war efforts. We have no other choice other than continue to defend ourselves. We were attacked. We did not attack anyone. We have no other choice but to keep defending ourselves. It is not easy.

MLS: How do you perceive the role of women in Congo? Looking at your example one would think that Congo is a very progressive country in terms of women's rights. Do you see women taking a more active role in politics and in trying to bring an end to the war?

Mitifu: Oh yes! Even under the previous government we have had women cabinet members. I am always proud to talk about it. The first woman minister in Congo was Madame Liyau in 1968. She was Minister for Social Affairs. We have had women in our government. Unfortunately there were not as many as one could wish. At the time we had very few women with university degrees. Today we have many women with college degrees in Congo. These women do participate actively in NGOs [non-governmental organizations]. There are many women who are militant. Right now we have four women in the government. We have five women ambassadors. They are posted at the Organization of African Unity, in Kampala, in Addis Ababa, in Washington. We also appointed a woman to Brussels which is one of our most important diplomatic posts. Of course I would like to see more women appointed.

MLS: How did the Congolese people receive your appointment?

Mitifu: We should not kid ourselves. As women we still have a very long way to go. We still have people in our society who think that women are not as competent as men. Generally speaking, women and men were enthusiastic at the news of my appointment. Women were very proud. Men were very encouraging. But you still have a small number of people who were very surprised that the president had appointed a woman to Washington and who believed that during this time of war there should be a muscle in Washington, a man. There is still a long struggle ahead for women. As you stay longer in this line of work, you feel that the women constantly have to prove themselves. It is still a man's world. Far more is expected of women. However, women should by no means be discouraged by those kinds of attitudes coming from a small minority of people. We should continue working hard and pave the way for other women who are aspiring to that kind of profession.

MLS: Is a woman's way of handling diplomacy different from a man's way of handling diplomacy?

Mitifu: I am sure it has to be different. I am not saying that it is systematically different. It is a matter of personality. We have our ways of tackling problems. I am a bit reluctant to provide a blanket answer. I do not handle diplomacy like all the women diplomats and vice versa. I am sure that a woman has special qualities that allow her to have a different approach. Different does not mean less efficient.

MLS: What is next in your career?

Mitifu: You might be surprised to hear that my next move will probably be to go back to academia, back to the classroom. I love teaching. I will go back to teaching, perhaps with a different approach, but I am going back to teaching.

MLS: Thank you Ambassador Mitifu.

AMBASSADOR SONIA PICADO
OF COSTA RICA

"A Funny Thing Happened on the Way to Washington" could be the title of a book written on Ambassador Sonia Picado of Costa Rica. The voluble envoy explains in the following interview some of the unexpected twists of fate in her career. In her world of intricate wrought iron, white walls against terra cotta, and petits fours served on delicate china, a reception hosted by Ambassador Picado is a true delight. It invariably combines the elegance of her Central American country and her eclectic attention for details. Inevitably it does away with the conformist stuffiness often found at other Washington receptions. The law professor's style is more high brow and less high nose, allowing every guest to relax in a convivial atmosphere where issues are more important than the jargon in which they are framed.

If her entertaining distinguishes itself, so does the country she represents. Costa Rica is the only country in the Americas that does not have an army. The Ambassador is very proud of that fact. It is one of her marketing assets. In this country of 3.5 million inhabitants a budget that neighboring countries might have used for the army is used on social development. It has paid off. Costa Rica has the highest literacy rate in the Americas. The "no guns, many books" combination has allowed Costa Rica to enjoy democracy for much of its history, an exception in a region plagued by civil wars and political unrest during much of its history. One of the reasons for Costa Rica's success at democracy since its independence in 1821 is that the majority of its population has not been subjected to marginalization. A large majority of Costa Ricans are descended from Europeans who were not marginalized and benefited early on from an equitable land distribution unlike the remaining ten percent of the population of African descent. When dictatorship tried to rear its ugly head in 1917–18, it failed on Costa Rican soil—so did the two-month "civil war" of 1949.

I met with Sonia Picado during the winter of 1996 to talk about her role as Ambassador of the country that she wants to regard as a model in its region. I found in her someone extremely eager to share her experience and quite a conversationalist!

MLS: What brought you to the world of diplomacy?

Ambassador Picado: I had worked for the political campaign. The president came to see me two days after the elections to discuss possibilities of collaborating, especially taking into consideration my international experience as director of the InterAmerican Institute of Human Rights and justice at the InterAmerican Court. In that capacity I was an ambassador to the Organization of American States. Certainly it is very different from being ambassador to your country. When he mentioned the possibility of coming to Washington my first reaction was that I did not want to give up my human rights career. His response was "Costa Rica and human rights have always come together. You can work for both!" Actually it has proven a very good experience to serve my country in such capacities. I have done a lot of work with most of the countries in transition towards democracy in Latin America.

MLS: Which brings me to your experience in Washington. As an ambassador to Washington, D.C., in a setting where women ambassadors are a novelty, what has been your experience?

Picado: I am sure that the other women ambassadors have told you the same thing. It is very hard not having a "wife." [Laughter.] There are two reasons for that. One is simply that in addition to the other duties you have to take care of your house and fulfill your other duties by yourself. I call it the "home-made dish factor." I do not have small children. I am divorced. My children are in Costa Rica. Nevertheless, I do have to host receptions and entertain. In my case I happen to like to do it. I put a lot of personal input and touch into it. That is an extra task that the men do not do—period! Especially the Latin American ambassadors, they are not going to do it. The second point is that the wives also play a political role in Washington. There are many organizations such as the Neighbors Club in which the wives (spouses) of ambassadors meet with wives (spouses) of senators, members of Congress, cabinet members and that creates a network. They are mainly "women" activities, but very often they lead into activities with their husbands. This is an additional work. Very often I do go to these women's activities because, in the first place, I find a lot of interesting women involved in them and also because I think it is an important part of Washington's life. So, I have to play two roles in one and that keeps me extremely busy.

MLS: What are your views on the condition of women in Latin America and in Costa Rica in particular?

Picado: I have worked a lot with women issues. As a lawyer I have promoted a family code in Costa Rica in 1974. Costa Rica was lucky that in 1887 a civil code was adopted which was very advanced for its time. It included equal rights for men and women as far as civil rights are concerned. It also included divorce. It included the possibility of the father recognizing the child. The French law, the Roman law, as you know, did not give any position to women and children who were always under the protection of men. This went on in France until the 1960s and in Spain until the death of Franco. Women were not allowed to own property or to open a bank account or to come into a court. In the case of Costa Rica we did have a lot of these advantages, but that did not erase the machismo culture. The culture in Latin America, particularly the Catholic religion, in many ways promotes obedience on the part of women creating a lot of cultural values and stereotypes in which women play a submissive role under the protection of men which, of course, inhibits them and prevents them from doing work outside. I graduated in 1968 from law school. We were only two women then. Fortunately, today there are as many as 50 percent women in the same law school. Quite a difference!

However, I think the machismo in Latin America is part of that vertical culture I mentioned earlier where you have a culture of caudillos, a very strong army, and a very strong hierarchical church. Consequently, all this is reflected in the extent of the violence in homes. To make violence against women a human rights issue has taken many years, as you well know, and a lot of work from the United Nations and the world in general. I would say that the condition of women in Latin America, as a result, is improving. However, it is very difficult to talk about women's issues if you do not differentiate. It is very different for women in Latin America from the upper class or the bourgeois class in terms of what they can do or what they perceive they can accomplish and women from other social classes. Even in my country in the areas of [Guanacaste] and Limon, which are more iso-lated, close to 50 percent of the children are born without a father. There women have to work the land. They bear all the responsibilities for the kids. I do believe that it is very important that we work on shared issues and on the rights of women in terms of family planning.

MLS: Is machismo subsiding or is it so intertwined with the culture that it is looked upon as one of its quasi-permanent fixtures?

Picado: It is still very present. . . . It is a way of thinking that a man is superior, the man is king of the house and leader of the community. You do see women working in politics, but the ones who get the jobs are usually their husbands or the brother. Similarly, in the campesino families and also in the urban families preference is given to the male to attend a university, not to the woman. It is changing because the world is changing. Many women have to go out and work. Once they are economically independent and exposed to the world, they no longer accept the position of the slave at home. That is helping them change their mentality and understand that their daughters have to be educated also. This is something that is not only taking place in Latin America; it is a worldwide phenomenon. It is linked to economic issues, to the globalization of culture, to the globalization of trade. The world has become small and women are looking at it from a different perspective. Men, too, need women to work at their sides and expect them to be stronger. I think this is creating one of the most prob-lematic issues in our times. What is a family? Do the kids suffer from both parents working? We do not have enough daycare centers. The whole society is changing. I think we women have to be very alert in how to approach these changes and at the same time raise a family and become more knowl-edgeable and less submissive.

MLS: Personally, in your own life did you have to encounter and confront this machismo and how? At which level? In which way, shape or form? Are there specific examples or was it a smooth sail?

Picado: Definitely not! I come from a home in which I got a lot of support from my parents who believe very much in education. At that time it was very unusual for a woman to study law. Only two women out of forty students were part of my graduating class when I graduated in 1968. This seems like ages ago, but in terms of history it is really a short time. The law faculty was really a male place! As I have said in an article, I have had two divorces. In many ways I think I have paid a high price for the right to think. I don't think my husbands were supportive of my work. There are many ways to make things difficult. When I first started to study law, I had to raise two children. I was not allowed to drive. So I had to take a bus very early in the morning. I had to get things ready before leaving. But then my mother moved in and helped with the kids. But still, there was this whole social environment opposed to women studying.

MLS: At that time, it was not viewed in a good light for women to drive in Costa Rica, let alone initiate a divorce?

Picado: Right! There was no divorce on mutual consent; so I had to incur a cost. It was not clearly spelled out that I could not do it, but there were so many ways to make things difficult not only on the part of my husband but of society in general. I remember walking into a dinner party one day, a small dinner party, and a gentleman I did not even know screamed at me across the room "So you are going to the university and aren't you ashamed of leaving your home to go to a place that is not for ladies." And he was not even an acquaintance of mine. This shows how the social environment was in general. However, if you were a nurse or a teacher, you were alright. Law or engineering or any other career were out of the question for women. So things have changed very rapidly. As I said, I have paid a very high price for the right to think, for the right to do things that are good, and at the same time be responsible for my family. It requires a tremendous amount of strength to be a woman who wants to accomplish something. You do get a guilty complex for not being at home. Everybody makes you feel badly about it. At the same time, you have to perform well because, otherwise, men think that because you are a woman you cannot do it. It is very difficult.

MLS: Your children, were they supportive?

Picado: I have two children from my first marriage. The first, my daughter, is a career woman. She is now living a lot of the things I lived myself. Which means that in spite of the fact that things have changed, they do remain the same. She had all of our support to study in Boston and in Washington, D.C. at George Washington University. She obtained a master's in museology. She is an expert in education. She also had to make her work compatible with her life at home. My son is a computer engineer and is very supportive. I am very lucky in that respect. But it's not a short story. I divorced and it was a very difficult divorce. When you want a divorce, you lose financially. I found out that it is the man that usually holds the privilege of keeping the capital. So, it is another sacrifice you have to pay when you want a divorce.

MLS: Is it still this way today?

Picado: It is changing of course. Now the law has changed. I contributed to change the law. In 1974 when we worked on the family code, we introduced the concept of divorce on mutual agreement. Women are beginning to look out more for themselves and also to earn money and to make sure that that money is theirs. We have more protection now, but it is still more difficult for women than for men. When I remarried I took care of three more children with my second husband. So for five years I did not work. At a certain point, I had five teenagers at home. I was married to my second husband for sixteen years. During that time, I was offered a political position with every single change in the government. But I was not able to accept because my second husband did not want to hear about it. He used to say "you can have an academic life, but not a political life."

When I became dean of the law school, he resented that also very much too. I think he resented all along my work in human rights also. So, at a certain point you wonder why. If you have been supporting them through thick and thin at every stage in life, through their different works, doing both your own work and helping them in theirs, you cannot help wondering why you cannot get support. This is part of their mentality. I think it is in spite of them that we achieve. It is something they cannot accept. And it is bad for them and bad for us women.

MLS: When did you make that decision that it had to be your career or your marriage?

Picado: I did not make the decision. He made it. At a certain point I was very successful at the Court. I was very successful in my human rights work. I had to travel. He did not like the fact that I had to travel. In all those years of marriage I had never once been alone with a man for [a business] lunch; I was very protective of the marriage. At one point he said that the only way he would accept staying in the marriage would be if I gave up my work and stayed home. Let me put it this way, you cannot accept to go against yourself. I had sacrificed already my political career. I had raised his children during those five years. My father's was the best law firm in the country. I had stopped working for my father. I assumed the career of professor. I thought it was very unfair. I think at a certain point it becomes a question of self-respect.

MLS: What do your two previous husbands think of your current career and of your appointment as ambassador to Washington? Do you have any feedback from them?

Picado: You are going to laugh at this. With both of my former husbands I keep a very good relationship. We talk on the phone. It has been good for the children. It has been good for everybody. My second husband is now the vice-president of the country. He never allowed me to have a political career, but he did further ,his. I even have to talk to him for work related matters. At this point we are divorced and there is not much he can say about my career. I don't think he is too happy about it either. My first husband is an engineer. He gave up on me—literally. Since my children are grown up and I am divorced, my daily life does not interfere with my duties as ambassador. I have devised my life very much as a family program. My mother is eighty-five. She came to Washington with two of my children when I presented my credentials to President Clinton. The president was extremely lovely to her. Last Christmas I invited my children with their kids to visit. I think they should take advantage of the fact that I am in Washington to visit the museums, see the snow and experience some of the traditions the city has to offer and that are different from ours. My granddaughter who is seven came to a day camp for six weeks here. I have two grandchildren from my daughter. When I talk about my grandchildren, I naturally include my stepchildren's kids and there are eight of them.

MLS: Can you talk about some of the women you regard as role models, either because of their political engagement in Latin America or elsewhere or because of their contributions in any other field?

Picado: I have been very privileged to call myself a friend of Betty Friedan. I met her here. I read her book, *Feminine Mystique*, when I was in law school in the 1960s. Her book influenced me a lot. I attended high school in Washington. The fact that I saw so many women among my classmates that were going to college gave me the strength to go on and fight for my own career. Betty Friedan with whom I talk as often as I can is so up-to-date. She is now working on family values because she says that it cannot become a political symbol. Increasingly, it is an economic problem for women. Increasingly, it is women who have to make the decisions in the family. Increasingly, family values are linked to women's issues. I feel very close to that issue working in Latin America. She mentions how women have to work even with a guilty complex. Many women can relate to that.

Let me tell you that in general women here in Washington are really interesting. For example, watching what Hillary Clinton had to go through was tremendous. I really admire Janet Reno, Donna Shalala. On the Republican side, Elizabeth Dole has had a remarkable career in a different style. I saw her at the Republican Convention. She was by far the most interesting figure. In Latin America it is more difficult. I admire Violetta Chamorro a lot. We are very good friends. One of the two things I have here (pointing to an award), one is Violetta Chamorro's. She gave me the highest honor for my work in the elections in Nicaragua. I respect her. I know her work. I think she has done wonders for Nicaragua. I do feel, however, that in most cases even Violetta had to take the flag of the party because her husband had died. More and more women in Latin America are respected when they are the daughters of or the widows of. We have to find our own profile!

MLS: Isn't it like that all over the world whether in the Phillippines or Pakistan?

Picado: Very much so! And look what happened to Geraldine Ferraro here. Often women that do not have the support of a husband or a father have a much harder time. Having said that, that does not diminish the work that Violetta has done. In many ways, being able to bring peace to Nicaragua is in itself a great accomplishment and I have a lot of respect for that. But women have to find their own profile in Latin America.

MLS: What are some of the inroads that women have made in various fields in your country? How have these accomplishments inspired you?

Picado: A very close friend of mine, a woman I respect a lot, Elizabeth Odio, is the only Latin American at the Hague in the Yugoslavian war crimes tribunal. She has been Minister of Justice twice. She is a woman who had to fight politically for her own position. In law there have been women who have done a great job. I also believe that in many cases the role of the First Lady is very difficult. Nowadays they are expected to play an important role. Many of them are very capable women. However, the society wants to see them as ornaments and does not want to give them credit for who they really are. I can point out the case of Oscar Arias' wife Margarita. These are very strong, very capable women, career women with a hard time doing their own work because they were subjected to their husbands. Costa Rica now has a woman vice president, an economist. She is also in her own right quite accomplished.

I also respect very much the sister of President Figueres, Muni Figueres. She was a candidate to the vice presidency. She did not make it at that particular point. She is now working at the InterAmerican Bank. There are a lot of strong women in Costa Rica because Costa Ricans are open in new ways. Costa Rican women are also breaking the tradition of just staying home.

MLS: What do you wish for women in your country and for women in Latin America in general?

Picado: Every human being deserves respect, respect in terms of human rights, political rights, liberty, to live life free of not only fear, but also of economic deprivation. I have repeatedly said that the main violation of human rights in Latin America is poverty. And women are the poorest of the poor, as you well know. We cannot talk about men or women having a dignified life if they don't have the mininum basis in education and health. I am proud that my country has the second place in human development in the Americas and the highest literacy index in Latin America, one of the highest in health. I am very proud of that. Costa Rica does not have an army. The fact that we do not have an army has a lot to do with improvement in health and education. Men and women in the Americas deserve to have a better standard of living, especially in those areas in which so many of our co-citizens live.

MLS: There will be a forum soon at the InterAmerican Development Bank on the alleviation of poverty in Latin America, particularly in the black communities.

Picado: Yes I have been invited. I will be at another seminar, but I will send someone from the embassy. At this point it is the key issue to discuss. We cannot keep on taking economic measures that are widening the gap between rich and poor, thus affecting women more, because again we are the ones who are more deprived of everything.

MLS: In the United States race issues are very much tied to economic issues. To which extent is this also a concern in Latin America?

Picado: That varies from country to country. Costa Rica has a much more homogeneous population. We were very poor, very isolated, and the Spaniard came and settled down. On the contrary Guatemala has 70 percent of indigenous population and they are definitely a marginalized population. Wherever there are indigenous populations in Latin America, they are marginalized. It is one of the poorest populations in Latin America. In my country when the railroad was built, a lot of black people came, especially from Jamaica. They live in Limon and they have been quite isolated. I think that Costa Rica did not want to feel as though it was discriminating, but I think we end up discriminating. Now a lot more attention had been given to the province. It is still a very poor province. We have had bad luck in the province. It was doing very well at some point and then we had this earthquake that destroyed a lot of buildings—hotels that were doing well in tourism. I believe there is much more we can do and that we have to do. So, to your question I answer yes, race and economics are a concern. Our indigenous population is very small. It is larger in Panama and quite isolated from the rest of the population.

MLS: Is it simply a matter of taking them out of that enclave which is reflected in their economic status?

Picado: Yes. In the case of the indigenous population I think it is a bit more confusing than that. In a way you do not want to impose your values on them. On the other hand, if you keep them isolated, they are prevented from getting health care services, from getting an education. They live in very isolated areas of the country where the roads came very late—just at the port of Panama. They have more in common as a community (they think more in terms of community) with Panamanians in rural areas than they do with the rest of the country. But I think that is changing.

MLS: Is it a matter of finding a happy medium where they can preserve their culture and improve their standard of living to the extent that it will no longer be an "us" versus "them" society?

Picado: Yes, in the case of the black population in Limon, the fact that they spoke English isolated them even more. Right now, what is spoken is a blend of both languages. That in itself is a problem. As a university professor, I found especially in law they had a lot of problems with the language. Bilingual education should be an option. Costa Rica is making a commitment; right now all first graders are taking either English or French. It is going to be all bilingual education. We are strengthening this. Limon should be given priority in this endeavor. They are already bilingual, but at this point they are speaking neither correct English nor correct Spanish. That handicaps them in every respect.

MLS: What is the biggest hurdle you had to overcome as a woman ambassador?

[Long pause]

Picado: I would not say there are really tremendous hurdles. As soon as I mention that I am the ambassador, people think I am the wife of the ambassador. The question that immediately follows is "When are we going to meet the ambassador?" If I am with a male colleague, they immediately assume that he is the ambassador and not I. I would say that, in general, more and more people feel embarrassed at the confusion. They do not do it in bad taste. There are very few women ambassadors. The task of an ambassador here is difficult because Washington is a city that is very political. You have to read the *Washington Post*, the *New York Times*, the *Washington Times*, the *Wall Street Journal* by 11:00. This is a small embassy. We all have to do a little bit of everything. At the same time, I lead the residence. I often come back late or ready for dinner. Everything has to be working. Life here is very focused on political correctness. You have to cope with it. In general, I have found people quite supportive. People like Josette Shiner, the co-editor of the *Washington Times*, have been very supportive of our work. I find that very fortunate.

MLS: What is a typical day for you at the embassy and at the residence?

Picado: I am not an early riser. However, I have tried to refuse working breakfasts. I like to have some time of my own. As a woman ambassador, not having "a wife," you have two jobs. There is a wonderful Filipino couple who lives in the residence. During the week-end, Rosy and I plan ahead for the dinners or the luncheons. If I have guests at home, that is a bit more complicated because I have to have breakfast with them. Otherwise I have fruit in my room, walk on my treadmill. In general it is very important for women ambassadors to take care of their appearance.

MLS: Most of my students have commented on that, on the fact that the women ambassadors tend to fill a room with their presence, more so than their male counterparts because they add a lot of grace to the post. I am only quoting my students here.

Picado: That's a very nice comment. You have to send a message, you know. Again, there are few of us. Usually the world demands more of a woman in a position that has been traditionally filled by men. They expect you to do it well. You have to prove that you are not just a pretty face, but you also have to be a pretty face. By pretty face, I mean that you have to look good, you have to have a good level of presence, not worry about your appearance, but invest some time in it. And it is time consuming also. I usually leave my house around half past nine and arrive here at 10:00. The embassy opens from ten to six. I never leave the others unless I have a meeting. I have a meeting this afternoon for example on Women and Development at 6:00. I intend to and I like to keep involved in women's issues and in human rights issues. I don't come back to the residence unless I have to change for a reception. Very often I stay here in the office. When I come to the office, I like to read the Costa Rican newspapers on the internet. On weekends at home I have a look at *La Nación* on the internet. Also, I have staff meetings on some of the most important news. I have a lot of working luncheons. If I don't go out, I love to have lunch here with the people of the embassy because I think that it is a family time with your own people. The rest of the day is spent in different meetings on a host of issues. Ambassadors now-adays have to invest a lot of time on trade issues, on legal issues. Globalization means for small countries getting hit in the head very often. We have had some big legal battles in Washington. So depending on what the issues are, you go to Congress or not. You don't go to a member of Congress just to tell him or her "Here I am. Costa Rica is a lovely country; we would like to see you." You have to have a direct and specific issue to visit senators and Congress, otherwise they don't have the time, especially during a campaign year. We do a lot of work in the area of promoting the country. I do a lot of traveling. I have recently visited Fort Worth, the Chamber of Commerce. I have lectured in Dayton, Ohio, in Chicago, in New York, among others. In most of these lectures I talk about sustainable development. In many instances I also lecture on what I have come to regard as my own causes, women's rights and human rights.

MLS: Among all your colleagues here in Washington, is there a particular person that you think stands out or whom you admire for his or her accomplishments?

Picado: Certainly Enrique Iglesias, the president of the InterAmerican Bank, has certainly opened up the Bank to such conferences as the Conference on Poverty Alleviation in Latin America. From an administration of justice standpoint, he has done a lot for our country. I feel privileged to know him and to be his friend. I think that the group of women ambassadors in general has been very interesting to know and very supportive and so have my Latin American colleagues. I would have liked to meet more ambassadors from other regions. Unfortunately the diplomatic corps here in Washington is large. We do not have that many gatherings. We tend to congregate within the same region. That is a shame because we never have the opportunity to talk to the Africans or to the Arab world. I have met with a lot of them which I liked very much. For instance, the Egyptian ambassador and his wife are lovely people. That is one of the things that I like about the women's groups. They are interregional and give you the opportunity to meet with other people. I would say that there are many interesting people in Washington and to name just two or three would be unfair. I have tremendous respect for Pablo Tarso Flecha de Lima, the Brazilian ambassador. After his surgery he recovered beautifully and has shown courage and leadership. He is very good and we all respect him for that. I could go on and on. From the Caribbean there is an excellent ambassador from Saint Lucia, Ambassador Edmunds [the predecessor of Sonia M. Johnny]. He has also shown strong leadership. He is now the second man in the Court. One of the beauties of being a diplomat in Washington is that your colleagues are interesting people and are leaders in themselves. So it is very pleasant working with them.

MLS: Before becoming an ambassador you already had a successful career. Is this new role as an ambassador a growing process? Are you growing with the role?

Picado: I am enjoying talking to you. Yes, it is a growing process. In life it is important to open your eyes to other careers. I have repeatedly said that I am taking these four years in Washington as a Ph.D. in a lot of things I never thought I would have to worry about, like bananas, and cellular telephones and legal cases here. They have forced me almost to hurry back to my law career because, even though I am not carrying the cases myself, I have to deal a lot with lawyers and with some of the issues that are brought before us. For example, we had a long case in expropriation. We have taken it to ICSIT (the International Tribunal of the World Bank). It has forced me to look from a different perspective at a lot of the issues you tend to focus on as a specialty. For example, I do attend meetings of the World Bank, of the International Monetary Fund when my delegation is in town, not to do the negotiations of course because I am not an economist, but it is very interesting to look at these institutions for their leadership and even to be able to also criticize what they are doing. You have not been a human rights person and work a lot with NGOs to sit idle to what is going on. Working with the government has given me a different perspective that I find enriching. In life you always learn from other human beings. You can always make a new experience a rich one—working for my country, introducing my country to the United States at a time when we are not strategically important has been rewarding. When the world was divided between communism and capitalism, we were strategically important because we were in the middle of a region that was very controversial and very difficult. At this point what we have to offer is our policy of environment. I have a lot of respect for my president. I do not think you can be ambassador to Washington if you do not have a linkage with your president directly. We are committed to have at least 25 percent of our territory as an environmentally friendly society. We believe you cannot have sustainable development if you do not invest in education and health and that is our main priority. For example, we are having meetings this week on telemedicine. We are trying to coordinate our efforts with clinics in the United States to connect our hospitals to the program of telemedicine in order to help our people. Computers in every school including the poorest is also our priority because it is a technical world and unless we improve the education of our children, we will not be able to be citizens of the first world but fall into the fourth world. In these endeavors I am very supportive. I try to do my best to influence and to carry out those programs. So, in total, it is a very enriching experience.

MLS: Is there one particular issue that catches your attention more than others or that you would much rather focus on?

Picado: Definitely, for example, working for the telemedicine program. I am really convinced that we can improve health care delivery in Costa Rica. With the combined technologies of computers, televisions, software, and telephone in a small country like Costa Rica, central hospital diagnosis can be provided of, let's say, a woman in the countryside. Such a program has tremendous human value. It will touch mainly women who cannot come to the capital. It takes women in rural areas three or four hours to come to a major city and from there to reach the capital; it is usually a full day traveling. Very often to find a specialist they have to wait three or more months. They usually cannot afford the care or have four or five children they cannot leave behind. Who do you leave them with? You were talking about Limon, about Guanacaste. People in these areas are faced with those issues.

MLS: I found that out as a consultant working on poverty alleviation that some of the requests for funds were related to transportation of patients to the capital.

Picado: In the case of Costa Rica, since we have electricity and telephones covering the whole country, we can work to improve health care delivery and can be a pilot project and a testing ground for, let's say, Nicaragua or other countries that have more problems. I am very Central American in my approach. We alone are three and a half million; together we are thirty million. I am very lucky to serve simultaneously with Ambassador Sol, another woman ambassador, from El Salvador. We both feel strongly that we have to work together for the development of our countries. If we can have this program in Costa Rica and build a network instead of creating more hospitals and becoming more bureaucratic, this could make our hospitals more efficient and allow us to have, let's say, heart transplants with the assistance of the Cleveland Clinic. What difference does the Cleveland Clinic make! We have excellent doctors, but essentially we do not have the amount of money for research; neither do we have the equipment that you have in the United States. We can all share this knowledge. I relate more to programs that have human beings as recipients and the possibilities of improving their lives is very important.

MLS: As an ambassador, do you see your role more as a negotiator, a moderator, a facilitator, or do see yourself more in a monitoring role?

Picado: All of the above. I do a lot of promotion because, even when I touch on women's issues, I am promoting my country. I am saying here is Costa Rica speaking. I like that idea. In spite of the fact that my country is small, we have many things to promote and to be proud of. For example, it is wonderful to say that we do not have an army. I feel very proud of that! It is one of my promotion tools. Certainly we are negotiators. When we had the banana suit to keep the brand to Costa Rica, we had three or more investigations. Also Senator Dole tried to pass a resolution taking away regarding Costa Rica and Colombia, CbI and parity. It was extremely hard battling it in the Senate and in Congress. We had to immerse ourselves into that and it gave me the opportunity to go to Congress almost every day to explain our position and to find ways to protect my country's best interest. It is a very complex issue. It would take a long time to talk about it. It all started when the Europeans passed 404 which is a quota system to protect the Caribbean productions and their ex-colonies' productions. We fought at the GATT against the 404, because we think that if there is free trade, there ought to be free trade for everybody. In spite of certain facts the Europeans kept the resolution. We accepted the framework agreement which is part of the quota equivalent to the amount of production (Costa Rica is the second producer of bananas in the world). Chiquita brand accuses the Europeans here in Washington in spite of the fact that the United States does not produce bananas. It has to grow them in Hawaii. Of course we got a lot of support from the Caribbean countries. They want to keep the 404. A solution will have to be reached at the WTO (World Trade Organization). I think that now the Caribbean countries have a lot of reasons to protect their industry. But I also don't think it makes sense to protect it within a globalization of trade. If we are not honoring the agreements, I think we all have to come to an agreement that is beneficial to all. Certainly, to do what Chiquita did, which is to come and get political interest by being the largest individual donor to both campaigns, I don't think that's the way to do it. I find it hard to explain in such a short time such a difficult problem. The situation has been very difficult for all of us involved.

It was a pleasure talking to you. Being a university professor, I always enjoy talking to other colleagues and to students. I enjoy being among students. I am going to Georgetown for an informal sandwich lunch tomorrow. It enriches you to talk about these experiences. What we have gone through as women is very important, but it is also important to talk about our work. Very often some of the interviews done on women in high positions focus too much on the personal matters. It is important to say that we are where we are because we have worked hard. We are here in spite of all those obstacles. We are here because we have done a good job! What I admire the most about my women colleagues is the excellent professional careers they have had prior to their appointments.

MLS: Rumor has it in Washington that they even have a stronger track record than their male counterparts.

Picado: In many cases it is true! In many cases it is true! It is a wonderful idea to sit with them and to find out what their experience has been. Women do have to work harder. This is a common thing. You are right. I hope that comes out in your book. Many of us are divorced, some had to forego marriage, others have had very difficult experiences in their personal lives. But, in spite of that, it is important to mention that they are achievers.

MLS: I hope that this is what will come out. On that note what do you think is your most important achievement?

Picado [without hesitation]: The United Nations' Human Rights Award of 1993. Working with the NGO community in the 1980s in human rights, working at the Court, working with indigenous people, working with poor women in the Americas, that is by far my greatest achievement. Of course in my personal life, raising my children from two different homes, putting them together and having a family, a family of which I am very proud, is the complement of that work.

MLS: Thank you for your time Ambassador Picado.

AMBASSADOR
ERATO KOZAKOU-MARCOULLIS
OF THE REPUBLIC OF CYPRUS

Copper Island

They reach me from afar
the feathery waves
of your surrounding shores.
I shower my heart in the warmth
of your brightful sea,
in the dazzle of light
that swings over your sky.
The breath of time
eternal,
engraved wide wrinkles
on the scarlet soil of your body.

Footprints,
millennial remnants,
marble memories,
encircle
your indelible ruins.
Eteocyprian,
I feel your image
on the stony silence of Khirokitia,
in the domes you carved.
You First,
initial vein,
first pulse
on the ancient body.
Blessed Island they named you,
womb of copper,
Aeria.
In the depths of your earth
restlessly roam the shadows.
Tearful Aphrodite strolls,
mythical figures embrace,
engraved on the roots
Tefkros
Onesilos
Evagoras.
Profound the passage of fire
left anguish and wounds.
Here is the bitter crossroads
interlinking three worlds.
Ships unloading the ashes
with spears reaping the fields.
Copper island
wounded island
My Homeland.

—Erato Kozakou-Marcoullis

According to mythology, a long time ago near the historic town of
Pafos on the south coast of Cyprus, a goddess was born out of the
foam of the sea, Aphrodite, the Greek goddess of love and beauty. If
you wonder at the end of this poem why Aphrodite is tearful, the
answer is simple. The goddess of love had too many suitors, far too
many conquerors. And so did her birthplace, Cyprus, during its 9,000-

year-long history and civilization. Remains of the oldest known set-tlement in Cyprus date from 7000 B.C. During the Bronze Age the island was known for its copper exploitation and trade which brought wealth and prosperity to the island. The Mycenaean Greeks originally colonized Cyprus as early as 1500 B.C. During the twelfth and elev-enth centuries B.C. mass waves of Achaean Greeks came to settle on the island, spreading the Greek language, religion and customs. First the conquerors were the Egyptians, the Assyrians, the Persians, and the Romans and after the division of the Roman Empire, Cyprus came under the Eastern Roman Empire, known as Byzantium. Then came the English king, Richard the Lionheart in 1191, who married Princess Berengaria of Navarre at Limassol where she was crowned queen of England. A year later Richard sold the island to the Knights Templar who resold it to the French Guy de Lusignan, deposed King of Jerusalem. Under the Lusignan Dynasty the Catholic Church of-ficially replaced the Greek Orthodox Church, but the latter managed to survive. The last queen of Cyprus, Catherina Cornaro, ceded the island to Venice in 1489. In 1571 the island was conquered by the Ottomans who ruled Cyprus until 1878 when the island was leased to the British. In 1923, under the Treaty of Lauzanne, Turkey relin-quished all rights to Cyprus and in 1925 Cyprus became a Crown Colony.

The sober and luminescent poem written by Cypriot ambassador to Washington, Erato Kozakou-Marcoullis, captures the beauty and the rich ancient cultural heritage of this island at the crossroads be-tween Europe, Africa and Asia. Today Aphrodite keeps her chin up and has a lot to smile about. The Cypriot population of 741,000, consisting of 82 percent Greek Cypriots and 18 percent Turkish Cyp-riots, enjoys a high standard of living reflected in its U.S. $13,600 per capita income and highlighted in a 60 percent home ownership (20 percent in the 1960s). The Cypriot merchant fleet ranks fifth in the world. And as Ambassador Kozakou-Marcoullis always proudly plugs in, Cyprus has one of the highest literacy rates in the world and ranks third in the proportion of University graduates. What is more remarkable about Cyprus's feat in education is the fact that it opened its very first University only in 1992. What is its secret then? Edu-cating its youth abroad, usually in the various European capitals and the United States, after giving them a solid foundation at home. This accounts for the eclecticism and cosmopolitan mind frame of the usu-ally polyglot Cypriot youth.

Another factor in Cyprus's growing prosperity is tourism. Over 2 million tourists flock from all over the world to enjoy the intense Mediterranean climate and marvel at the prehistoric settlements, the archaic statuary and pottery, the ancient Greek temples, Roman theatres and villas, the early Christian basilicas, Byzantine churches and monasteries, the Crusader castles, Gothic churches, Venetian fortifications and Islamic architecture of this large outdoor museum. The good side of the conquest coin is the multitude of cultural influences left on the island. Cypriots are particularly proud of the way they arranged these layers of culture creatively, crafting something uniquely Cypriot. Add to those layers a layer of hospitality coupled with a superb cuisine and divine wine and a high standard of service and you have your recipe for a successful tourism industry. Other sectors of the economy have also banked on and benefited from the know-how of the population. Its strategic location, coupled with its developed socioeconomic infrastructure, telecommunications, sophisticated banking system, quality of professional services and a favorable economic and business environment, has made Cyprus an ideal center for international business.

But this snapshot of the island nation bathing in the Mediterranean Sea, geographically closer to Africa and the Middle East but turned towards Europe would be flawed if its struggle of the past decades were omitted. From the early 1900s until the 1950s the Greek Cypriot majority aimed at uniting the island with Greece. The movement culminated in the formation of EOKA (Ethniki Organosis Kypriakou Agonos or National Organization of Cypriot Struggle) targeting British colonial rule. The outcome of the anti-colonial struggle in the 1950s was the independence of Cyprus proclaimed in 1960. The first elected president of Cyprus was Archbishop Makarios III and the first vice-president Dr. Fazil Kutchuk. Intercommunal violence broke out in 1963 and Turkey threatened to intervene. A United Nations Peace Keeping Force was sent to Cyprus in 1964 in the interest of preserving international peace and security and to help restore law and order. But then came "Operation Atila" or the Turkish military invasion of Cyprus in 1974 and the occupation of 37 percent of the territory of the island Republic. As with all military interventions, immeasurable human suffering and material loss ensued pushing the nascent republic to the brink of total collapse. For example, in the aftermath of the war Cyprus had lost 70 percent of its economic potential and 65 percent of its hotels. Its newly inaugurated airport had suffered severe damages and was rendered inaccessible to the government.

Today there are still 35,000 Turkish troops on Cypriot soil and the 200,000 Greek Cypriots (one-third of the population), who were evicted from their homes during the intervention, remain refugees in their own country. The purely humanitarian problem of the missing Cypriots still remains unresolved. Tens of thousands of settlers, mostly from Anatolia, have been transferred to the occupied part of Cyprus which in 1983 was unilaterally declared a separate state, the self-styled "Turkish Republic of Northern Cyprus," an entity not recognized by any country other than Turkey. The United Nations Security Council "considered the declaration as legally invalid and called for its withdrawal." It further "called upon all States not to recognize the purported state of the 'Turkish Republic of Northern Cyprus' set up by secessionist acts and called upon them not to facilitate or in any way assist the secessionist entity" (SC Res. 541 [1983] and 550 [1984]). Many ancient historical sites have been plundered and Nicosia, the capital, remains the only divided capital in the world.

Through the adoption of numerous resolutions, the Security Council of the United Nations "reaffirmed that the status quo is unacceptable" and established the parameters for a just and viable solution: "A Cyprus settlement must be based on a State of Cyprus with a single sovereignty and international personality and a single citizenship, with its independence and territorial integrity safeguarded, and comprising two politically equal communities as described by the relevant Security Council resolutions, in a bi-communal and bi-zonal federation, and that such a settlement must exclude union in whole or in part with any other country or any form of partition or secession" (SC Res. 1251 [1999]). Accession to the European Union, earmarked for 2003, is also believed to act as a catalyst for the solution of the Cyprus problem. It is clear that the accession of a united, demilitarized Cyprus would bring prosperity and security for all Cypriots. Whilst a solution prior to accession is the goal, it is not, however, as the Helsinki EU Summit declared in December 1999, a precondition for accession.

In order to move towards demilitarization, seal the peace and enter the European Union, Cyprus has to play its best cards. On the international scene the island's major asset is its savvy diplomatic corps.

Although steeped in patriarchal traditions, Cyprus did not hesitate to call on a woman to represent it in Washington. Educated at the University of Helsinki, Finland where she obtained a Ph.D. in the social sciences and at the University of Athens, Greece where she received a degree of law and political science, Ambassador Erato Kozakou Marcoullis is one of the world's most seasoned diplomats. The list is impressive: Consul of Cyprus in New York (1982–83), Member of the Permanent Mission of Cyprus to the United Nations in New York (1983–88), First Political Division on the Cyprus Question (1989–93), Director of the Office of the Permanent Secretary at the Ministry of Foreign Affairs (1993–96), Ambassador Extraordinary and Plenipotentiary to Sweden and also accredited to Norway, Finland, Denmark, Iceland, Estonia, Latvia and Lithuania. As of September 1998 she is the Ambassador Extraordinary and Plenipotentiary to the United States of America. She is also accredited as High Commissioner to Canada and is Ambassador designate to Brazil and High Commissioner designate to Bahamas, Barbados, Jamaica and Guyana.

I visited Ambassador Erato Kozakou-Marcoullis in the winter of 1999. Her embassy is discretely tucked on R Street on the uphill side where finding parking is a true sport. The flag shows a yellow map of Cyprus underlined by two olive branches against a white background. By staying away from the usual geometric designs the Cypriots have managed to add a warm inviting note to something as official as a flag. Ambassador Erato Kozakou-Marcoullis greets me in this large light wood patrician house with blue and pink saroukh rugs with a big hug and smile as bright as her sun shaped broach. Her demeanor is frank, straightforward and untampered by conformist distance and conventional stiffness. I feel as though I have known her a very long time. Once I sit down and am offered Cypriot coffee, I begin to imagine the place overlooking some cave or an ancient site in Famagusta or Limassol and the ambassador/poet writing a poem.

The interview is preceded by a lesson in various Mediterranean coffees. I pay more attention to the beautiful china than to the coffee which, in my lay appreciation of coffee, tastes like Turkish coffee or even like the one I had at the embassy of Macedonia. In my cup of coffee the foam has the shape of the map of Italy. The Ambassador remarks "If you were in Cyprus people would interpret this as a sign that you will either travel to Italy or have some type of connection with Italy."

MLS: The *Washington Post* describes the diplomatic corps as a "men's club." What has been your experience so far in Washington?

Ambassador Marcoullis: If one reads the diplomatic list it is obvious that from 180 embassies and missions in Washington, D.C. there are only eleven women ambassadors out of a total number of 172 missions. This is of course a very small number. To a great extent it is a man's world as far as Washington, D.C. is concerned. This is not the case as far as some of the European posts are concerned. For example in Sweden, there were fourteen women ambassadors out of ninety. I am glad to see that there is a steady increase in the number of women ambassadors in Washington, D.C. Out of eight, three years ago, we have now reached the number of eleven. This is a very positive sign.

MLS: What are some of the pluses and minuses in being a woman ambassador in Washington?

Marcoullis: I personally do not see any minuses. I only see pluses. Not because I am always a positive thinker in my approach. Being a woman ambassador is . . . first of all I do not see any difference being a woman ambassador. We are all diplomats and we are trying to do our job the best way we can to represent and serve the interests of our country in the country where we are posted. The distinct plus that I would see is that being a woman and being among a small group of women ambassadors is a very positive sign for my country. There is a very positive reaction, not only on the part of my other colleagues, but also particularly from people from the administration and in the wider American society about the fact that my country has appointed a woman in this so very important post. Otherwise, there is no difference. I am treated the same way as my male colleagues.

MLS: If I asked whether your life as a diplomat conflicts with your personal life would you take it as an unfair question that would not have been asked of your male colleagues?

Marcoullis: The life of a diplomat is difficult whether you are a man or a woman. It involves a lot of traveling. It involves being transferred from one post to the other. I know a number of male colleagues who have been separated from their families. That is also my situation. My husband is in Cyprus. He is a medical doctor, an oncologist/hematologist. He has a distinguished medical career in Cyprus. It is not possible for him to move around with me. I was really fortunate to have had his full support throughout my career. I think this is important whether you are a female or a male diplomat, especially an ambassador. Responsibilities are carried through more effectively if you have the support of your family. I have one son who is studying in the United States. He does visit me. Now it is much easier that we are in the same country. When I was in Sweden all three of us lived in three different countries.

MLS: What was the reaction of your compatriots at the news of your appointment?

Marcoullis: From the expressions of congratulations I have received, it was a very positive reaction, particularly on the part of women. Many women expressed their pleasure and satisfaction of the fact that a woman was selected to become ambassador to Washington. I still receive a lot of expressions of satisfaction and pride of the fact that a woman is representing them in this challenging post. This is the first time that a woman represents Cyprus in the United States. However, we have five other female ambassadors posted in very important posts: Rome, Strasbourg, Prague, New Delhi, and Beijing. We have six women ambassadors out of a total of thirty-two, if we count three consulates it is a total of thirty-five. It is one of the highest proportions of women ambassadors in the world. Being a small country we do not have as many diplomatic missions abroad as larger countries.

MLS: When was the first woman appointed ambassador in Cyprus?

Marcoullis: Cyprus does not have a long record. This is a very recent phenomenon. The first woman ambassador from Cyprus was appointed in 1993. She was appointed as ambassador to Beijing. Currently she is Cyprus's ambassador to Rome. She paved the way for others. Mrs. Kleopas set a good example showing that women can do the job. She was a good example for us to follow. After her appointment, came my appointment and the other appointments. Always someone has to pave the way. In Cyprus we do not have political appointments. We are all career diplomats. Women entered the diplomatic service in Cyprus quite late. This is primarily the reason why there were no women ambassadors prior to 1993. They had not reached the necessary level at the diplomatic service to enable them to be eligible for an ambassadorial appointment. Now that there are quite a number of women who have reached that level, it is logically a time for women to be appointed.

MLS: Did the ratio of women graduating from universities play a role in women moving to diplomatic careers, Cyprus having a high percentage of educated women?

Marcoullis: In general, Cyprus has one of the highest records in the world for university graduates. Out of the university graduates, the majority are women. Education is very important for the Cypriots. Cypriot women have a tendency to study more than in other countries. This has played a very important role in the transformation of our society and in enabling women to participate in areas traditionally occupied by men. Of course, there are still many obstacles and traditional attitudes and women are still not represented well in decision-making positions, but we are getting there.

MLS: Do you foresee an increase in the number of women ambassadors?

Marcoullis: Yes. In fact, during the last recruitment we had, the vast majority of the recruits were women. The year before they were fifty-fifty. More and more women choose the diplomatic service as their career. This will lead gradually to the appointment of more women in the future.

MLS: What was your husband's reaction at the news of your appointment?

Marcoullis: He was very glad. He was very glad both for the first appointment as ambassador to Sweden and for the present appointment. He has always been very supportive. He is a true feminist and he believes in me. He has always been with me, supporting what I am doing. Without his support and encouragement I could not have managed to reach so high.

MLS: Is it a tendency among Cypriot men to support their spouses in their career?

Marcoullis: The young generation (insisting), the young generation yes. Certainly because in their generation young men and women study together and they appreciate the fact that women are studying and devoting so much of their youth in higher education. The mentality and the attitudes are so different in the young generation from the older generation.

MLS: You are representing a country that is located in a rather (to use an expression used before by Secretary Albright) "dangerous neighborhood." Is there a specific challenge in representing Cyprus in the United States?

Marcoullis: Certainly there is a particular challenge. First of all, as you know, we have a very serious problem. This problem is, of course, the occupation of 37 percent of the territory of Cyprus by Turkey and the forcible division of the country and the people that has been going on for a quarter of a century. My most important task in this country as the ambassador of Cyprus is to try to project our point of view on the situation. Most of my time is devoted to this issue rather than other bilateral issues, which, of course, are important, such as economic and trade ties. Some of my colleagues are devoting more time to those issues. My particular challenge is to see how best I can explain our point of view on the situation to the administration, to the Congress, to the think tanks, to state and local authorities, to the universities, to the media. My message is very simple and very clear. That twenty-five years of forcible division of the country and the people, twenty-five years of suffering and pain, are twenty-five years too long. A solution is long overdue. The United States as the only remaining superpower could play a very important role in this direction and we count a lot on this country's active involvement. The fact that we are in a region that is very critical is also a reason to attract attention to a solution of the Cyprus problem because we believe that such a solution could be a source of stability and peace for the whole region. Now that efforts to move the peace process forward in the Middle East, another hot-bed of tension in the area, are on the right track, if there is a similar movement to solve the Cyprus problem, then we will have two issues that have created tension for such a long time become bridges of peace and prosperity. Of course, that will be to the interest of the countries and the peoples in the area, but also to the interest of the United States. Also our special bond with Europe poses a challenge. We are among the six candidate countries that have started negotiations for accession to the European Union. Our special relationship with the EU and the very friendly ties we maintain with both Israel and all the Arab countries in the area are a very important factor in using Cyprus as a bridge between Europe and the Middle East. These are some of the challenges I try to project.

MLS: Did the Turkish invasion and occupation of 37 percent of Cyprus on July 20, 1974, hamper or slow down Cypriot integration in the European Union? Although you serve in a non-European country, how would you like the host country to perceive Cyprus on the diplomatic and political scene in Europe?

Marcoullis: The Turkish invasion and occupation of 1974 has certainly hampered and slowed down the integration of Cyprus in the European Union. Socioeconomic development, which was rapid during the years that followed the independence in 1960, was utterly disrupted by the Turkish military intervention and the occupation of one third of the territory. The area occupied was the most productive and developed part of Cyprus, particularly for agriculture (control of 41 percent of livestock and 48 percent of agricultural exports) and tourism (seizure of 65 percent of hotel and tourist establishments). The only deep-water port of Famagusta, that handled 83 percent of the cargo, was occupied and the only International Airport in Nicosia was heavily destroyed and now lies closed in the buffer zone. An additional factor for the slow down of the economic development was the forcible displacement of one third of the population and the seizure of their lands and properties in the occupied areas. Cyprus had already signed an Association Agreement with the then European Economic Community in 1972 but the catastrophic effects of the invasion on the economy delayed the implementation of the Agreement and particularly its second stage for a Customs Union. The government of Cyprus submitted its application for membership of the European Communities on July 4, 1990, when economic recovery from the devastating effects of the invasion was achieved. The road towards membership was opened and the developments towards that end are now rapidly on their way. Cyprus, as you know, started accession negotiations in March 1998 and substantive negotiations in November of the same year. In fact Cyprus is leading the group of six candidate countries in its harmonization with the Acquis Communautaire. The United States, although not a member of the European Union, has openly supported Cyprus' EU accession process and we are grateful for that. Cyprus has been a very active member of all intergovernmental organizations within Europe in which we belong culturally, politically and economically. Membership of Cyprus in the European Union would be to the benefit of all the people of Cyprus, particularly to the benefit of the Turkish Cypriot community. It would also be to the benefit of peace, stability and prosperity not only for Cyprus itself, but also for the whole region. These are the benefits that I try to explain to all my interlocutors here in the host country and I believe that they are well received.

MLS: Cyprus' international issues concern Britain, Greece and Turkey. Describe the relations you wish existed between Cyprus and these three countries.

Marcoullis: All three countries, Britain, Greece and Turkey are guarantor powers of the independence of the Republic of Cyprus. According to the Treaty of Guarantee of 1960, these three countries undertook by their signature to guarantee the independence, sovereignty and territorial integrity of the Republic of Cyprus. Regrettably, one of the guarantor powers, Turkey violated with its invasion the very independence, sovereignty and territorial integrity of Cyprus that it undertook to guarantee. She continues to violate it as a result of the occupation of 37 percent of Cypriot territory by Turkish troops. We would certainly want this unacceptable situation to come to an end. We would certainly want to see Turkey complying with the many binding resolutions of the UN Security Council that call for the withdrawal of its troops, the return of the refugees and respect for the sovereignty, independence, territorial integrity and unity of Cyprus. With Britain and Greece we maintain excellent relations and cooperation in all spheres. We would certainly like to see such relations develop also with Turkey in the future. For this to happen, of course, Turkey must withdraw its occupation troops from our territories and cooperate for a solution that would allow the reunification of the country and its people, in a bizonal and bicommunal federation, as agreed by the leaders of the two communities in 1977 and 1979 and as endorsed by the international community in numerous United Nations resolutions. Cyprus could then be a source of peace, stability and prosperity for the whole region.

MLS: Cyprus is turned towards Europe. Talks have begun in late 1998 regarding full membership in the Union by the year 2003. But your role in Washington is nevertheless very important. What are the most challenging aspects of your role as an ambassador of Cyprus to the sole superpower presenting Cyprus within the European context?

Marcoullis: Our journey to membership of the European Union is irreversible. Actual membership could be around 2003 or 2004 depending, of course, on the specific decisions of the European Union countries. Cyprus will be ready much earlier, anyway. We have taken our role of preparing for membership very seriously and we are working very hard to harmonize our legislation with the European Union Acquis. Our only problem is the political problem of the forcible division of Cyprus. We hope that by that time, through the efforts of the international community, particularly of the only superpower, the United States, a solution will be found and Cyprus will join the EU as a reunified country. We shall do our utmost to achieve that through the cooperation and political will that we have consistently shown. But, if by the time of the next enlargement, a solution of the political problem is not within reach because of the lack of political will of the Turkish side, then it would be unfair and unjust to victimize Cyprus for Turkey's intransigence. From now until the next enlargement we have plenty of time and we hope that the United States, that has been so instrumental in bringing other international problems towards a solution, will also put its political weight and exert its influence to convince Turkey to cooperate. Such a contribution on the part of the United States towards the realization of a just and viable solution of the Cyprus problem, also would be a contribution towards a smooth and complete enlargement of the European Union. Such a development would be to the benefit of everyone, the EU itself, the United States and all countries in the region, including Turkey and its European orientation.

MLS: Your embassy participates in Cypriot cultural activities in Washington in part as a way to promote tourism. What is your outlook on the future of tourism in Cyprus?

Marcoullis: Cyprus has a 9,000-year-old history and civilization and a cultural heritage for which we are very proud. One of my tasks in this country is to project this aspect of Cyprus through different lectures, exhibitions and other activities in Washington and in other states. Cyprus, being a small country, is not known to many Americans. I try to reach out to the people and to make known not only this cultural wealth that Cyprus has to offer to a visitor, ranging from Neolithic sites of the 7th and 4th millennium B.C., ancient theaters of the Greek and Roman periods, Byzantine churches of the 6th century A.D., mosaics, frescoes and icons of magnificent artistry, Gothic churches and Muslim mosques of later periods, but also the natural beauties of sandy beaches, high mountains and lively traditional villages. This cultural and natural richness is the primary attraction for the 2.4 million tourists that arrive to the island each year. Tourism from the United States is not to the extent we would desire, only about 35,000 a year. The majority of tourists come from the United Kingdom, the Nordic and other European

countries. We would wish to see more Americans visit Cyprus and our tourist office in New York is working towards attracting more visitors who could
combine their trip to Cyprus with a visit to Israel, Egypt and other countries
in the region.

MLS: Of all the roles an ambassador fulfills, that of a negotiator, a mediator,
a promoter, which role do you enjoy the most and why?

Marcoullis: Definitely, the role of a promoter. Being an outward personality
by nature, I enjoy meeting and communicating with people and informing
them about my country, its history, its people, its attractions and its poten-
tials. It gives me great satisfaction each time I reach out and my message
goes through. This is why I consider my task as a diplomat and particularly
as an ambassador as a mission and not merely as a profession or simply a
career. The more people I reach the more favorable climate I create about
my country. The more interest I spark, the closer I feel I am to meeting my
goals in this post.

MLS: What is the most delicate aspect of your job as an envoy to Washington?

Marcoullis: Cyprus is a small country. The United States is the only remaining superpower with a different perspective of the world, shaped in line
with its own strategic and other interests. One of my most delicate tasks is
to find the right way to convince my interlocutors in Washington and in
other parts of the country, that a solution of the problem of Cyprus and
reunification of the island would be to the interest not only of the people
of Cyprus themselves and peace and stability in the whole region, but also
to the interest of the United States. I am very cognizant of the difference
in size and political weight in the international scene between our two countries, but I am confident that our message is well received because it is based
on the same values of freedom, democracy, human rights and the rule of
law that the United States is all about.

MLS: Can you tell about the inroads that women in your country and in
your part of the world have made in various fields and about the extent to
which these accomplishments inspired you?

Marcoullis: Definitely southern Europe, where Cyprus lies, has not yet
reached the levels of women's equality achieved by northern Europe, particularly the Nordic countries. I was fortunate to be accredited to all five
Nordic countries and I can say without any hesitation that they have paved
the way for the rest of the world to follow on women's issues. In southern
Europe the advances have been remarkable, especially after World War II,
but still a lot of work lies ahead. Cyprus followed the same path with con-

siderable strides, particularly after independence in 1960. A decisive factor
was the high standard of education of women and the rapid development
of the economy which, despite the heavy blow it suffered as a result of the
Turkish invasion, it was able to recover and flourish again. Women are now
present and active in every profession and there is full equality before the
law. Where we are still lacking is representation of women in decision-
making positions. Although in the very first Cabinet formed after the establishment of the Republic in 1960, a female Minister was named Minister of
Justice, there is presently no woman included in the Council of Ministers.
That first woman, Mrs. Stella Souliotis, who later became Attorney General
of the Republic and Adviser to the President in the intercommunal talks,
was my role model when I was growing up and I sincerely believe that the
appointment of more women in decision-making positions will act as a catalyst for opening up the society and getting rid of stereotypes and traditional
attitudes.

MLS: What are the accomplishments you are the most proud of in your
career?

Marcoullis: Generally, the fact that I succeed to communicate with people
and get my message through in most of the cases. I am also a good listener
and try to perceive the others' point of view. In my work I try to be me-
thodical, something I inherited from my mother, time conscious, prepare
well for every meeting or project and always go beyond the limits of my
potential, missing no opportunity. At the same time I always try to be hu-
mane with my colleagues and staff because I strongly believe that a friendly
environment is the most important ingredient of success. As far as any specific accomplishments that make me proud, I cannot really isolate some from
the rest. I feel as accomplishments all the cases in which I succeeded one
way or the other to strengthen the image of my country and, especially, to
convince people that the shameful division of my country and our people
should come to an end and make them friends of Cyprus.

MLS: Do you believe that women's approach to diplomacy is different from
men?

Marcoullis: No. It is not a matter of man's or woman's approach. It is,
rather, a matter of personal style and character. It is a matter of being a
communicator or a closed personality, an outward or inward looking person.
It is also a matter of being a positive or negative thinker, an optimist or
pessimist. I do not really believe in stereotypes about men's and women's
approaches. The same way one approaches life, irrespective of gender, depending on one's character, the same way one approaches diplomacy.

MLS: What do you want your legacy to be once you leave this post?

Marcoullis: Being the first woman ambassador from my country to be ever appointed as ambassador to the United States, I want to leave behind me a good mark so that I will set a good example for the rest of the women in my country. I wish my legacy to be one of praise not for myself but for women in general, so that it may be obviously proved—what should not have been necessary to be proved in the first place—that women are as equally good as men in all spheres of professional life. I feel this as a great responsibility and I will certainly do my utmost to see that this task is successfully accomplished. I feel indebted to the president of Cyprus for entrusting me with this important mission and I shall do my utmost to meet his expectations.

MLS: You have landed one of the most prestigious posts in diplomacy. What's next careerwise?

Marcoullis: I really do not know. It may seem difficult to believe, but I never make plans or put targets for my career. I, rather, try to concentrate on the present and especially on how to best fulfil my tasks. If you excel in what you do, be it in diplomacy, art, medicine or any other profession, you will inevitably succeed and advance careerwise. My present post entails many challenges but also many responsibilities. I have set a number of goals and I shall try to achieve them the best way I can and the best way I can serve my country's interests. I intend to work hard in order to reach them by the end of my tenure. This is where I want to concentrate at present. What comes next will come as a welcome surprise. . . .

AMBASSADOR IVONNE A-BAKI
OF ECUADOR

© Photo by Albert. Reproduced with
permission.

On a road in Lebanon she hit his car in an accident. It was love at first
sight, or should we say at first crash. A year later they were married. She
was only sixteen. Her husband's family, the A-Bakis from Lebanon,
had a burning passion for politics. And so did her family in Ecuador. So
young Ivonne, a straight-A student who completed high school at age
fifteen grew up with politics. If one were to give her biography a title, it
would be one with a literary ring to it, "War and Peace." When the war
broke out in Lebanon, she became an unwilling witness to its horrors
and vowed to become an advocate for peace. And so she did. Becoming a major peacebroker in the settlement of her country's border dis-

pute with Peru is one in a long list of her accomplishments. Her whole
life is a class act combining eclecticism, peace activism, vision, charm,
great parenting skills, a passion for languages—she speaks seven of
them—and for art. Along the road she studied art at the Sorbonne in
Paris, gathered a degree in architecture from the Arab University in
Beirut and a master's degree from the Harvard School of Government
while raising her three children.

I met with the incredible Ambassador A-Baki in her embassy in the
summer of 1999. Her office is a wonderful art gallery filled with her
own paintings. I asked her about the significance of the painting located across her imposing desk.

It is a painting called "Bureaucracy." It is about bureaucracy in Latin America and in Ecuador. It is about the vicious circles of power. The people try
to make a difference and to go through these circles of power. Those in
power would not let them reach the upper circles. Only very few of them,
the stronger ones manage to reach the circles of power. But they are so few
that they get absorbed and assimilated into the system. But since I am an
optimist, the symbolic green dominant color evokes the hope of change. If
you do not have hope, you lose everything.

Her explanations accompanied with ample gestures are in French, one
of our common languages. The diplomat, world renowned artist and
grandmother with the toned and shapely figure of a tango dancer has
such an appetite for life that words come gushing out of her mouth. In
her precipitous rhythm she switches from one language to the other.

She explains the next painting in perfect German, her eyes glitter-
ing. "This painting is about the ascension of a woman. She has tried
everything on earth and now she is ascending to connect to another
level," she begins. It is apparent that the painting is also about her
and her own introspection.

The very dramatic Ambassador A-Baki comes to Washington at a
crucial time to represent a country ridden with debt and poverty.
Ecuador, a nation of twelve million inhabitants is currently going
through one of its worst financial crises. To represent them in Washington, Ecuadorians have put their faith in this complex intellectual
with a passion for life, their beacon of hope.

MLS: Since the discovery of oil in the 1970s there have been some tensions
with neighboring Peru. These have been solved. Now what role do you see
your country having in its region?

Ambassador A-Baki: I am glad that you asked this question. First let me say that our border dispute with Peru (which has been resolved) went back to the independence days in the nineteenth century. Oil has never been a source of conflict with Peru. I lived a long time in the Middle East. I believe that most of the countries that have oil have a problem. Studies have been conducted on the issue. Dependency is always a problem, particularly in the case of oil. In countries where there is oil there is sometimes the feeling that there is nothing else do to except depending on the oil. Other activities that could balance the economy are not undertaken. A drop of oil can create a lot of chaos. Of course, Ecuador has also bananas, which is our number one export, and shrimp. It has many resources. In addition to the problem of the falling oil prices, we had the problem of El Niño which devastated completely the coastal area and stopped transportation. All the bridges were broken. We could not transport our products.

Countries that have oil should decide not to depend so much on oil because one never knows what can happen in the future. Oil is definitely a curse. Ecuador is an amazing country that has so much to give to the world. It has so many different regions. We have the Amazon. We have the Andes mountains. We have the coast and we have the Galapagos Islands. It is not a big country but it is a very peaceful one. We are not plagued with narco traffic and guerrilla problems. It does not mean that Ecuador is totally immune to them. Ecuador has a lot of untapped potential. I see Ecuador as a country that can be an example to others if it [were] well administered. It is a place where environment plays an important role because it has a huge Amazon area.

MLS: How would you like the international community to view your country?

A-Baki: I am trying to get the message across that Ecuador is a place that the international community should see as an example of how different kinds of people are living together peacefully. We do have many political problems. If they were to be solved and if we were to be self-sufficient, Ecuador could be an example. It would be a place of unity. It could be a paradise.

MLS: How do you perceive your role in Washington, D.C.? Do you see your role as being that of a promoter, a negotiator, a mediator?

A-Baki: When I was appointed here I viewed my role as that of a promoter of Ecuador. I saw Ecuador as an oasis in the region. But the economic problems worsened. Now I mainly negotiate with the World Bank, the InterAmerican Development Bank (IDB), the International Monetary Fund (IMF), the State Department, with Treasury, with the White House to help Ecuador overcome the situation it is going through which is the worst ever. We are now facing a combination of problems—the effects of El Niño, the falling oil prices, the structural problems of the past and the global economic problems that affect Brazil and had their ripple effects on Ecuador. The social impact is devastating. Poverty is rampant. A country that is so rich is living the worst situation ever because of poverty. When people start sifting through garbage, the situation is at its worst. America and any country for that matter cannot be indifferent to such situations because the world is so interconnected. If a situation worsens in one country, the entire region could be affected. That was the case with the cholera epidemic in Ecuador in 1991. It affected tourism. For us it meant a huge health problem. But it also affected the United States in the sense that it meant less bookings for American travel agents specialized in our region.

Latin America expects more support from the United States. The Americas should be more united, should be more stable and should rely on a strong middle class. There should be a strong middle class in the Americas. In Ecuador we do not have a strong middle class. Our poverty level is very high. One percent of our population owns 40 percent of the resources. Our annual income per capita is a reasonable $1,070 but most of it is due to the wealthy one percent. More than 75 percent of our population lives below the poverty level. This is really sad. In the Americas we should support each other and think of the whole continent rather than in terms of individual countries. That is where the role of women could be used more. Men are great politicians and negotiators but women see things in a different way. Men and women should work in tandem. They complement each other in their work. Women try to unite instead of separate. Therefore, there should be more women in diplomacy, in politics, in key positions. Women are mothers. How can you imagine that you as a mother, you have a child and you see another child that is dying in front of you? You will not accept that situation. You will do everything to help out. That is the role of women. Women tend to see the whole instead of the part.

MLS: In Washington you devote more time to which aspect of your work?

A-Baki: It is like having a patient in front of you that is dying. You call the doctor and the doctor says "Let the nurse check the heart rate and when the heart rate reaches a certain level, and only then, call me." When the doctor finally comes, it is too late; the patient is dead. What do you need the doctor for? We need immediate attention. Of course, with the United States relations are very dynamic and every day there are important issues in the political, commercial and cultural aspects that have to be dealt with. I would love to devote more time to cultural events. I do cultural events promoting Ecuadorian art and music. I believe that art—all kinds of art—is a way of going beyond conflict. It is a means of conflict resolution. We have showcased the cultural potential of Ecuador, tourism and other aspects of our country.

MLS: What is the most challenging aspect of your work? Is it making American lawmakers understand what your country is going through? Is it making the World Bank or the IMF see your point of view? Is it obtaining a good deal on a loan for your country?

A-Baki: It is all of the above. At the moment, the main objective is trying to secure an agreement with the IMF so we can get funds from the IDB and the World Bank.

MLS: What is the most delicate aspect of your work?

A-Baki: Trying to convey to the American government and to multilateral institutions in Washington the efforts being made by the government I represent to strengthen democracy, combat poverty and eliminate corruption. It is crucial that we obtain their full support so we can achieve these objectives. Ecuador is divided into the coast and the mountains. Our Congress is also divided between the coastal area and the mountain area. We do not have a majority in the Congress. There are divisions. There are often frictions. It is difficult to pass any law in our Congress. The President would love to comply with the IMF, but those laws would not pass in the Congress. If you cannot pass those bills, what do you do? Do you dissolve the Congress and go against democracy or do you choose to negotiate? Our president is trying to keep democracy; so we negotiate and try to get the most out of negotiation. That is what I am trying to convey here.

MLS: Is democracy too often too loosely applied? Is it used as a buzz word? Shouldn't there be some variations on the theme of democracy?

A-Baki: I agree with you. Democracy is a word that is too loosely applied. It is a concept that should be applied according to the individual needs of each country. It should be molded by the cultural system of each country. You have to go according to what you are. You cannot bring something that works in one place and apply it to another place hoping it might also work there. It is a step-by-step process. Democracy is a very good concept. The example of the United States is an amazing one, but it does not mean that this system will work in every place the way it does here. The success of democracy depends on the people. It depends on education. It depends on opening up. Without all these ingredients there can be no real democracy.

MLS: Should there be variations of democracy or various levels of democracy?

A-Baki: There should be variations that are universally accepted.

MLS: To which extent would you adhere to the motto "trade not aid"?

A-Baki: The aid that we are getting is not grants. It is all credit. Even for the phenomenon of El Niño which had such devastating effects, we did not get any grant. We are deep in debt. We never got grants. Our country is very rich in resources but is now going through a very difficult time. I am working with the Congress and trying to make them see that. Other countries obtained aid when they were ravaged by hurricane Mitch. We did not. We are still feeling the effects of El Niño. Trade and investment are of course key elements in the promotion of growth and development.

MLS: Bananas are the main crop of export. However it is a sector that is very volatile, is very much under siege, and that has known some very difficult times due to falling prices and due to the banana war. Can you describe where your country fits in that agri-war?

A-Baki: Ecuador is the largest exporter of bananas in the world. We have 5,000 independent growers. Ten percent of our population depends on the banana industry. We have major companies involved in the international trade of bananas. For all those reasons Ecuador has played a pivotal role in the banana controversy with the EU. We want fair access to that market in a WTO compatible fashion.

MLS: How important are foreign languages in diplomacy?

A-Baki: Languages are extremely important in diplomacy. Their knowledge allows the understanding of culture. Knowledge of foreign languages is about connecting. It is about understanding. It is not just about applying some rule. Before applying any rule to a people, one has to understand its culture first and foremost. All the rules exist because of a lack of communication. The three misses—miscommunication, misunderstanding, misinterpretation—plague us. It is because we do not understand the people and their culture that we have miscommunication and conflict in the world. We have to understand how the others think before doing anything. That again is the role of women. Men tend to be more power oriented. Maybe it has to do with the way they were brought up to provide, to bring the bread, to fight, to defend. Women tend to be more analytical. The heart and the brain have to work together. To have that kind of understanding you have to understand the human. To understand the human you have to understand the culture, the language and the belief system in which the human operates. You have to give love and communicate. The word love has been so often misused. Love is a word that should be used more and generate pride. If we do not love, we know nothing in the world. It is love that connects us as humans.

Languages are extremely important in diplomacy and otherwise. I often hear people who have visited France say of the French "they are such snobs." It is not true; the French are not snobs. When people do not know the language of the country they visit, they experience a barrier. In diplomacy it is very important to speak fluently the language of the host country in order to remove barriers. It is a better way of negotiating especially when you have such a good command of the language that you can appreciate all its nuances and have a good accent. There is a saying that in translation something is always lost. Similarly, the negotiator who has to bring along a translator loses big time.

MLS: You speak Arabic, French, English, German, Spanish, Italian and some Russian. How does the knowledge of foreign languages make a difference?

A Baki: That's correct. I believe that so many conflicts could be avoided by focusing on the knowledge of foreign languages and the appreciation of various cultures. What is negotiation? It is communication, understanding, and common interest in solving a problem. When communication is facilitated by thorough knowledge of a common language, it is a win-win situation. Without good communication the negotiation process takes much longer. It takes more effort. The outcome is less obvious. It is a lost opportunity.

MLS: Negotiating through an interpreter is obviously very different from having full command of the language and communicating directly.

A-Baki: It is like going to the movies and enjoying a film through subtitles. It is not a direct contact.

MLS: Which accomplishment are you the most proud of?

A-Baki: My children. I have three children—two boys and a girl. I married extremely young. I was sixteen when I got married. I have three [children] that I am very proud of. The best things you can give your children are good values and a very good education. Once they have that they can be thrown into the world. My eldest son, Mohammad, lives in New York. He works for Merrill Lynch. He did his undergraduate studies in Princeton and a Ph.D. in economics at Yale. My other son, Faisal, studied at Harvard. He is an economist. He is working now in Ecuador. My daughter, Tatiana, also graduated from Harvard. She has a degree in Philosophy, in German and French literature. I am pleased about the balance they have in their lives. They have developed not only technical skills but also their artistic side. They love music, art, poetry. They all have these sides which is the right balance. It enables them to connect with people. I learn from my children. Children teach you so much. I talk to them every day on the phone. It is not only important to give them much but also to listen to them. It is crucial to listen to the new generation, to their needs. We would be in a better position if we could only listen to the youth. We do not give enough attention to how they think. And they are so perceptive of everything.

MLS: Is Washington your first post?

A-Baki: I am not a career diplomat. I am a political appointee. As an ambassador Washington is my first post. I was honorary Consul General to Lebanon for fourteen years, all through the war. I was Consul General to Boston. These were political posts. I consider diplomacy my career. Most of my life I have worked as a diplomat.

As a consul in Lebanon I lived the war. That is why I care so much for peace. When you listen to war, when you live it, when you are a witness to what happens, to people dying in front of you, when you realize that you are unable to do more, that the politicians are dividing instead of reaching a solution, that the process of finding a solution takes forever, then you understand that it is your role to try to work more towards peace. As an artist I was using art for political issues. My art is very political. Then at Harvard I learned the art of politics.

MLS: You are the first woman ambassador of Ecuador?

A-Baki: I am the first Ecuadorian woman ambassador to Washington. There are very few women ambassadors in Ecuador. You can count them on one hand. This is a recent phenomenon.

MLS: What is the extent of the involvement of women in politics in your country?

A-Baki: Now in this government women have taken an active role. It is recent. I was amazed to see that. In Ecuador we recently had a woman vice-president in the previous government, Rosalia Artiaga. She ran as candidate for president. There were two women in fact running as presidential candidates. We have several women in Congress who are very active. In the new government we have, for the first time, women in cabinet positions. The Minister of Finance is a woman; so are the Ministers of Environment, of Education and of Tourism. It is a sudden change, a move forward. I think it is very progressive. I was one that was often criticizing the absence of women on the political scene. I lived in Lebanon where women were also not very visible in politics. "What is stopping us from being more and doing more in politics?" I often asked myself. I think we have reached a time when women are realizing that they too can be movers and shakers. It is not useful to say that "It is a man's world and the men are not letting us achieve." It is a matter of us women deciding that we are ready and have the motivation. Women should encourage each other. Often the enemy of a woman is another woman. We should encourage and promote each other. This is precisely why I was so happy to find out about the work you are doing for the advancement of women. That's the way to have women feel more secure about their role. Women always think they are second. They should feel equal. We have an equal right. Our role is even more important because we raise the generations. We are the mothers which is the most difficult and the most important role ever. Why should we feel intimidated about anything else when we have the most important role. Who brought up these "important" men? It is usually the mother. So why should we be intimidated of being out there and showing our feelings that are different? We do not have to compete with men. We do not have to become men. We have to stay women and feminine and show our feelings in our own words and not try to be hard and tough, just to be accepted in this men's world. We women should not confuse toughness and inner strength. Men tend to want to appear tough. Inner strength is, however, more crucial and women should remember that.

MLS: Women have accomplished a lot recently in Ecuador. What do you wish women in Ecuador?

A-Baki: I wish they would even accomplish more. That is one of my main issues. I have co-founded a foundation in Ecuador with another woman who is now the Consul in Boston. The foundation is called "Beyond Boundaries Foundation." This foundation started two years ago to help Ecuador. Our main goals are the preservation of culture and motivating women. In order to preserve culture you need the input of women. We started our work in Esmeralda which is a black community in Ecuador. The community was ridden with diseases and lack of education. What we found was amazing. Women there were born leaders. They were the leaders that were pushing to make a difference. If you start motivating women who already have leadership in them, the results are amazing. Everything is already inside of us. It is by motivating, by encouraging, by educating, by giving someone a chance that you create an amazing difference. We do mostly motivational work. Diseases affect so much the region that we also have to help in public health. You cannot achieve motivation if health and education are not taken care of. So we went back to the basics and dealt with those two issues.

If we had more involvement of women in the political arena, it would be helpful not only for Ecuador but for the whole region. The other countries should do the same and they are doing it. Colombia, Peru, Venezuela, all over Latin America you see more woman involvement than before.

Have you noticed that non-governmental organizations (NGOs) are now in a way reaching the role of government. Who is usually heading the NGOs? Women. Women could not be out there in the world of politics so they have taken over the NGOs. Now the NGOs are taken seriously. In many countries to get something done you go through an NGO. NGOs are a form of parallel government.

MLS: Do you believe that women have a different approach to diplomacy?

A-Baki: I will say "yes" and "no." You cannot generalize. If a woman could be really who she is, she would have a different approach. Sometimes we are not doing what we think we should do. Deep inside a woman would have a different approach to diplomacy. It would be an approach that includes more her heart, her feelings, her genuine interest in the people. Sometimes we do not follow that route—and I include myself in it—because we think it is not the right moment because we think that we lose.

MLS: And also perhaps because there is already a pre-established world that is already organized mostly by men and where women have to fit in.

A-Baki: That's true. If women were together more, we would make the changes that are needed in this established male order. It is so difficult. How can a woman alone affect change in a system that was long established by men. As a group women have a different approach. It will take some time. I notice when we the women ambassadors to Washington meet as a group, it is an amazingly different energy. If you were to ask me at that moment whether we see things differently, I would say "yes." When I am in my group of ambassadors from Latin America where I am currently the only woman, I see myself as sometimes accepting their male way of dealing with issues. The parameters are already set and you can break but so many of them.

To give you a concrete example, when women are asked to make a choice to allocate funds to an education project or to a technology project, they would usually choose to allocate funds to the more people oriented project, in this case to education. Men would invariably choose technology. That has been my observation. Men are more "toy" oriented. No matter how much technology we have, if we do not have the right education, we will not have a strong society. Look at the state of the economy in the world now. Yet we have so many economists but there are still huge disparities and a great deal of poverty. Why? Because we are putting the money in things that are not essential. We should be more people oriented. We should worry about providing a strong basis and creating a strong middle class all over the world. Male politicians are beginning to see that because they have gone too far. I hope it is not too late.

Women will make a difference in the future. They will not invest so much in armament, bombs and other such technologies. What is power? Does power mean concentrating on having more of that when we still have people dying of hunger in the majority of the world?

I am sure there are quite a few studies on the topic. I am not sure whether the behavior of men has to do with socialization or with their testosterone levels. It has perhaps to do with the way they were brought up to provide, to bring the bread, to fight, to defend.

Women are very suited for politics because, as I said, women are more people oriented. And it is the people who elect the politicians.

MLS: Who are some of your role models?

A-Baki: Mahatma Gandhi. Gandhi is important to me because he made a difference without title. I would also say Socrates because he died for the people and was convinced that everything is inside the individual and that it is through questioning that things will come out. Of course I admire Simon Bolivar because he wanted to unite the Americas. I admire Vaclav Havel because he is a combination of politics and art. All these people have made a difference.

If I were to talk about women role models, I would tend to admire women who have made a difference while retaining their feminity. I could not really evoke Margaret Thatcher or Golda Meir, although they made a tremendous difference, because they are women in male molds. Indira Gandhi was certainly a role model for me. So was Evita Peron. Evita was for the people, but her ambition grew out of revenge over her past. When you get to certain positions you have to put the past to rest and forget about your issues of anger when you want to accomplish something. But overall I admire her. She made a big difference. I admire Benazir Bhutto. She tried very hard and what happened to her political life is a bit sad. In general I tend to admire less women who have inherited the mantle of their fathers or their husbands. Joan of Arc and Cleopatra, I certainly admire. Mariam, the wife of prophet Mohammed, was a wonderful figure. Why is it that now we do not have more larger than life women figures emerging?

MLS: Out of 190 countries you can count on one hand the number of women presidents. How do you think women will fare in the next century?

A-Baki: I see the twenty-first century as the century of the advancement of women. Women will be more visible. They will be more secure and will not be afraid. Most women do not get in the political arena because of their family. They feel that they will lose. The reality is that if they do not go out there they will lose their families, their countries and the world.

MLS: Many said the same thing about the 1920s when women in many countries were acquiring the right to vote. It was a time of hope for women. There was momentum. Then things sort of fizzled out.

A-Baki: It was different then. We have come a long way. Change takes time. Now the thing is more ripe and ready.

MLS: What do you think of large conferences on the advancement of women such as the Beijing conference?

A-Baki: You are going to get upset with me, but I do not think much of those conferences. I gave a talk about the Beijing conference. If I were the organizer of such a conference, I would not put the word "women" in the title. I would use the title "Conference for Social Change" for example. I would still gather a majority of women at that conference. By using the word "women" we are showing that we still have to prove something. The Women's Museum of the Arts here I would call it "Smithsonian Part I" or "Smithsonian Part II." When you go to large museums in France or anywhere else, you see museums that are full of art by men. There is not a single painting by women except for rare cases like that of Mary Cassatt. These museums are not called "The Men Museum of the Arts." Why do we have to use the word? Are we trying to affect social change just for ourselves or is it for the betterment of the society at large, for everyone? Men have to see and appreciate what we do. Initially, we needed to use the word "women." We are moving towards a new phase where the word "women" will not be needed. It will happen naturally.

MLS: What would you like your legacy to be?

A-Baki: I live the moment very intensely. I used to be a very goal-oriented person. When I was very young I had so many goals in front of me. I wanted to be an artist, a politician. But then war broke out in Lebanon and I witnessed its horrors. It changed completely the way I saw things. I enjoy the process of doing things, not the goal. Seeing friends and relatives die in the war made me realize how much I had to work to affect change in the country, in the world. Reducing poverty, bringing happiness to children's faces, improving education are the things that matter to me. Getting a position for the sake of it is not what I want. If my position as ambassador allows me to make a difference, I am glad. Focusing on the real issues rather than on the title is the way to go. It is far more rewarding. That is why I appreciate so much Gandhi's way. Titles come and go. Titles do not bring respect to the individual; they bring respect to the position. Real leaders are followed not because of their titles but because of what they believe in, because of what they are. That's real leadership!

MLS: What is next in your career?

A-Baki: I really do not know. I wish I could tell you. I do not know what tomorrow is going to be like. I know I have a program, a mission here. I enjoy very much what I am doing now. I have a passion for it. I wake up in the morning enthusiastic. The day I would wake up without that passion would be the day I would stop what I am doing and go paint.

What I really would like is to know myself more. I would be able to have more of that inner connection and have this inner freedom that is so important in order to be a better person. The more you try to reach your inner soul the more you realize that it is far away. I would like to have that connection with myself which is in fact the connection with a higher level of thought. You learn that through people. When you have seen the suffering of others you realize that there is something more inside of you that you do not know. That's my goal. Learning about that inner strength, that inner freedom that is untapped to a certain degree and that allows us to do so much. We are so obsessed by external things—material things, positions. We forget about our internal richness. We discover the stars and we do not know our inner star yet.

MLS: Thank you, Ambassador A-Baki, for the pearls of wisdom.

AMBASSADOR ANA CRISTINA SOL
OF EL SALVADOR

Her story is intricately linked to the history of El Salvador. On a larger scale it is also the story, all too common, of a Central American republic with an obscene gap between the rich and the poor, caught in the cold war and then left out in the cold in the aftermath of a standoff between two giants. As late as the mid-1990s 89 percent of the population (Mestizos and Amerindians) owned only approximately one quarter of the land, tiny plots used for meager subsistence farming of rice, maize and beans. A minority of white families owned more than a third of the land, large plantations exporting coffee. Add to this enormous disparity the human rights abuses and the backing of the elite by the military and you have the perfect recipe for civil war. The results speak volumes: at least 80,000 dead, 550,000 displaced and 500,000 in exile.

As the civil war ravaged the country between 1979 and 1992 a glimmer of hope appeared in 1984 in the persona of Christian Democrat José Napoleon Duarte, elected president in the first democratic elections of the country. But he could not find a panacea for the deeply wounded nation. He faced the fate of other moderate and democratically-elected Central American presidents before him whether Jacobo Arbenz of Guatemala or Juan Bosch of the Dominican Republic. Tensions soon mounted between the main left-wing opposition, the Liberation Front (FMLN) and the right wing, the National Republican Alliance (ARENA). The FMLN inspired by the Sandenistas of Nicaragua had hoped to redistribute wealth through armed struggle. ARENA's goal was to keep the wealth in the hands of those who had it. For the small farmer plagued by malnutrition and beleaguered by illiteracy, it was not about some Marxist theory invented in some far-away country and not even about Sandinista concepts developed next door. It was simply a matter of survival. But until the 1980s, in the corridors of power of Washington worlds apart from the daily heart-wrenching poverty and glaring underdevelopment of a Central American nation, for some the choice is clear—support the Salvadoran right wing military regimes and very conservative figures such as Roberto d' Aubuisson in order to prevent communism from creeping over the U.S. borders. However, American democracy and the faith of Americans in it are much stronger than credited and the brutality that reigned in the country raised eyebrows in many capitals and outraged many Americans. The outcry had culminated in 1980 when the popular Roman Catholic Archbishop Oscar Romero, the Salvadoran voice of human rights, was assassinated allegedly by the right wing while conducting mass.

In the late 1990s the country that the Pipils Indians, cousins of the Aztecs, proudly called "Cuscatlan" (The Land of the Jewels) is now picking up the fragments left by the war. Some of the fragments are hard to work with, hard to forge into a jewel. However Salvadorans have every reason to be hopeful. Although a large majority is still illiterate and undernourished, sound reform programs such as EDUCO and ESCUELA SALUDABLE have contributed to lower the illiteracy rate. Unemployment is at 15 percent and inflation has been in the single digits for several years. Other reforms are undertaken to reduce the reliance on aid from relatives abroad. In general

Salvadorans have undertaken enormous efforts to get out of war and go forward into the age of information and globalization. To usher in the peace process, Alfredo Cristiani was elected, an ARENA candidate, but a more moderate and forward-looking president.

I met Ambassador Ana Cristina Sol in 1996 at her embassy located a stone's throw away from the large Salvadoran community of Adams Morgan. She welcomes me, a motherly boteroesque figure with a pleasant smile.

MLS: Good morning Ambassador Sol.

Ambassador Sol [interrupting]: Ana Cristina.

MLS: Ana Cristina, could you describe the evolution of your diplomatic career. I understand you started your career in France. What was this experience like?

Sol: Yes, I started my career in France in 1989 as a political appointee of the president to France, Portugal, and the UNESCO [United Nations Educational, Scientific and Cultural Organization]. That was in October of 1989. I got the acceptance from France in July, but I could not leave before. I had to fix all my things. In December they asked me to go to Belgium to the then European community, now European Union. So, since then I had an embassy encompassing five different posts: France, Portugal, Belgium (three bilateral embassies), UNESCO and the European Union, and that was very interesting! Two years after that I asked to be relieved of the post to UNESCO because it took much of my time. What I have found is that in a bilateral that is very active (for example the United States) it is very difficult to go to general assemblies at a multilateral one like UNESCO that last three or four weeks because you cannot leave the rest without day to day attention. So I was left with the four posts.

MLS: That was in fact your first appointment as an ambassador and you were responsible for five posts.

Sol: That is very common among our countries because we do not have enough money to have ambassadors in every country that we have relations with. So you have concurrences, you are ambassador to one country, but travel to the other. So that is very common. I had actually two posts. One post was France, Portugal, UNESCO; the other post was Belgium and the European Union. For a while it was not as hard. Because while we were at war there were not many programs of cooperation with El Salvador in any of the countries, especially in Europe. So there was not all that much technical work. It was more of a political, social work, public relations work. As soon as we signed the peace accords, and even before, when we started to

show that it was a serious accord and that we were going to reach an end
to that war, then it really started picking up and the European Community
started a very intense program with El Salvador. Then it became really hard.
I had to go back and forth a lot.

MLS: What was your training prior to becoming a diplomat?

Sol: Actually, I was a mother. We had moved to Arizona from El Salvador
in 1979. Our children had to go to school in a place where they would not
be so threatened like they were in El Salvador. At that time El Salvador had
a lot of problems. Sometimes the children could not go to school because
there was a bomb somewhere about to explode. So they were missing a lot
of school days. We moved to Arizona so that they could attend school in a
peaceful environment. We also had three kidnappings in our family. My
father was kidnapped in 1975, my brother-in-law in 1979, and my sister
was kidnapped in Miami in 1982 by a Salvadoran man and a Guatemalan
couple. . . . Both my father and brother-in-law were kidnapped by the FPL
[Popular Liberation Front; one of the five groups of the FMLN]. They
returned my brother-in-law after more than a month of captivity. He had
been shot in the leg. It was a very cruel kidnapping. He was 72 years old.
He had been brutalized and it left an indelible mark on him. They took
over a radio station the day they released him. They said that they had
released him because the family had paid the ransom, but that he had shot
the leader of the operation. When they kidnapped him, they broke down
the door of his home. He went into his room to get a gun. He came out
and shot the chief of the operation. That leader of the operation I understand was a woman. They said that they wanted to get even. They wanted
revenge. They said that they would take revenge on one of our children.
That is why we all left with the children. We took all of them out of the
country. We had a home in Arizona. We used to go there often and we
loved Arizona. So we moved there. I was totally dedicated to my two children and six others I had brought with me from El Salvador, the children
of my brother-in-law, sister-in-law and best friends. I raised a total of eight
children. It took all my time. When I went to Arizona State University
(ASU), they really felt that I had abandoned them. After two years the
children asked me to go back to being a mother. So I did. As the kids grew
up I began to work in Arizona. I worked for a travel agency from my home.
We had special services to big companies. Then I did some work in real
estate. I had a real estate license. I kept myself busy, but my main business
has always been in El Salvador.

MLS: Was your family very active politically?

Sol: No. As a matter of fact, I am the only one in my family who is active
politically. The kidnappings in my family were for the purpose of getting

money. They were not politically motivated. Most of the political kidnappings end tragically. My father was an agriculturer who never got involved
in politics. He was very reserved and a very private man. His only sin was
to have worked hard and made money. My brother-in-law was a banker, a
self-made man who started as a clerk in Bank of America and ended up
founding the largest and most respected bank of El Salvador. He was a very
serious man, very well respected, very socially conscious. He was the first
man in El Salvador to create a credit program for the women of the market.
They did not have a credit rating, so they could not get loans. His bank
was the first one to provide them with small loans, microcredit. My brother-
in-law was a very special man. He did not have an office at the bank. He
had a desk in the middle of the bank so that everyone could have access to
him. For us it was a big shock that he would be kidnapped. After going
through all that, we started a new life in Arizona. We lived there for ten
years. My kids are American citizens. We have wonderful friends in Arizona.
Arizona is a second home to us.

MLS: How were you appointed ambassador and why Paris?

Sol: Nine days after the inauguration of President Alfredo Cristiani, his Minister of the Presidency was assassinated. José Antonio Rodriguez-Porth was
a very respected attorney in El Salvador, as well as a political analyst. He
was a very close friend of mine, and also my attorney. So I went to El
Salvador for his funeral.

It was during my stay that one evening a member of the party started
asking me if I would accept an ambassadorship. I took it as a big joke
because at that time there had never been a woman ambassador in El Salvador. But we continued talking and joking until someone remarked that I
spoke French—so France seemed the logical place. I actually forgot all about
this conversation until a week later when they called me in the name of
President Cristiani to know if I would accept a post in Paris. It was a great
shock to me, but when I talked to my children, they were very supportive.
So I decided to accept.

My paternal grandmother was French. I learned French at the age of five
in France. I had already lived in France with my parents twice. First when
I was five and then at seventeen. We were there a total of four years. I felt
I knew enough about the country and its people to perform well in my new
job.

MLS: Was your family in France on business?

Sol: My father was a coffee and coconut grower. He was also one of the
oldest dealers, if not the oldest dealer, of John Deere tractors and Caterpillar
tractors. So our travels involved both business and pleasure. He had a co-

conut plantation on an island. My father invented a machine to take away the husk of the coconut. He did it with scraps of metal. He never patented it. A lot of people came to see it, from American companies. He started with coconut coil and then went into shredded coconut. We used to sell coconut to Peter Paul Mounds here in the States. He was about to go into coconut milk production when he was kidnapped. He also wanted to produce car seats. Oh my father was a very special man! He had what he used to call a three-tier plantation with coconuts, cocoa and lemons and cattle underneath that. Yes my father was very ingenious and to answer your question, yes he was always traveling on business.

MLS: When you went to Paris, that was prior to the kidnappings, did he visit?

Sol: Oh yes, that was prior to the kidnappings. He commuted, if you can call such a long distance a commute and visited us every two to three months and spent three weeks with us. My mother loved France! So he did it to please her. He spoiled her. My mother was his second wife. I have three brothers and sisters from his first marriage. Wonderful! We really get along. I would never call them half-brothers. We all love each other very much and are very close.

MLS: How did you embrace that new career in Paris?

Sol: Not very well at first. It was difficult to adjust from being a business woman to being a diplomat in the country where diplomacy was invented! War in El Salvador had intensified. The FMLN had launched an attack on the capital city of San Salvador.

I was representing a conservative government while the government of President François Mitterand had attempted to sign a joint declaration with Mexico accepting the FMLN as a belligerent force with control of part of the Salvadorean territory.

No, things were not easy at first in France! And to top it all, we practically had an all-woman embassy, with the exception of the driver, and none of us were mature of age or had any diplomatic experience. Oh boy did I make a lot of mistakes!

MLS: Like what?

Sol: Lack of experience! Most of all the worst mistake I made was thinking I could change things in France, that I could get what others had not been able to get. I was so sure that if I really worked hard, I would succeed. It was very hard to accept that El Salvador was not liked in France, except by few people. It was very hard on me. I could not understand that. So, I really had to study and read and remember a lot of things that had happened and try to understand why people felt that way. It was not until then that I could start working in an effective way. At first I was so busy feeling sorry for my country and for myself for not being accepted that I was not doing a good job. But then came a big change. The government in France realized that I was there to work. At the time I was much younger and a hundred pounds thinner. When I arrived, they thought I was there to play. I had a minister counselor who was 23 years old, a beautiful young woman.

MLS: So they thought it was the beauty pageant of El Salvador descending on Paris?

Sol: Exactly! Seriously, I was invited to every cocktail party in Paris, but never to serious meetings. That was a shock to me because I did not expect to find that degree of "macho attitude" in France, but it is there! Everywhere I went they would ask where my husband, the ambassador was. I always enjoyed seeing their surprised faces when I told them I was the ambassador.

But these things do not bother me in the least. Eventually, people are brought to recognize one's work if it is well done. And I concentrated on doing my work well. I made many mistakes at first. Oh, many mistakes!

MLS: Was that your first victory in diplomacy?

Sol: Definitely, victory for El Salvador. President Cristiani made very sure that peace would never be considered anybody's victory. That is one of the most positive things that made this peace work. There were never winners and losers. He was very emphatic in saying "It is because of the people of El Salvador that we have gotten this peace. Had they not wanted it, it would not have been possible, no matter that the United Nations and no matter how many other countries helped." You cannot really achieve peace unless the people are ready. He was very emphatic on that. He brought everybody into the same boat. Everybody felt part of the peace process. So I would not call it a personal victory.

MLS: What brought you to Washington as an ambassador? How did your countrymen and women react to your appointment?

Sol: Washington—because I had already been here for a few years. When I went back to El Salvador I hinted that I wanted to be closer to home. I had told the President directly. He replied to me that they were making some changes in the diplomatic corps and would like me to come back. "There are a few posts we would like to offer you," he said. I went back. I had a broken foot and was wearing a cast. It was the most terrible trip. It is hard traveling with a cast. I waited and waited—witnessed people being nominated and sent to different places. I was just waiting. After awhile I called my minister and told him "I am really not doing anything here. Let me go back to my work in Belgium and call me when you reach a decision."

I packed and was ready to leave. The day before I was ready to leave, the foreign minister came to my house some time before lunch. He said, "President Cristiani would like you to go to the United States." For us it is the most important embassy in the world because of the connections that we have. Both times that I have been sent with the diplomatic service I have been very surprised. First, because I was El Salvador's only woman ambassador and then because they sent me to the most delicate or important post. I was obviously very honored and very pleased. I had a few impediments I had to take care of. I went to take care of them immediately. I had a lot of things I needed to take care of before coming to the United States. First of all I had an American citizenship. I had to renounce the American citizenship. It was hard. I love the United States. I was always thankful to the United States that gave us refuge. Maybe refuge is not the right word because we were never refugees. We were able to be here when my children needed to be. They got a wonderful education. They are American citizens. They would never change their citizenship. So it was a very emotional moment, and yet I had more chances of helping the relations between our countries being an ambassador. I had to wrestle with my personal sentiments. I went to the American embassy where I had some friends. I told them about it. They all knew [laughing exuberantly] I was going to be sent to the United States. I was the only one who was caught by surprise.

MLS: Your countrymen already knew about it and welcomed it?

Sol: I have been very lucky to be very popular as an ambassador. It meant taking care of the community. I love to be very close to the Salvadorian community. I started that when I was in France. I never expected that I would have the chance to be posted here where most of our countrymen are.

MLS: Here in Washington you are only a stone's throw away from the community in Adams Morgan.

Sol: The entire first floor now is a department for the community. We have four people working just on relations with the community. We give them legal support, legal advice on how to legalize their status. Many Salvadorians, if they want to be here, they want to do it legally. They do not want to have to hide from the authorities. The people have responded tremendously. We have the entire community with us.

MLS: Is the diplomatic corps a "men's club" as the *Washington Post* puts it?

Sol: I never had any problems with any of my male colleagues in any of the countries that I have been. I never felt that, here in Washington especially. In the Latin American diplomatic corps, there are two women—both from

Central America, Costa Rica and myself. I don't think the Ambassador of Costa Rica had any problems either. I think it is a lot of perception from our side. I have never felt that. Yet you can call it a men's club because it has an overwhelming majority of men. I truly cannot say that I feel any different than if I were a man.

MLS: Now a sexist question. Do you find that your duties as an ambassador conflict with your other roles as a mother, as a wife?

Sol: It would have very much had I had small children. It is not a job I would have liked to do as my children were growing up because I am such a mother hen. I pay such close attention to my children. I would have been miserable not to be able to give them the same attention. Currently, I am divorced. I don't think my husband would have been able to stand by me. The hours are very long.

MLS: Did you divorce during your appointment?

Sol: I divorced twice. I have two wonderful friends in my ex-husbands and in their new wives. My children are very close to both of them. They see my second husband as a second father. My daughter just got married. Something beautiful happened. My first husband was to walk our daughter down the aisle to the altar. Right as they were entering the church, I had somebody call my second husband who was seated in the first row because my daughter wanted him there. He was asked to walk with my daughter half of the aisle and her own father walked her down the other half. That is how close we are. Thank goodness I married two good men! The fact that our marriage did not succeed did not leave any hard feelings in either of us and we have been able to have a larger family as a result. It would have been very hard. Maybe it's because of the way we handle it. I am very passionate about that.

MLS: Were there any options for you to remarry? Would it have been a big obstacle to your work?

Sol: No. It depends on the person you are married to. I just really have not had time. I have friends. Here in Washington I have very little private life. If the kids do not remember me and arrange something with me, I do not do anything special on weekends for instance.

MLS: Really? Why?

Sol: Because I am tired. I like to rest on weekends. In Europe I had a very active private life. I had friends with whom I went out to dinner. I mean just friends, not diplomatic obligations. Very good friends who still call me from Europe. I had a very good relationship with my colleagues from Central America and Latin America and their wives.

MLS: Can you tell us about the inroads that women have made in your country and in your region?

Sol: Women in El Salvador have achieved a lot. They are very much involved in education. We had our first woman Minister of Education a long time ago. She was excellent! I just met with her as a matter of fact. Women decided a long time ago in El Salvador that the fields they wanted to be involved in public life were education and the protection of children's rights. Women have held both posts for the longest time. In politics they have come a long way. Right now we have a Minister of Education who has been there for two terms (two presidents) or eight years. We had a Ministry of Planning last time, but the Ministry of Planning disappeared in El Salvador. The former Minister of Planning is now the president of the new university, a business university. It is a graduate institution. Sixty percent of the students of that university are on scholarship. That was the goal of that university. They recruit the very best students from each and every small town in El Salvador and bring them to San Salvador. We have congresswomen. Right now the sister of the President is in town. She was a congresswoman. She is not running at the present time because her brother is president. She became congresswoman before he ran. The president of the National Assembly is a woman and the vice president is a woman. We have an ombudsman for Human Rights in the World who is a woman. The former vice minister of Foreign Affairs is a woman. Currently she is the president of the Social Investment Bank. The vice minister of Health, head of the ombudsman office, director of the Social Security Institute, director of the National Pension Fund, the director of the Social Investment Fund are women. In the Judicial Branch we have two of the magistrates of the Supreme Court that are women. I remember when Justice O'Connor was named to the Supreme Court here. I was in Arizona at the time. I told you about the president and the vice president of the Assembly. One is from the official party. The other one is from the opposition party. In their professional lives women have really made progress. Women used to study only to become secretaries, in other words, three years instead of five years of secondary school. That was it! They could be a very good secretary even an executive secretary, but that was as far as they would go. Now you find them in all the fields. We have wonderful doctors and attorneys. They accomplished it in a very positive way without having to riot. Many of these women are role models for other women and have fought for laws to protect women and render men more responsible. We still have a lot of irresponsible men! Salaries for men and women are now equal in most fields. In the military we now have a woman lieutenant in the infantry. It is harder to have high ranking women in the military. We do have a woman general, General de Alien. Initially, she was in the medical field.

Another achievement is related to the name issue. I was very surprised!

When my daughter got married, she confessed "I really don't want to hurt my fiancé, but I want to keep my name." My question was "Is it possible here?" She informed me that in the new law of the family that was passed and promoted by our First Lady there are all these beautiful things for women; women can do whatever they want, just like here. My daughter kept her name. In El Salvador the change was not such a trauma because we had never lost our names in the first place. We were always called by our maiden names followed by the name of the husband. When you divorce in El Salvador, you automatically go back to your maiden name. It is different in the United States. My second divorce took place in the United States where I actually had to tell the judge that I wanted to go back to my maiden name. They kept asking me why. I had to sign reams of documents about it. For us it is different. Your name remains your name. If you want to keep your husband's, I guess you can, but no one does. That is why my children have a different name.

MLS: How have the accomplishments of women inspired you?

Sol: I am bad with these kinds of interviews. I have never made an issue of the fact that I am a woman. I admire any person who can achieve something in their lives. It does not necessarily mean that I admire more a woman than a man. I do however admire all those women who have gone through a lot of adversities and still succeed. But then there are men who have done that too for different reasons. I do not know of any accomplishment that has inspired me solely because it was accomplished by a woman. A lot of people have inspired me. Some are men; some are women. My father, for example, was a big figure for me. My attitude comes from having a mother who was sick and very fragile. My father and I were always taking care of her. So my father became the figure that I looked [up to]. My mother was the person I took care of. She could not take care of me. Maybe that is deep down the reason why I do not make an issue of this question.

MLS: What are the accomplishments you are the most proud of in your career.

Sol: My children. You asked about career and they are not my career, I know! My children are the one thing I am the most proud of in my life. I can't even start explaining to you what they are like. They are hard working, bright, sweet. My son lives in Boston. He works for ATT Solutions, a consulting company. My daughter lives in El Salvador and works for Unilever Co. They both achieved a lot. In my career the thing I am the most proud of is being an ambassador without having had any training for it whatsoever. I have been able to do things for my country that I always wanted to do, but maybe I was going about them the wrong way. I was going through the political route. I never thought that diplomacy could permit me the same tools I needed to accomplish these things for my country. This is something that I am proud of and happy about. Now that I have found the way, I hope that after being an ambassador I can continue doing them.

MLS: What do you wish for women and men in your country?

Sol: Education—99.9 percent of the problems we had in El Salvador in the past were due to lack of education. Education for me is . . . [pausing to reflect]. I am going to tell you a story. I do not know whether you would want to publish it or not. Maybe you will not want to publish it. It is my own story and I will make it short. I was never formally educated. I educated myself. As you see in my curriculum vitae there are no degrees because I never got a degree. My father was a bit of a macho, a lot of a macho. He was fifty years older than I. I was the baby and he never wanted to let go of me. He was convinced that women should not study too much because, otherwise, they would not find a husband. Ever since I could remember, he used to say "What are you taking Latin for?" I ended up taking four years of Latin. Children sometimes like to go against their parents. In my case it was good for me. I went against him and studied a lot because my father thought it was not important. But I was never able to go further because he would never let me go to a private school. When I finished high school and expressed the wish to go to a college, he opposed the idea. He wanted to find a women's college. I could not find a women's college where I could study architecture. I wanted to be an architect. I had been going steady with the man who became my first husband since I was fourteen. To prevent my marriage, he sent me to Europe with my mother right after high school. Actually he sent me to Europe right before my final exams so I never graduated from high school. So when I went to the Sorbonne, to l'École du Louvre in France. I could not register as a real student; I had to audit because I did not have a high school diploma. That bothered me my whole life. When I went to Arizona, grown up with kids and all, I got my GED and finally was able to go to a university. I have known how hard it has been to try to learn. I have taken every course possible. I was just in Boston taking Professor Michael Porter's course on competitivity and productivity because I was never able to formally learn these things. I know what it is not to have the opportunity. I would like for everyone to have that opportunity. Those who do not want to take it should be spanked. I have spent my whole life trying to make children study. Right now my housekeeper lives with me with her two children; one of my assistants is also temporarily living with me with her two daughters. These kids, whenever they get one bad grade, they hear me. They cannot talk on the phone with their friends and cannot watch TV until they improve their grades. A lot of people do not understand what opens up to you when you are able to study. Life changes completely. The problems that we have in El Salvador would not exist if our people were educated. The problems that our people here that have emigrated to the United States are having are due to lack of education. The reasons that Americans do not want us here is because they say if you come from Ireland or from Spain or France you are perceived as educated. Our people are being discriminated against because they are not educated. When I am no longer ambassador, I shall work on a project that promotes education. I am not going to be a teacher; I do not have the required degrees to do that, but in some way I will go back and educate the people. It is the greatest gift you can give someone.

I am completely convinced that you fight poverty by creating wealth with education. Even though I am not an economist I have been working very hard in the economic sector of my country. As we have been able to straighten up our economy up to a certain point, people are starting to be less poor. You have people in our economies whose only reason for not creating wealth is their lack of education. It is a cycle which I want to contribute to break. I want to teach people to help themselves. We have an association of the Salvadorians of Los Angeles. They were telling me that they felt they had ruined their families by sending them money and not having them invest it. You create a dependent group of people that expects money. That is not good for the people. Right now we are working on projects with our communities and the World Bank to use the moneys that they send as collateral to microenterprise projects to make their families get off their chairs, stop watching TV and start working again in the microenterprises. From here, they can help them promote their folk art products. They cannot have it both ways.

MLS: On the same subject of education, you and Ambassador Pamela Harriman have a lot in common, particularly lack of formal education. I am very curious as to how you accumulated all this knowledge necessary to run an embassy. Did you have advisors?

Sol: Now I do. In Paris I did not. I was in embassies where there were only four of us, such as in France. In Belgium I opened the embassy. Little by little I read a lot on the subject. I have not read a fiction book in the last seven years. All I kept getting were these documents that these kids gave me. I still have problems reading economic reports because no one has taught me how. I am trying to read Michael Porter's book. I tried to read it on my way from Boston. It is quite a complicated book! I mentioned it to my son because he uses it as a textbook. He told me "Try to go beyond the words." That's right it is the only way to pay attention.

I met Pamela Harriman. She came as ambassador to France when I had not left yet. She was a remarkable woman. As a matter of fact, I just sent a letter to her family. I did meet her. I was very familiar with the work she had done without a formal education. Being politically savvy does help.

Sometimes when you don't understand something, you can turn it around into politics to give you time to go find out what they are talking about. You also tend to be more intense in what you are studying because you are an adult. You try to get knowledge from everyone. I was talking to students at Howard University the other day in the presence of all of my ambassador colleagues. My colleagues have master's and doctorate degrees. At that meeting I felt, "Oh now you are on." I wanted to get through to those kids how lucky they are to be there. These two years at Arizona State. . . . You cannot imagine how much they represented to me. I was just like a kid absorbing it all! If I had a chance, I could go right back.

MLS: It is never too late to get that diploma. Thank you for the interview, Ambassador Sol.

AMBASSADOR EUNICE BULANE OF THE KINGDOM OF LESOTHO

Her piercing voice, her southern drawl, southern African that is, fills the conference hall of Howard University and tells the saga of her country, the landlocked kingdom of Lesotho in southern Africa. The topic is the role of women in political life and in development. Ambassador Eunice Bulane enlightens the students on Lesotho's role in harboring African National Congress (ANC) political refugees from South Africa during the brutal apartheid regime. She paints, in broad strokes, the plight of Lesotho men leaving their homes to find work in the diamond and gold mines of South Africa. Lesotho women cannot be left out of the political process because "women are more educated than men in Lesotho" explains the ambassador. There are reasons for this. Many men, at least 10 percent of the 1.9 million inhabitants, work as miners in neighboring South Africa. Being a miner under apartheid South Africa meant moving to a forbidden city, a segregated citadel of horror made of a million concrete bunk-beds. No women were allowed. It meant not seeing one's family for four months at a time. It meant descending miles into the entrails of the earth on an over-crowded elevator with no breathing room and with twenty-five other miners as one—like sardines. It meant working hard in the dark on those rocks armed only with a flashlight, lungs absorbing dust and ears ringing constantly with explosions. A hard-earned pittance was sent home. One could not survive on these mea-ger earnings in salary in South Africa in Johannesburg, but converted into Malotis, Lesotho's currency, these South African rands allowed the women and children a mere subsistence living back home. Losing one's life in a mine explosion meant sending one's oldest son as a replacement. The product of such labor invariably found its way to adorn the body of some being a world away.

"Lesotho has suffered in more ways than one from the effects of apartheid in South Africa," emphasizes Ambassador Bulane. Its mere geographical location makes it economically dependent on South Af-rica. The rulers of the racist apartheid regime in South Africa had no scruples over exploiting this dependence in order to deter Lesotho from receiving ANC political refugees. In 1986 South Africa contrib-uted to the overthrow of the government of Prime Minister Lebua Jonathan (who had been in power since independence in 1966) thus ushering in the military rulers with whom they maintained good re-lations. The economic blockade previously imposed by South Africa had crippled Lesotho's already fragile economy.

In post-apartheid southern Africa, the complexity of politics is heightened by the fact that Lesotho is a kingdom, although the role of the king today is purely ceremonial. South Africa, Botswana and Zimbabwe had to intervene in order to reinstate Prime Minister Mokhele, parliamentary rule and King Moshoeshoe II, the descen-dent of Moshoeshoe I. King Moshoeshoe I can be considered the father of Lesotho. In early 19th century, the fearless soldier had pro-vided leadership and guidance to his people fighting against the Zulus and the Boers alike. He carved a nation for his people out of the mountains around the Thaba Bosiu (Mountain of Night), a territory the size of Belgium. To preserve his kingdom against continuous Boer threats, he placed it temporarily under British protectorate in

1868, remaining in power as the de facto ruler. In the post-apartheid era, the struggle for power opposed the Basotho Congress Party (BCP) which apparently obtained a landslide victory and the Basotho National Party (BNP). The years 1993 and 1994 involved disturbances for the kingdom. Its population lives on subsistence farming and continues to migrate to South Africa for work. In 1991 alone, remittances from migrant workers in South Africa constituted 70 percent of Lesotho's domestic output. Lesotho's largest mines were closed in 1982, although some diamond mining continues today.

Lesotho is still recovering from South Africa's economic blockade. However, it is banking on many developments. The Lesotho Highlands Development dam project will provide the power necessary for industrial development. The burgeoning tourism offers such attractions as skiing, excursions to the country's spectacular gorges and gambling in the casinos of Maseru (the capital). Further Lesotho has one of the three highest literacy rates in Africa (68 percent for women and 44 percent for men).

I met Ambassador Bulane at the embassy to discuss with her among other things the role of women in the economy of Lesotho, the Basotho culture and the work of her embassy. In contrast with its neighbors, the embassy of Lesotho on Massachusetts Avenue does not quite look ambassadorial. In the absence of the white, blue and green flag with its asymmetric design and its yellow warrior emblem, one would mistake it for a middle-class red brick private home. In the sleepy building days are punctuated by the ring of the telephone. Perhaps telephone calls come from those rare Americans curious about this small kingdom or inquiring about visas or a call from Prime Minister Mokhele asking the ambassador to attend a conference in southern Africa. The ambassador greets me in a rather bare conference room. A stern and almost shy woman wearing glasses, she reminds one of the typical southern African head mistresses from a school in the Transvaal. Educated abroad, fluent in French, Russian and Sesotho, she pursued her graduate studies in electrical engineering in the former Soviet Union. It is easy to imagine the importance of her future role in her country.

MLS: What are some of the inroads and what is some of the progress women have made in your country? What is the average daily life of a Lesotho woman or of a Lesotho man like?

Ambassador Bulane: We have more women in the countryside than men. Most of our Mosotho men go to South Africa to work the mines and do other jobs. At the same time, our Mosotho women are more educated than our men in numbers. They also are more highly educated than men. Why? Because the cattle is usually taken care of by young boys. This means that a young girl would start school at the age of five while a young boy would start attending school later. So it is women who have the opportunity to learn earlier and they continue their studies much longer than men because, in most cases, young boys grow up to take care of their families. If the father dies, the young boy would have to leave school and work somewhere to maintain the family. But then rural women would take care of the house-hold. She would be responsible for the tilling of the soil, taking care of children, children's education. She would have to take care of everything because men would be out working in South Africa. At the same time, we have educated women in our country who would be executive managers in the industry or who occupy high level posts in our government, although we do not have many women in the parliament. We only have six women members out of thirty-six. Two women ministers and three women ambas-sadors at the same time. We have a woman ambassador in Bonn, in Canada and in the United States. On the whole, women contribute a lot to the development of the country and try by the same token to uplift others. For example, we have an association of women lawyers who represent women in civil rights and educate the Lesotho public to respect women leaders and civil rights. This association is called FIDA. Also, we have a lot of women waiting outside. Women far outnumber men (72 percent women). It has to do with the fact that men go to South Africa and that their life spans are much shorter because they tend to work underground in the mines; they develop all sorts of complicated illnesses of the lungs. On the other hand, there are not many women going to South Africa. The few women that go to South Africa are professionals. Once embarked on their careers there they live better in South Africa than at home.

MLS: How did apartheid in South Africa affect Lesotho?

Bulane: Lesotho has always been a refuge for South African freedom fight-ers. Most of the South African leaders were educated in Lesotho. Some of the ANC leaders were educated in Lesotho. We had a university which was an integrated university with high standards of learning. Lesotho also was affected directly by apartheid. We lost lives and our economy was affected. There has always been interdependence between Lesotho and South Africa because we are landlocked and South Africa is highly industrialized. We supply South Africa with manpower. Not only people who work in the mines but also educated people contribute to the South African economy.

MLS: Is there a brain drain that impacts negatively on the Lesotho economy?

Bulane: We did not feel it as much when there was still apartheid. Now the system in South Africa has changed. Some of the youth want to migrate there. It might be economically advantageous for some in Lesotho to migrate, but at the same time South Africa's hands are full. South Africa has its own concerns.

MLS: People from Lesotho went to South Africa mostly as manpower and South African leaders went to Lesotho to be educated, but how did apartheid itself affect people in Lesotho?

Bulane: Lesotho was a British protectorate until 1966 when we got our independence. It had never been part of South Africa. The cultures are slightly different. Lesotho has a monarchy which also makes it different. The cultures are slightly different. We are two distinct countries. To answer your question I would say that those who migrated to South Africa during apartheid were more directly affected in their daily lives.

MLS: What are some of the aspects of Lesotho culture you are the most proud of?

Bulane: Lesotho music. It dominates the music scene in the whole of southern Africa. The music of South Africa in large measure originated in Lesotho. The Lesotho staccato! You find it in Mozambique, in South Africa, but originally it is from Lesotho.

At this point the ambassador even sang for me and what a beautiful voice she has! She allowed me to appreciate the different sounds of Lesotho music. While she sings nostalgic of her country, her face loses the stern headmistress characteristic I found in her earlier. She treats me with a sample of "clicks." In her velvet Makeba staccato she sings of the beauty of her country and of the hope of its youth.

MLS: Out of 180 ambassadors there are only ten women here in Washington. Is the diplomatic corps a "men's club"?

Bulane: I don't think it is a men's club because women are outnumbered by men. What is important is that we are accepted by the American government. We do mix with our male colleagues, we do exchange ideas with them and we are accepted by them.

MLS: What was the reaction of your countrymen and women at the news of your appointment to Washington?

Bulane: My countrymen and women were happy for me, although I was reluctant to accept the appointment. I thought it would not fit with my career because I am an electrical engineer. Close relatives encouraged me. I am happy that I accepted the appointment.

MLS: Was it difficult for you to make the change from an electrical engineer to a diplomat?

Bulane: In all my active life I worked for the Lesotho Electricity Corporation. I started as an engineer and ended up Deputy Managing Director of the Corporation. I liked my work very much. I felt very comfortable. However, I do not regret having accepted the post of ambassador. At first it was difficult to adjust. But I acclimatized and I am quite comfortable at the moment. I enjoy the post which I have held for two years, since January 1995.

MLS: In the two years of your tenure here, have you witnessed many changes in the relations between your country and the United States?

Bulane: Yes, there has been changes. We work much closer with the government. American investment is increasing. We are doing a lot to promote our country and our efforts have, in some instances, been met with success.

MLS: Would you like to talk about your family life?

Bulane: I am a widow. My husband passed away in early 1994. My only son passed away at the age of five. That brought me to do a lot of soul-searching.

MLS: A hypothetical question. How would your husband have welcomed your appointment to Washington?

Bulane: He would have supported it. He was always very encouraging of contributions to the development of my country.

MLS: Can you name a few things women have achieved in your country and of which you are most proud?

Bulane: There are women in our country who obtained graduate degrees in the early 1930s which is very rare. They obtained their degree from a university at home and later went to Britain. We had a university even before our independence. It was called the University of Botswana Lesotho and Swaziland (UBLS). Its name has changed since then. Among our famous women there was a scientist who was also an adviser to the king. She was not a formally educated woman. She was very gifted and talented. Her name was Line Mantsopa. She died in the 1930's. She was a healer and a successful traditional doctor that many in the south wanted to consult. She was not part of the royal family, of course, but she was part of their circle. As I said, we do have members of parliament, but we have not had a woman Prime Minister for example. We do have very capable women, but they do not apply themselves enough to reach that level. It is also due to tradition. Some women still accept the tradition that dictates that men should always lead. Probably they believe that they should not demonstrate their capability. I wish we could join hands and prove to our society that we can do more.

MLS: What is the best approach to overcome what appears to some as "the yoke of tradition" and demonstrate capability?

Bulane: I think first and foremost they should join hands together, discuss, share ideas and reach a consensus about the appropriate approach to show their capability to the nation, to the society. Then tell the society they have been ignored. We should say loudly, "Give us the opportunity and the whole country would benefit."

MLS: When you look at western women and their concerns, sexual harassment, equal pay for equal work, where do these concerns intersect with those of Lesotho women?

Bulane: By and large, they are the same. In many western countries a woman cannot open an account without the husband's approval. Many people argue that there is a big hiatus between western women and women in a country like Lesotho. I would argue that the concerns are the same. What makes things different is culture.

MLS: Sometimes western women think that they enjoy more freedom, more sexual freedom. Is this all a fallacy?

Bulane: This so called "freedom" exists in African countries, but it is promoted by poverty. Some women go to extremes to survive, to support their families.

MLS: What are some of the accomplishments you are the most proud of in your career as an electrical engineer and in your career as an ambassador?

Bulane: In my career as an electrical engineer I am proud that I did engineering and was successful at it and contributed to the development of my country. It is, as you know, a male dominated field. There are approximately ten women engineers in my country, that includes electrical, civil, and other branches of engineering. As an ambassador I think that women are better negotiators than men. Personally, I have achieved some success in promoting investment in my country. But I must confess that it took me a little while to acclimatize to the town before achieving what I just described.

MLS: Most ambassadors I have talked to deplore the fact that in Washington ambassadors tend to congregate and to meet each other on a regional basis. They usually wish for more interregional contacts. There is a lot of bilateral interaction going on, but very little multilateral interaction, unlike other posts such as Paris for example.

Bulane: I also wish there were a more multilateral approach to diplomacy here. The more you talk to people, the more you exchange ideas with others the more you benefit. We do meet as women bimonthly to exchange ideas and consult each other. The Women Ambassadors conference held at Howard University and of which you are the Director is certainly a wonderful opportunity to interact with the American public. I am also grateful for the wonderful articles that were written by the *Washington Post* and the article "The World and I" giving us more exposure. There is also a group of women ambassadors in post at the United Nations. It has been very beneficial interacting with them.

MLS: What do you wish for women in Lesotho?

Bulane: I wish women in Lesotho be granted the opportunity to contribute more to the development of their country. I don't think that men will simply invite women to participate more. I think women should get organized. We should ask ourselves what we want to do with our lives and look at our capabilities. Map out our strategy for a better future. I do not want to see my country dependent on aid. I want to see my country flourish.

MLS: How much damage has aid done to your country?

Bulane: Aid has made us dependent. I think now it is time to be independent. Investment is what we want. We want to improve our life style. We want to flourish and be happy. I think people should improve their lot; they should work hard. Begging should be discouraged. Relatively speaking, we have few beggars on an individual basis. Overall as a continent, we should not be begging.

MLS: Thank you very much, Ambassador Bulane.

AMBASSADOR
RACHEL GBENYON-DIGGS
OF LIBERIA

"We want the world to know that we are not war mongers." In this beehive of an embassy the walls are thin. One can hear Ambassador Gbenyon-Diggs on the telephone. The freshly upholstered stately sofas in the hallway where I am waiting for the ambassador catch one by surprise after having noticed the odd and undefined chipped blue and brown paint of the exterior of the embassy. However, the one-family home turned embassy will soon be a fixture of the past, the symbol of a nation at war. Liberia will show its new face, the face of a nation at peace, on 16th Street in northwest Washington in its new chancery. For the time being, the new chancery located one block away is under construction, pretty much like the country itself, picking up pieces after the war. Liberians do not want to be reminded of war times, so, Ambassador Gbenyon-Diggs will host the festivities of the national holiday at the new site under a tent. Already on the embassy's answering machine a proud voice announces the celebration of the 152nd anniversary of the founding of Liberia.

When Liberia was recognized as an independent nation in 1847, it became Africa's oldest republic. Its relationship with the United States is historically unique. Liberia was founded by freed slaves coming from the United States. The name of the country, evocative of liberty, is a reminder of the role of African Americans in the birth of that nation. Another symbolic name, Monrovia, that of the capital named after American President James Monroe. Since 1822, African Americans have migrated intermittently to the land of liberty forming an elite minority that ruled the country for many decades. The Americo Liberian elite intermarried with other ethnic groups and ruled the country in the same fashion as a southern state in the United States. They knew no other model of government. In 1980 a military coup brought Samuel Doe to power. His rule ended in 1989 in a civil war opposing various army factions. In August of 1990 the troops of the Economic Community of the West African States (ECOWAS) moved in to implement a cease fire and usher in a provisional government headed by Dr. Amos Sawyer. Later, in a rare move two individuals declared themselves President—Charles Taylor and Harry Moniba. Outbreaks of fighting plagued the country forcing many Liberians to seek refuge in neighboring Ivory Coast and Guinea. It took a woman, Mrs. Ruth Sando Perry, interim president, first woman president on the continent, to bring the warring factions together and put a stop to the war. Once her mission was accomplished, elections took place and Charles Taylor headed the country.

In Washington, it also took a woman to bring cohesion to the Liberian community and rebuild its embassy. I met the dynamic ambassador with the perfect pearly smile during the summer of 1999. Ambassador Gbenyon-Diggs, a graduate of the University of Geneva School of Interpreters, appears to be a woman of the world at peace with herself and the world and in symbiosis with her continent. It is easy to figure out why some call her "the African queen." She does look very regal!

I was ushered into her office by the hospitable and resourceful Veda Simpson, her assistant.

MLS: When people think of Liberia today the first epithet that comes to mind is "war torn" and not the image of the first recognized independent state in Africa or the first African nation to be led—even if for a fleeting moment—by a woman. You have been in Washington a staunch advocate and savvy lobbyist for the reconstruction of your country. Explain that position. How do you want Americans to perceive Liberia today?

Ambassador Gbenyon-Diggs: Liberia's past peaceful history and stability surely demonstrate that there should be structures put in place for countries in post-conflict situation. As you rightly said, Liberia was a peace maker, the stabilizer and promoter of democracy and human rights and women's rights. And then we started on a downhill trend which brings to mind two things that countries in Africa need to ward against—proliferation of arms and poverty. In countries where there is a high rate of illiteracy some people tend to feel that it is much easier to get what they want by the point of a gun rather than through hard work. In Washington I have been advocating that Liberia's past could reflect its future. There are things that the international community needs to take a closer look at. Certainly Liberia could be a pilot project for post-conflict development and also for the non-proliferation of arms in poverty stricken countries.

MLS: The civil war claimed at least 150,000 lives in 1994 alone and displaced a least a third of the population in Guinea and Ivory Coast. What was the most challenging aspect of your role as an ambassador trying to convince American lawmakers who might have never set foot in Liberia of the necessity to rebuild it?

Gbenyon-Diggs: I try very hard to let people see the big picture. Usually, they look at the picture and compartmentalize which does not help Liberia. We feel that if the United States has any role in Liberia's successes, it definitely has a role in its failures. We looked to the United States for guidance. We looked to the United States as a role model. The one devastating advice we took from the United States was that we should arm. Our forces for many years had a militia in Liberia, but they were not armed. Based on what we perceived as cold war politics, we acquired weapons. The United States did put some pressure on Liberia to militarize in 1978. This brought us complete devastation. Because of this, we say to them you must help these people to resettle. Our major problem is repatriation at this time. First, it is very difficult to get the necessary security apparatus in place to assure people that when they come back they will be secure. Secondly, it is very costly to repatriate people and to resettle. We put out a reconstruction program last year. The international donors were very supportive of it. What is ironic is that because of a bilateral incident with the United States, the United States put pressure on the international community to withhold all assistance to the Liberian people. Because, as I see it, the government is there to implement the wishes of the people and look out for the well-being of the people. This has been my major quest in Congress with lawmakers. You have to empower people to be able to speak out for themselves and say "this is the kind of government we want." You need to help promote and build the institutions that will empower people. My plea has not fallen on very fertile ground. It is an extremely difficult lesson to drive home and to tell the United States that in promoting the people, in alleviating poverty, they are helping to build democracy.

MLS: In the early 1800s 10,000 African Americans moved to Liberia and formed an elite that remained in power until the 1980 coup led by Sergeant Samuel Doe. By [some] historical accounts, the relationship between the Americo Liberians and other groups in Liberia has been a bit rocky. Do you agree with that characterization? Could you describe your delicate task as an ambassador in reminding American lawmakers and the administration of the strong historical ties with Liberia and linking these ties to the relationship that Liberia and America should establish today?

Gbenyon-Diggs: It is a delicate task. But what we are faced with today in Liberia is that the majority of our population is American Liberian. Liberians ran off from Liberia since the 1980s. It has been twenty years. Many of them have lived in America, have had children and grandchildren. Those are all Americans. What is unfortunate for these people, unless we resolve these differences, these American Liberians will go back and be faced with the same situation that the freed slaves went back to. We tell the United States that there are myths that have been perpetuated over time about our population. First, let us look at this historically. These freed slaves left here over 133 years before the coup. How could such a small number of slaves remain in power in a country of 2 million and there be no mixing or no intercommunal marriages or interrelationships. So it was a myth. It was a myth that there were people who were perceived either by their names or their features to be of a certain group. Ironically, the "indigenous" person who took over Liberia was called Samuel Doe. So what is not American about that name? Who is or is not of American descent is very fuzzy in Liberia. In Liberia by asking people who their mother or father is, we challenge anyone to find who is or is not an "indigenous" Liberian. If anyone asked me whether there was a class distinction, I would say certainly because the missionaries brought education to Liberia. The government was so small and impoverished that it could not afford to educate the people. Our "indigenous" cultures did not approve of education. "A woman should know her place and stay in it." We were an agricultural society. So the boys went out farming and there was some resistance to disrupting our cultural life to merge it with this American way of life. So few were the educated and other groups remained illiterate. I think that this is the genesis of our crisis in Liberia. If you were educated you were perceived to be an Americo no matter what.

MLS: So "Americo" is indeed the term used in Liberia for African Americans who migrated to Liberia over a century ago.

Gbenyon-Diggs: The terms used are "Americo" or "Congo." "Congo" because many people came from the Congo. Liberia does not have indigenous tribes. Even the tribal people all migrated to Liberia. Only very small pockets of tribes are indigenous to Liberia. This is demonstrated by historians. This myth of the African Americans going back and suppressing the indigenous people in a master-servant relationship was done in the same devious vein as the myth put out that African Americans or blacks were "lazy, shiftless and no good." That myth was repeated so much that even blacks began to believe it. In the United States these were the slaves who built this country, built the railway, planted the cotton, nursed the children, tilled the farms and all of a sudden because of convenience or inconvenience they were portrayed as being "lazy, shiftless and no good." And I think that the same devious myth was perpetuated about Liberians. This is not the truth but this has caused much dissension in our land just as the black issue has caused much dissension in the United States.

MLS: At Howard University we had the pleasure of receiving your first lady, Mrs. Taylor, an extremely articulate and vocal advocate of the rebuilding of Liberia. What are some of the fruits of her advocacy?

Gbenyon-Diggs: Mrs. Taylor has tried very hard during her short term—the administration is barely two years old—to redeem the orphans. Liberia was left with many orphans during the war. She has taken on this issue as a bulwark. She has also done a lot of work in the area of empowerment of women. Men go to war and die. Women are the ones who are left with the grieving and the burdens of picking up the pieces. In the beginning of this new millennium, women are in a position where they have to be mothers and fathers. They have to educate the children, they have to nurture them, they have to provide for them financially; therefore, their backs need to be stronger. Mrs. Taylor is taking a strong role in promoting women and children's well-being and the economic empowerment of women through small projects. She has focused on education and more recently on health because good health allows one to take full advantage of education opportunities.

MLS: Of all the roles an ambassador fulfills—that of a negotiator, a mediator, a promoter—which role do you enjoy the most and why?

Gbenyon-Diggs: Actually I enjoy all of the roles. The negotiation skills need to be honed because you can never tell which issues come up. Africa is always at a disadvantage in negotiations because we enter into negotiations in a position of weakness. If we were trading partners of the United States or of the international community, we would be able to talk as partners. Whenever you enter a negotiation as the weaker or perceived as the weaker, it takes even greater skills to get to an even position. So that is a more difficult role. I enjoy the difficult aspect of my job. Women in Africa are born into hardship and brought up in hardship, so, are born negotiators.

MLS: The *Washington Post* describes the diplomatic corps in Washington as a "men's club." What has been your experience as a woman ambassador in Washington?

Gbenyon-Diggs: Men like women very much! [Laughter.] It is definitely a men's club, but they show much appreciation for women, not only the appearance of the woman, but they have begun to appreciate a woman's mind. Women have always played all of the roles that men play but silently in the background. All of the things that men do daily and get praise and adulation for, women do them silently without the recognition. When women are pushed out in the forefront, people realize that they have to look at women for their individuality. Many of the things that women achieve they have put a lot of hard work and energy in them. Men and women's roles should be in tandem like a relationship rather than women mimicking men. I do not have to do things like a man in order to be the best. This battle of the sexes should be put to rest or phased out in the new millennium and men and women should be equal partners.

MLS: Are there differences in the way men and women approach diplomacy?

Gbenyon-Diggs: Women are more apt to catch flies with honey rather than vinegar. The kind of "soft" approach they bring to issues is much needed. Women are always seeking solutions. Men discuss problems. Women try to solve them. Men would tend to say, "Let's discuss this problem." Women would say, "Let's solve this problem." When you are looking for a peaceful solution to any issue, your best bet is to place the issue in women's hands. It has to do with the way women are brought up. Women are taught that if they are abrupt, they cannot achieve anything. People hate women who are too abrupt or too forceful. Women end up getting their way through their upbringing, through negotiations and by not being hostile. These are precisely the qualities necessary for a diplomat. I wish that many men would take a "women course." Having said that, I should add that by and large every approach is individual—not male or female.

MLS: What was the reaction of your countrymen and women at the news of your appointment as ambassador to Washington?

Gbenyon-Diggs: I am not the first Liberian woman ambassador to Washington. My immediate predecessor, Eugenia Stevenson, is a woman. She was appointed Consul General to Bonn and to New York approximately fifteen years before she became ambassador. She was ambassador here until 1992. Liberia has had quite a few women in top positions. The first time that I heard of a woman Secretary of Defense or "Minister of War" as we say was in Liberia and that was in the early fifties. Her name was Etta Wright. When I spoke at your program at Howard University I mentioned Angie

Brooks-Randolph who was the first woman to become president of the General Assembly of the United Nations and that was in 1969. The head of our transitional government was a woman, Mrs. Ruth Sando Perry. She was the first and so far the only woman president in Africa. We had a woman candidate in our last presidential election, Mrs. Ellen Johnson-Sirleaf. We set another precedent when we posted women both at the United Nations in New York and in Washington as ambassadors. It is unusual for a country coming out of war to send women in those posts. One tends to associate war or post war with "strong men." The Liberians however are beginning to think that women can accomplish. So, the reaction of both men and women to my appointment was positive. They are accustomed to women representing their country.

MLS: Do you find that your duties as ambassador conflict with other roles in your private life since it is a twenty-four-hour job?

Gbenyon-Diggs: I am lucky that all of my children are grown. So, it is a comfortable time to be at post.

MLS: Can you tell about the inroads that women in your country and in your part of the world have made in various fields? How have they inspired you?

Gbenyon-Diggs: The most powerful inspiration was my mother who was an educator. She was head mistress of the all-boys school. She was very stern with her boys, very fair to her boys and very demanding of them. This was my first look into the world of what a woman's role could be and how influential a woman could be in shaping lives. I told you before that I grew up in Liberia with women who were ministers of education, of war, of justice. All of these women were role models. In general, women in Africa are always working, always cheerful; they are always negotiating something whether they are at the market place or anywhere else. We have a long lineage of female heroes. My own mentor is a lady called Fatima Massaquoi Fahnbulleh. She was the first Liberian that I knew who spoke several languages. She was a professor at the University of Liberia when I was there. She made such an impact on me that my choice of becoming a translator came from her. She wrote many children's books in Liberia. A real, real inspiration! Her father had set up a school at the University of Hamburg where the Liberian Vai language was taught and that was the language used as a code by the Germans during World War II. She also had been given a place in life, not a male place or a female place and she felt very comfortable in the world. I got a lot of inspiration from her. Consequently, I went to Geneva to study and became a professional translator.

I would like someday to find some of her books and have them reprinted. There are certain works, however, that might have been destroyed in the war and those, unfortunately, we will not be able to get back. She has a daughter who is also a writer. She and I often discuss ways to find some of her mother's projects and reprint them.

MLS: Inspired by Mrs. Fatima Massaquoi Fahnbulleh, you became a translator. Which languages do you work with and how do your linguistic skills enhance your performance as a diplomat?

Gbenyon-Diggs: I speak French, German and English fluently; some Italian and my Russian is getting a bit rusty. I speak French at home with my family. French is my best second language. I love the way languages connect people. As a translator, I do know that in translation or in interpretation something gets lost. Some feelings, some emotions, might get lost. Languages are the big love of my life. Languages are extremely important in diplomacy. They establish that immediate connection between negotiating partners that does not exist when an interpreter is involved. As you know as a very accomplished polyglot yourself, when you communicate in the language of your negotiating partner, there is more of a connection; you are entering their world. Communication is faster, easier and more in symbiosis. In diplomacy, speaking fluently the language of the host country should be a must and learning a language or languages is a lifelong commitment, not a three or four months crash course. In the United States most people feel that knowing one language is enough. In diplomacy negotiation skills are greatly enhanced by the knowledge of foreign languages.

MLS: What are the accomplishments you are the most proud of in your career?

Gbenyon-Diggs: I am very proud of having gotten our chancery off the auction block. Our embassy is being rebuilt on 16th Street. We are moving towards dedication in September. I am proud of having contributed to getting justice for our president and getting the charges against him in the United States dismissed. At the insistence of the military government, our president had embezzlement charges brought against him as a way of getting him back to Liberia which many people felt would be a certain death. He escaped from a prison in the United States pending extradition. Charges related to that had been pending in the United States. When I became ambassador it was one of my assignments. With the help of many dedicated Americans, we were able to get the charges dismissed. I also feel a sense of accomplishment because Liberians are beginning again to use their embassy as a center. I wish I could be prouder of building stronger relations between Liberia and the United States. Relations are on the mend but they are not where they should be. Perhaps I am impatient because you can do only so much in a year and a half. We now have an American ambassador appointed to Liberia after a long period of interruption since the war, since 1991. An ambassador was appointed but sent to Pakistan instead, so the current American ambassador will be the first one of the post war.

MLS: To which extent are the concerns of women in Liberia or in West Africa in general different from the concerns of women in the United States or other developed nations?

Gbenyon-Diggs: For us, daily life is a matter of life and death, a matter of survival. Women in Africa have so many major concerns that people take for granted here—health, education, everyday survival in war times, just about everything related to basic survival. Our child mortality is so high; we are concerned about the life and death of our children. While women here in the West worry about nails, their hair, their diet to remain or become slim, we worry about survival. I do not want to trivialize the concerns of women in the West. They too have important issues. But ours are far more pressing. Our concerns are life and death concerns.

In America and in other Western nations women have the right to vote and they sit on that right. In Africa we die for that right. We die on the way to the ballot box. In the United States the right to vote is taken for granted, and so is food on the table, electricity and all the amenities of life that are right there at the finger tips. When you are so blessed, there are many things you take for granted. We in Africa tend to look at all these amenities as blessings.

In Liberia we did get the right to vote before American women. The women's rights issues they have here in the United States, we in Liberia feel that we have already acquired these rights. There are some rights that American women push to us that are more culturally based like serving our husbands. By serving them we do not acquire the status of servant. It is absolutely not a submissive act. It is an act of friendship. In our culture you serve your husband the same way you serve a friend or a guest in your house. In Liberia the husband is looked upon as a friend and a guest in the wife's home. If you are not friends with your husband in your home, how can you invite guests into your home and treat them better than you would your own family?

MLS: In your culture is serving a position of strength then?

Gbenyon-Diggs: Exactly! What women learn is a life of service, like in nursing. You give a part of yourself to someone. Sometimes in international gatherings it becomes confusing when Western women look at service as a reduction of our rights as women. On the other hand, we in Africa feel that Western women have acquired a lot of rights but do not quite know what to do with those rights. American women, for example, have a lot of rights that they need to use. In our case in Liberia, when we have a right, we use it. In their case when they have a right, they put it aside and say, "Well I

have this right let me go get another right." And I think this has to do with
the fact that they are not fighting for the basics. In Africa, in Liberia, women
fight for the basics. We keep fighting until our basic rights are protected. A
prime example is the peace process. It is women, who saturated with the
insanity of the war, started the peace process. In Liberia women have been
the engine of the peace process.

In the United States when there are two or three women in government,
many feel that it is a great accomplishment. I feel that if we went out and
acquired the same rights we would use them more. American women do
have many rights and they can use their power to promote women. In the
case of First Lady Hillary Clinton, the fact that she may run for Senate in
New York creates such a commotion. It should be viewed as normal. Had
the roles been reversed and the husband of President Hillary Clinton were
to run for the Senate, it would be perceived as natural. In Liberia we have
five women senior senators out of thirteen, which is a higher proportion
than in the United States. And we are a country coming out of a war where
everything is military and macho. In the United States you can count on
one hand the number of women senators out of a total of ninety senators.
This is the type of situation I refer to when I say that American women
have rights, but they are more concerned with acquiring more rights rather
than using the rights they already have.

MLS: Can you elaborate on the crucial role of Liberian women in the peace
process?

Gbenyon-Diggs: During the war women formed coalitions of women's
groups to lobby all the war lords. Women started to lobby ECOWAS, lob-
bied the international community. Their plea was "We have the right to live.
We have the right not to have our sons, daughters and husbands killed."
Women would leave their homes in large groups, go to churches, to the
legislators, canvassing the country, starting the whole peace process. In fact,
they continue this work until today. This is based on this very visible fact
that a woman was chosen to lead the transitional government. Many are
saying that had it not been a woman, we would not have peace in Liberia
today.

MLS: What do you think of the president of the transitional government,
Mrs. Ruth Sando Perry?

Gbenyon-Diggs: She is one of Liberia's greatest. We attended the same
school together. She has the energy and the drive. She was at the right place
at the right time. She is currently involved in charity work.

MLS: I was fortunate to be one of the organizers of her trip to Washington
three years ago. She told us that she was in Nigeria attending a conference

when someone summoned her in the hotel lobby. A group of people informed her that she had to urgently return to Liberia. In Liberia she was informed that she had been unanimously selected by the Council of Elders as interim president. How proud are people in Liberia of the fact that the first woman president in modern day Africa is Liberian?

Gbenyon-Diggs: It registers. Women have taken such a strong role in public life in our country that we recognize this fact and accept it as normal. We knew she would do the job that she was put there to do and within the time frame that had been set. We were not expecting anything less. We expected her to stand tall, to move among men and move men towards peace. And she did exactly that.

MLS: What is the most delicate aspect of your job as an envoy to Washington?

Gbenyon-Diggs: It is getting across to the American people and to the American lawmakers that Africans played a very meaningful role in civilization. When they look at Africa today, they see poverty, they see debt, they see destruction, they see mayhem. I want them to see Africa's contribution to civilization. We had some of the richest kingdoms and some of the best universities in the world, Ile Ife is one example. The hieroglyphics, the use of papyrus, all of these things are African. This is the Africa that I want to present to the world. This is the Africa that I want American children to know about—the part that is lost in history, that is lost in writings. Yes, we do have a different culture, but our culture is as great as your culture. Therefore, we should not be portrayed or perceived as beggars. We should be in this whole global community as equal partners. Africa deserves to be an equal partner.

MLS: There is a disconnect between what is perceived as a glorious past and the sometimes heartwrenching reality of the present. Conflicts between Eritrea and Ethiopia, in the Congo, in Sudan, not to mention Rwanda, reinforce that disconnect. How do you convince Americans, not to mention Africans themselves, that all this chaos will be overcome and that Africa will be an equal partner?

Gbenyon-Diggs: The Africa Growth and Opportunity Act is an opportunity for Africa to showcase its potential. If we came to the table as equal trading partners, Americans and the entire international community would come to realize the potential of Africa. What we are trying to show the United States is that Africa is potentially the largest market in the next millennium. Wars, destruction and chaos are not inherent to Africa. They happen in world history, even in these United States they have had turmoil, civil unrest, a civil war and participated in world wars which Africa was dragged into. We have to portray our culture calmly, subtly, showing that we can be equal partners in trade, in education and that we have a contribution to bring if only they want to see it. A major portion of our destruction today comes from the West. Arms proliferation brought chaos to Liberia and throughout Africa. We do not produce the arms. We do not ship them. We do not manufacture the ships that take them to Africa. What we do is buy into the game that dictates that the most powerfully armed is the most powerful. When something goes out of control, we use those weapons to destroy ourselves. We should all work together to make the world a safer place. I often say to my president that Africa has become an industry. The industry consists of projects that are Africa-based or Africa-centered. If Africa were to straighten out, can you imagine the massive unemployment in the West? Large organizations such as the World Bank, the various Africa departments of the United Nations, the IMF, sections of the State Department, USAID employ many dealing with the problems of Africa. Should we straighten out our act, it would be a very scary thing for the West. We must impart that we can all work together for the betterment of Africa. Many of the organizations should contribute to help us tap into our potential rather than helping us keep our nose above water or encourage dependence.

Africa is always portrayed as a market of a high risk and high return. Investors push this high risk to get the high return. When we look at U.S. investment in Asia or Latin America, we notice that investment practices are different there. Africa is not any scarier or any riskier. Africa should get the same treatment.

MLS: Do you feel that investors and others look at things through the microscope of race?

Gbenyon-Diggs: It is not so much race as it is power. If you have power and you are a minority, it is scary. If only someone could conceive a plan where we would all get along and power would not be an issue!

MLS: In some cases large multilateral organizations such as the United Nations, the IMF or the World Bank have solved problems and in other cases they contributed to problems. Are they truly going to embark on a new course?

Gbenyon-Diggs: I think that they are all embarked on a new course. However, institutions such as those are very slow to move and to change. I remember when I was at the World Bank, they set up for the first time a Strategic Planning Department. It did not last very long because some of the ideas on how they could change would affect the power of some. It all boils down to power, the minority holding all the power. I believe that once Africa is looked upon as an equal partner, they will take into consideration more of the realities in formulating their policies. So far the policies were formulated and just circulated as if to say to Africa, "If you do not do it this way, you cannot be a member of the boys' club and if you are not a member of the boys' club, then you cannot be a player." Many African countries wanted to be players and, therefore, were pushed into becoming members. And we screamed. The World Bank took us into consideration during its structural adjustment programs, but louder African countries screamed "This is killing us!" So, they decided that they would put a human face on structural adjustment. It is taking some time. Prestigious organizations do not like to admit their mistakes. Mr. Wolfenson, the president of the World Bank, has requested that policy makers and directors go to Africa and stay there for at least two weeks to get a feel for the country they represent. This way they can get in tune with the types of policies that are necessary. I think good things will happen in the future. I am not one of these doomsday people who believe that the whole world will be destroyed. I believe in a renewal.

MLS: What do you want your legacy to be once you leave this post?

Gbenyon-Diggs: My wish is mostly for my country. I would like Liberia to be as strong as it was in the 1970s. We were then in a very comfortable relationship with the United States. Unlike other countries, we did not get massive financial support from the United States because we could do for ourselves. We were not so terribly aid dependent. We were respected in institutions such as the World Bank, the United Nations and in major world organizations. I do hope that my legacy will be to have opened up new horizons for Liberians living in the United States.

MLS: What's next career-wise?

Gbenyon-Diggs: I have promised the people in Minnesota that when I retire I will be a goat farmer. We went to Minnesota to visit Land-O-Lakes. Our hosts there took us to visit a goat farm that was run by one woman. She had volunteer help from a student, also a woman. When I saw this woman-powered goat farm, I was inspired in doing something that I could be in control of and that could bring in some money and all the calm in the world. I could be a goat farmer. That's the left side of my brain talking. The right side is saying, perhaps you could be a public speaker because some say that you touch them when you speak in public. I will see how I can combine being a goat farmer and an advocate for Africa as a public speaker.

MLS: I can see you combining both activities. Thank you, Madam Ambassador, for a thought-provoking conversation.

AMBASSADOR
ARLETTE CONZEMIUS
OF THE GRAND DUCHY OF
LUXEMBOURG

H.R.H. the Grand Duchess Charlotte of Luxembourg had created quite a stir when she moved with her entourage into the neighborhood currently known as Embassy Row. This was during World War II, in 1941. She had bought the limestone and brick manor from the daughter of Wisconsin Congressman Alexander Stewart. The price, a mere $40,000, almost a third of its assessed value. A bargain! Some were quite titillated over the spectacle of European royals in the American capital. However, Grand Duchess Charlotte of Luxembourg never entertained. She hardly lived there in fact. The Grand Duchess's mother, 80-year-old Dowager Grand Duchess Marie-Anne, spent the last year of her life there mourning the loss of a relative. After her death, the place became a Luxembourg legation and in 1955 a full-fledged embassy. In 1944 it was the first diplomatic institution to promptly celebrate the victory of the allies in a war where Luxembourg ranked third in highest percentage of human loss.

The current occupant of 2200 Massachusetts Avenue moved in far more discretely. Arlette Conzemius Pacoud, ambassador of the Grand Duchy of Luxembourg, also made history. Not as a blue blood royal but as the first female ambassador of her small European nation tucked among France, Belgium and Germany. She is accompanied by her supportive husband and their two sons, 14-year-old Antoine and 11-year-old Olivier, who immediately bring to mind Britain's Princes William and Harry.

Ambassador Conzemius' role is more that of a promoter rather than a negotiator, not an easy task when many in the host country think of Luxembourg as a "city" or a "region" located in France or Germany. The association is not too farfetched. Luxembourgers speak French, German and Letzebuergesh and describe their culture as "France meeting Germany in the heart of Europe." This is certainly reflected in their cuisine which combines German abundance and French accent.

In the long period of foreign sovereignty that stretches from 1443 under Philip the Good of Burgundy until 1814 under Napoleon I, Luxembourg was Burgundian, Spanish, French, Austrian and French again. Today, Luxembourg has it own dynasty, that of the house of Nassau headed by H.R.H. Grand Duke Jean. The small steel exporting Duchy of 400,900 inhabitants and about the size of Rhode Island has a big script in the European Union. It houses the European Court of Justice, the European Investment Bank, the European Court of Auditors, important services of the Commission of the European Union and the General Secretariat of the European Parliament.

The fact that the home of Jacques Santer, current president of the European Commission and former prime minister of the Grand Duchy, has chosen a woman to represent it is quite a milestone.

After serving as Deputy Chief of Mission in Washington in 1989, as a member of the Luxembourg delegation to the United Nations and as ambassador to the Council of Europe and to France, Ambassador Arlette Conzemius presented her credentials to President Clinton on September 10, 1998.

I met her one afternoon in March of 1999 at the stately mansion-turned-embassy, the work of architects Bruce Price and Paris-trained Jules Henri de Silbour, who had also designed Howard University's

Science Hall. After ascending a spectacular staircase enhanced by splendid Persian rugs, I was ushered into her dark-paneled office fit for a president. She appeared petite, soberly chic in her champagne-colored suit.

Ambassador Conzemius: When I joined the Ministry of Foreign Affairs in 1981, the minister of Foreign Affairs was a woman. Her name was Colette Flesch. She is one of our most prominent women in politics. Educated in the United States, her first public achievement was to participate in the Olympic Games that took place in Melbourne, Australia. Her specialty was fencing and this expertise must have been useful when she had to fight her way through politics. She became a long time mayor of the City of Luxembourg before joining the national government.

For the last twenty years, there have been women in key positions in Luxembourg—the mayor of the City of Luxembourg, the speaker of Parliament, the leaders of two of our major political parties (Liberals and Christian Democrats). But these women represent more an exception than the rule or a trend. The fact that some women made it to the top does not mean that it is easy for the majority of women to follow.

MLS: There is always a need to have a certain degree of fortitude to accede to these positions. Can you describe what these women have in common in terms of character that appeals to your compatriots?

Conzemius: Women who want to make it to the top must be very hard-working and when they aim at becoming political leaders, I guess they must also be quite tough. They must certainly have a degree of fortitude and a deep commitment to compete with their male colleagues. Many women shy away from political life because they are not ready for the rigors of campaigning or the burden on their family life. Therefore, those who make it in politics should really be commended and supported.

MLS: In some cultures grace, good looks on one hand and competence, intelligence on the other hand are perceived as incompatible, especially as they apply to women. Obviously, Luxembourg does not follow that pattern.

Conzemius: What really matters is the personality of the individual. Women who succeed in politics must prove that they are competent and that they are capable of doing the job. Appearance is only one part of the person. But just as it is the case for male politicians, some women politicians are more charismatic than others.

MLS: In which field is it more difficult for women to gain access in Luxembourg?

Conzemius: Politics, diplomacy and banking are certainly among those fields, but even these sectors are opening up. Women are already very well represented in the judicial sector, in academia as well as in the medical community. As I mentioned earlier, we do have women in government and in our civil service, but they are often concentrated in specific sectors. We do lack civil servants at very high levels, but there are quite a few now coming up. Basically, we are not as far as some of the Scandinavian countries but the last years have seen important changes. Slowly, women are entering all the spheres of life and as they reach higher levels, they are getting leading positions.

MLS: How vital is the quota system envisaged by your country and by western Europe in general with regard to giving women more access to political offices?

Conzemius: The system of quotas is being discussed in many European countries. The idea behind this is that sometimes positive measures are needed to attract women or minorities to certain careers. Women enjoy the same political and civil rights as men, but that does not mean that they are equally represented in parliament or in government. Those who believe in the quota system think that it is necessary, in a provisional phase, to create favorable conditions that will encourage political participation of women. I personally think that measures of that type can play a useful role. Any system that can improve the representation of women should be encouraged because we need to hear the voices of women in all realms of society.

MLS: What is the mandate of the Ministry for Women's Rights which interestingly covers issues affecting women and the "handicapped"?

Conzemius: The establishment of this new ministry in 1996 was an important initiative. The Ministry's mandate is to promote real equality between women and men de jure but also de facto. This means that you have to change the mentalities by educating and informing people about the gender problematic.

MLS: What is the biggest hurdle you had to overcome as a woman in your career in general and as ambassador to Washington, D.C.?

Conzemius: The fact that a woman held the post of foreign minister when I applied to join the Foreign Service was both helpful and an inspiration for my career. I was only the third woman to join the diplomatic service. When I first approached the Ministry, I was bluntly told that although I had the required degrees and obviously the right training, as a woman I was not very welcome because women had too many family problems that would prevent them from accepting assignments abroad.

The first challenge for me was to be accepted in the Foreign Service. I then had to prove that a woman not only could do as well as the men, but that in certain cases, she could even do better. I was conscious of the fact that I would be judged not only as a professional but also as a woman working in what was essentially a man's world. I am glad to be able to tell you that women are now doing quite well. In 1993 I became the first woman ambassador, two more were appointed last year and there has been a huge increase in the recruitment of young women in recent years. To some degree this reflects a willingness to reduce the imbalance in the numbers, but also the fact that women do very well on the exams.

MLS: You were for five years the only woman ambassador from your country and the first one as well.

Conzemius: Yes it was a spectacular appointment in a way because there had never been a woman ambassador in my country. In a way our government realized it was an asset to appoint the first woman ambassador. I was at a point in my career when I was the only one who could become ambassador, but now there is a consensus that our countries can no longer ignore women. So, for the country it is a kind of positive promotion also.

I was appointed first to Strasbourg and I was wondering about the next step. I never realized they would assign me to one of the biggest embassies. Meanwhile, in the last diplomatic movements there are two more women appointed ambassadors to two important posts—one is ambassador to China and the other ambassador to the United Nations and to Geneva. Also, in the last recruitment after the foreign service exam, many women were admitted. Some male colleagues are starting to say that it is too much. Women are doing very well on the exam and this is changing the diplomatic service. Now we are exceptions; however, as we get a more balanced foreign service in general, there will be more women. We were a bit late in comparison to the United States, Canada or to Scandinavian countries, but there is a general movement in Europe now to promote women. It becomes more normal. As I said, women can no longer be ignored because the fact is that they are doing well academically. They are getting better results than the men on their exams. So there comes a point when they cannot just be ignored.

The fact in this country that Mrs. Albright was appointed Secretary of State will help women in general in the diplomatic service. It might encourage countries to appoint women. All women in such positions will have an impact on bringing other women in the field of diplomacy and will take women from the usual sectors like social affairs and family affairs into foreign affairs or defense. It would normalize the picture and promote women to get into these sectors.

MLS: Can you tell me about the accomplishment you are the most proud of in your career? In your role as ambassador, you are a negotiator, a mediator, an interlocutor. Which role befits you the most?

Conzemius: When you are assigned to a multilateral diplomatic post, negotiation skills are indispensable. At the United Nations in New York, at the European Union in Brussels or at the Council of Europe in Strasbourg, a diplomat represents his or her country and tries to promote national interests while taking into account the global objectives of the organization. I enjoy multilateral work because it is always very stimulating to interact with colleagues from many different countries on issues of common interest. When delegates disagree on certain issues, negotiations start and that's when a diplomat has to demonstrate his or her skills. I have experienced very interesting times when Luxembourg was holding the presidency of the European Union Council. In that capacity, you have to chair meetings with experts from all fifteen member states of the EU and this is a unique opportunity for a smaller country to put an imprint on European foreign policy. When you are chairing, mediation is important as you need to fulfill certain objectives while taking into account the positions of many different countries. It was always a very fulfilling task for me to try to propose compromise solutions that would be acceptable to all parties.

MLS: In Washington you end up devoting more time to which aspect of your work?

Conzemius: In a bilateral posting like Washington, I have less opportunities to negotiate since I mainly concentrate on contacts with the administration, Congress or the business community.

MLS: What is a typical day like at the embassy for you?

Conzemius: Every day is different and that is what I enjoy the most about this posting. In Washington my primary objective is to work with the administration and the Congress. When I travel through the country, I try to meet people from many different circles and inform them about my country. Through the contacts I get, I try to initiate new projects in the economic, cultural and academic fields between the United States and Luxembourg. Of course there are many social events in my schedule because most of the diplomatic activity does not take place in your office but in the outside world.

MLS: What is your primary objective in representing Luxembourg in the United States?

Conzemius: Luxembourg has a strong relationship with the United States that dates back to the two world wars. People in Luxembourg have not forgotten that their country was liberated twice by American troops and that

5,000 American soldiers are buried in the American Cemetery in Luxembourg with their leader, General Patton, amongst them. Luxembourg is a founding member of NATO, the United Nations and of most international organizations. There are important American investments in Luxembourg and many cultural projects have been undertaken. Since we are privileged to have such a good bilateral relationship, my task is made relatively easy. I can concentrate on developing new links between our countries in many different areas—business, academia, culture. These new projects will create further links between our people and insure the continuation of our good relationship for the future. By promoting Luxembourg in this country, I hope to contribute to the consolidation of our links. On the official level, I try to develop even further the cordial relationship between our countries and, in a broader context, the relations between Europe and the United States.

MLS: How do you envision your career five or ten years from now?

Conzemius: I am a career diplomat. Washington being the "highest post," some people wonder whether I am going to retire after this (laughter). This would be premature! I see myself continuing my career as a diplomat. Washington is a very important post, but we also have interesting posts in Europe in our neighboring countries. The European Union is becoming more and more important every day. I certainly don't see this as the end of my career. Many people say that after Washington it is very difficult to readjust to other countries because it is true that much is happening here and it is such a rich country.

MLS: I am asking this question because usually Washington is the highest post and after Washington the next logical step is Secretary of State or Minister of Foreign Affairs.

Conzemius: In our government we have a clear separation between diplomatic career and political career. I am not an elected person. Those that are appointed to ministerial posts are appointed through political affiliation. No, I don't see that as a possibility.

MLS: Was becoming an ambassador a dream of yours early in life?

Conzemius: No, I did not dream of becoming an ambassador and I did not have any exposure to diplomatic life as a child. I had a big interest in international issues, especially in history and in international relations, and expected to work for an organization like the European Union or the United Nations. I attended two schools that specialize in international relations, but after graduation, my first choice was to go into international banking. Although this was an interesting experience, I did not remain in that sector for very long. I took the foreign service exam and was admitted into the diplomatic service. I never regretted my decision and still think that it gave me a very fulfilling professional activity.

MLS: Other diplomats or politicians in your family?

Conzemius: I do not come from a family of diplomats. My father was a veterinarian. I was born in Zaire. At the end of his forties my father decided to venture out to the then colonies, to the Belgian Congo. I lived there for four years. My mother was at home; she was a homemaker, but she was very involved in my father's work. She was working also although not having her own career. She was the person who influenced me and always told me I should have my own career.

MLS: Did your father also have a strong influence on your upbringing?

Conzemius: Both my parents were very supportive and have encouraged me in my wish to embrace a career. They left to my own decision what I would study. They really did not influence my choices. I ended up doing what I thought I would like. I was pretty much on my own for that I did not know where to look for a model in that respect. It was not obvious, especially when I had completed my studies and was looking for my first job. It was rather difficult because the society in Luxembourg was kind of traditional. I had studied in the United States for a year at Tufts University and this American experience increased my determination to have a career just as all my male colleagues would. When I came back to Luxembourg, I expected it to be easy. It was not. I had to realize that nobody was simply waiting for me. As a woman, particularly in banking, it was not all that easy.

MLS: Apparently it is not easy for women around the world to enter diplomacy. Is the diplomatic corps still strictly a "men's club"?

Conzemius: I think this is right. It is a men's club. When you just look at the figures, we are approximately 180 ambassadors in Washington. We are reaching record numbers with only twelve women ambassadors at the very present time. That is still a very low number. But it is increasing, which is an indication that things might change. In the traditional ambassadorial couple, the man is the ambassador and his wife handles the social functions. That is still very much the case.

MLS: How does your husband feel about your duties? Does he fulfill the role that traditionally the wives of male ambassadors would fulfill handling social functions?

Conzemius: For a couple trying to combine two careers is always a challenge. When one of the partners is a diplomat, this is even more difficult because the other one has to find ways to pursue his or her own career while taking into account the successive transfers that are inherent to diplomatic life. In our case, my husband was able to find a consulting job that he can accomplish from almost any location, provided that he has a computer and a fax machine. He deliberately organizes his work in a way that allows him to be flexible. His duties involve quite a bit of traveling, but when he is in town, he accompanies me to a number of social functions. He tries to combine his professional life with the social obligations we have in our diplomatic life. The fact alone that he joins so many social functions is very helpful for me because we can do this as a couple. It is easier to manage a group of people when there are two of you rather than when you are on your own. We actually both enjoy attending events where we get to meet new people.

Sometimes my husband confronts some uncommon situations. He recently attended a tea for the spouses of ambassadors. Of course all the spouses were wives. At that gathering they tended to speak of ambassador's wives, not of ambassador's spouses. In other postings and even in our association of diplomat spouses in Luxembourg, when they address letters to myself or to my husband, there is always a mention of "wife" in reference to the ambassador's spouse. This has to change.

MLS: And your sons? How do they adjust to diplomatic life?

Conzemius: The only life they know is the life of a diplomatic family. For the last fifteen years, we have been moving from one post to the other and they have enjoyed living in different countries. Of course, the hard thing for them is to leave their friends, but they try to maintain contacts with most of them. My children have always had a mother who worked. Of course, my job is very demanding and I am always careful to have somebody at home who could take care of them and make sure that they have all the attention they need and the necessary support for their studies. Like all the working mothers, I try to compensate my absences with quality time whenever I can. We attach a great importance to family life and try to reserve time for common activities. The prospect of coming to Washington was certainly exciting to them. I do not know whether they realize the importance of the post as such. They were in Washington as small kids and had fond memories of their life in the capital of the United States where I was posted from 1989–93 as Deputy Chief of Mission. They are adjusting well, attending the French Lycée.

One issue for diplomatic families with children is social obligations. Children don't like it when we are out too often. This is true especially of younger children. Older children might actually enjoy it.

MLS: What are some of the pluses and minuses of being a woman ambassador?

Conzemius: I do not believe that it makes a difference whether you are a man or a woman ambassador. When you represent your country abroad, you have an official function with duties and obligations and these are not gender related. All the ambassadors in Washington do their utmost to best represent their countries in the United States, to present their governments' views and to foster bilateral relations. Of course, every ambassador has his or her style and personality and that certainly can make a difference.

There might be a slight advantage for women in terms of public relations because we are such a small number and there is a certain interest for this group. This is bound to change when the number of women increases and people become more used to women representing their countries at all levels.

MLS: One plus is the diversity that exists in the group of women ambassadors. The other groups tend to be regional. This one is interregional.

Conzemius: It is one group that is certainly very diverse. The women ambassadors come from almost all continents. This allows us to get different perspectives on the subjects we discuss during our meetings. Since the diplomatic community in Washington is very large, it is almost impossible to get to know all your colleagues. Normally, you develop contacts mostly inside your regional groupings. In my case this means that I meet frequently with colleagues from other European countries. I do not have many opportunities to work with ambassadors from other regions and that is one of the reasons why I enjoy meeting with my female colleagues. The other reason, of course, is that we get opportunities as a group that we might not have individually. We invite distinguished guest speakers to our events and try to organize what could become the equivalent for women of "the old boys' network."

MLS: Washington is such a politically charged city where there are so many circles. How easy or difficult is it in getting to know the various political circles in Washington and understanding how they interact?

Conzemius: As you said, Washington is a very politically charged city. It is also very oriented towards U.S. policy. Members of Congress and Senators, for example, work primarily for their constituency and do not have much time to spend with foreign diplomats. But Washington is a very rich city in many aspects. It is a place where power, business, culture and academia meet and thus diplomats have many opportunities for contacts. People in this town are very open, internationally minded and there are countless events where diplomats are welcomed. It is, therefore, not difficult to meet people, but it takes time to develop a network of persons who will help your endeavors.

MLS: How different is it in that respect to your country's political circles?

Conzemius: The sheer size of my country makes it more accessible. We are located in the heart of Europe and very much committed to European integration. Our economy is very open and very much dependent on foreign trade. We attach a high importance to maintaining and further strengthening our international relations. It is therefore quite easy for a foreign ambassador in Luxembourg to meet people, even at the highest level, in all circles of political, economic and cultural life.

MLS: What was the reaction of your compatriots at the news of your appointment?

Conzemius: The usual set of reactions when a woman gets an important post. People are very supportive. They find that it is a great achievement and are very happy for you. There are others who would invariably say "Oh, she just got it because she is a woman!" The emphasis is more on the fact that you are a woman and not on your capacity. For a man the gender question would not even be raised.

MLS: The Deputy Minister of Foreign Affairs in your country is a woman. To which extent does her appointment help the promotion of women in the foreign service? How does her appointment help shape the public perception of women in the foreign service?

Conzemius: After our June 1999 elections, a new government will be formed. In the last government the Deputy Minister of Foreign Affairs was a woman who is very committed to women's rights. She was very active in that respect and that certainly made a difference. The fact in this country that Mrs. Albright was appointed Secretary of State will help women in general in the diplomatic service. It might encourage countries to appoint women as ambassadors.

MLS: How have women faired in your country as cabinet members and in political life in general?

Conzemius: In Luxembourg, it is not before 1969 that the first woman, Madeleine Frieden, became Minister of Education. The number of women remained very low for many years but the situation is now improving. In our present government, which consists of eleven members, we have three women ministers and one woman deputy minister. Some of the sectors they are responsible for could be considered typical for women: family, women's rights, social security, education. But, they are also in charge of the Departments of Transportation and Communications and serve as Deputy Minister of Foreign Affairs and Development Assistance.

In Luxembourg women acquired political and civil rights quite a long time ago. The right to vote was obtained in 1919 and in the October elections of the same year the first woman was elected to Parliament. But after this, it took almost fifty years before another woman was elected as Parliamentarian, in 1965. The fact that women have equal rights does not mean that they have been able to attain a satisfactory level of participation in the political process, not to speak about equality or parity.

MLS: I asked you about the reaction of your compatriots to your appointment. What about your husband's reaction?

Conzemius: He was very pleased and welcomed the news of my appointment which was unexpected. He immediately tried to figure out the practical arrangements concerning his own job. We felt that it was a big opportunity for the whole family, worth some sacrifices.

I attended a social function where there were many people from Washington. There were round tables. The only persons to have name cards were the ambassadors. There was a name plate indicating the "Ambassador of Luxembourg." To show you that everyone expected the ambassador to be a man, when I arrived there were ladies sitting on the left and on the right of that seat. They were kind of disappointed when they saw that I was the ambassador and that we would be three women sitting together. Someone kindly moved.

MLS: I guess they were expecting a dashing looking man to take his seat! At one point in your country there was a debate on how to call you "Madame l'Ambassadrice" or "Madame l'Ambassadeur."

Conzemius: Yes. This is also a new debate. In the French language there is the question of whether to feminize titles. A few women ambassadors were called Madame "l'Ambassadeur." "Ambassadrice" was the term reserved for the wife of the ambassador. Increasingly there is a tendency to feminize titles. The issue is still being discussed. I think we should feminize whenever possible.

MLS: Thank you Madame "l'Ambassadrice."

AMBASSADOR
LJUBICA Z. ACEVSKA
OF THE REPUBLIC OF
MACEDONIA

They are walking briskly in the efficient metallic gray structure of the Ronald Reagan building. It is the last day of the NATO summit. He has a slight limp due to age—perhaps also due to the car bomb attack he survived in 1995. There is a winning quality about her in a purplish fuchsia suit and black high heels. She is barely forty and already one of the stars of the diplomatic corps in Washington. Well-wishers shower him with compliments about her—her excellent work, her dynamism. Eighty-two-year-old popularly elected (78 percent of the vote) President Kiro Gligorov has many reasons to be proud of his ambassador to Washington, Ljubica Acevska. Her colleagues have a model, a predecessor, and have come to Washington to settle in existing embassies. Not so for the graduate in political science of

Ohio State University. She had to do everything from scratch. She could write a book on "How to Start an Embassy." She is revered as the "Mother of Macedonia."

Macedonia was born on September 8, 1991. For Macedonians the birth of the nation has been a long labor with many complications. Before its dissolution in 1767, the Ohrid Archbishopric was for over eight centuries the only institution which united the Orthodox Macedonians as a people and set the stage for their development as a nation. But who are the Macedonians? Referring to the Macedonians Karl Hron, an Austrian publicist, wrote in 1890, "In any case it may be shown from their history as well as from their language that the Macedonians are neither Serbs nor Bulgarians, but rather a separate ethnic group, namely the direct descendants of those earliest Slavic immigrants, who had settled in the Balkan peninsula long before the Serbian or the Bulgarian invasions and have not mixed with either of these two ethnic groups." If the Balkans have triggered many passions among larger European powers, Macedonia was often at the heart of those passions. Larger nations were often prompt to partition it or place the question of its independence on the back-burner. In the early 1870s there were Russian promises against the will of the Western European powers to seek self-determination for Macedonia. But these promises were soon broken once they conflicted with Russia's interest in creating a Greater Bulgarian state.

Neither the Conference of Ambassadors (1876–77) nor the Russo-Turkish war (1877–78) nor the treaties of San Stefano and Berlin brought about a significant change in the status of Macedonia. Subtle support for the Macedonian nationalists came however from an unexpected corner, the United States, which had no stake in the affairs of this small southern Balkan region. American diplomats were routinely informally briefed by American professors from Robert College in Constantinople. Close relations with American academics have become a tradition in Macedonian diplomacy and might explain Acevska's eagerness today to cover the American academic and think tank circuit in which she feels most at ease. The academic connection seems to have proven successful since the United States remained constant and consistent in its support of Macedonian independence.

In the 1870s the big Macedonist slogan was, "We have been freed from the Greeks? Should we submit to others?" The "others" that come to mind are the Bulgarians, the Turks and the Albanians. The room assigned to Macedonia for its briefing on this April 23, 1999, at the NATO summit is smaller than the rooms reserved for the bigger nations—perhaps commensurate with its youth and consistent with the NATO pecking order. Macedonia is the younger promising cousin invited to the adult table.

But, before reaching the table, Macedonia had to put up quite a fight. The uprisings of Kresna (1876–78), the actions of "Edinstvo" secretly forming a government are all part of the Macedonian saga. The climatic event, the 1903 Macedonian revolution, marked by the creation of the so-called Krushevo Republic, a milestone in the struggle for independence, proved the extent to which Macedonians were ready to fight for their national freedom. In 1904 in an attempt to echo the demands of the Macedonists, a British initiative was put on the diplomatic table. But under the rule of the Young Turks that initiative was stopped dead in its tracks. The British initiative would have given Macedonia a "special status in its natural and ethnic borders." On the other side of the Atlantic, U.S. President Theodore Roosevelt liked the idea. At the time the Europeans were against the formation of a new state in the Balkans.

At the NATO summit Acevska and Gligorov are aware of the fact that their unexpected and isolated friend of the 19th century is now the sole superpower of the planet. There is a sense of poetic justice to the whole saga. Back in 1911 U.S. diplomats tried to influence Balkan states to ease tensions. To no avail. The United States did not yet have the voice that comes with total "superpowerdom." Governed by their interests, European powers were in favor of the war. On October 8, 1912, the First Balkan War began with Montenegro, Serbia, Bulgaria, and Greece fighting the Ottoman Empire. Although Macedonians contributed to defeating the Turks, they were not yet able to secure their independence. The victorious Balkan Kingdoms convened in Bucharest in 1913 dividing the spoils and partitioning Macedonia into Northern Greece; Bulgaria awarded itself Pirin Macedonia; and Serbia received Vardar Macedonia which it rebaptized Southern Serbia.

At the beginning of the Paris Peace conference, Macedonia became the cause célèbre of a group of twenty-five intellectuals from Europe and the United States of America. Collectively they sent a memorandum on the Macedonian question to the president of the United States. In the famous memorandum they demanded the formation of an autonomous Macedonian state in "its natural and ethnic borders," from Lake Kostur to the Vardar estuary. One of the most vocal Americans on the issue was Professor George Herron who kept on urging President Wilson to at least put the question of the status of Macedonia on the agenda. There was even talk for a fleeting moment that an autonomous Macedonia could be placed under the protectorate of the United States. President Woodrow Wilson wanted at least an objective report on the southern Balkan "state."

Between the two world wars, manifestos and declarations hinted towards the independence of Macedonia. Macedonia joined the anti-Hitler coalition, the "Anti fascist Assembly of the National Liberation of Macedonia," and lost half of its troops in World War II. As was the case for many African nations World War II was a turning point for the Macedonians in terms of their struggle for independence. They suffered many casualties but freed some territories and drew attention on the issue of the assimilation (hellenization or Bulgarization) of Macedonians and their so-called "voluntary emigration."

Today as Ambassador Acevska always hastens to plug, "Macedonia is the only republic that broke away from the Republic of Yugoslavia peacefully through a referendum." For this southeastern European landlocked country slightly larger than Vermont, bordered to the south by Greece, north by Serbia, west by Albania and east by Bulgaria, being at peace with its neighbors is simply a question of survival in such a volatile neighborhood. President Gligorov's plan to sustain this peace is laid out in his "Macedonian Model of Peace and Security in the Balkans." If this peace has been sustained so far, it is certainly also thanks to his team of top-notch diplomats. And Ljubica Acevska is certainly the epicenter of that world-class diplomacy. In Georgetown by the harbor she runs a tight but efficient ship of an embassy.

Macedonia is walking a tight rope trying to keep the neighbors at bay while having good relations with them. This is what Macedonian officials coin the "positive equi-distance." Quite a balancing act! Not easy to achieve when one supports NATO against the northern neighbor. One of the reasons for that support—not too long ago Slobodan Milosevic was proposing to former Greek Prime Minister Mitsotakis a plan that would amount to the partition of Macedonia between Greece and Serbia. On the other hand, with Albania there are also issues regarding the prolific and less educated Albanian minority joined en masse by their refugee brethen from Kosovo. Close proximity with Kosovo does not make things easier. With Greece Macedonia has mended its issues. Among them were the flag and the name of the new Balkan nation. Greece considered "Macedonia" the name of an ancient province in Greece and did not want to yield it to the former Yugoslav Republic. Greece thought it had a historical right to the name. Greece imposed a blockade on Macedonia, thus cutting its vital access to sea.

So Acevska has far more challenges than most of her colleagues of the diplomatic corps. She had to do it all often single-handedly—contributing to the founding of her country, establishing an embassy in the most powerful nation, promoting Macedonia, finding a name for Macedonia, keeping Greece not too miffed about the choice of flag, explaining Macedonia to the Americans and promoting investment in Macedonia. As if that was not enough the war broke out in Kosovo, rendering Macedonia fidgety. The ambassador had to shift gears and explain diplomatically to Washington how Macedonia, barely able to keep its head above water, was unable to provide for all the Albanian refugees.

Acevska knows that in many ways the Republic of Macedonia is the key to peace in the Balkans. In part because her country is atypical of the Balkans and is undertaking reforms with some measure of success. On the lecture circuit, endowed with an attractive and elegant presence, she often explains the three international policy goals of Macedonia: a European orientation, friendly relations with the United States and good neighborliness and cooperation with the four neighboring countries. A dynamic combination of cogently brilliant arguments and impeccable camera-ready looks, she usually leaves audiences fascinated by the topic. She has a quality rare in Washington: she is as comfortable in historically black Howard University as she is in the predominantly European Georgetown setting. This allows her to bring her message to all ethnic groups in the United States. An excellent strategy for a country striving to be a model of multi-ethnic democracy. Macedonia's population of 2,000,900 breaks down as follows:

Population	Percentage
Macedonian	67
Albanian	23
Turkish	4
Serb	2
Gypsy	3
Other	1

From her fashionable wardrobe (somewhat tamed since her appointment) to decorative objects in her office the color purple dominates. I interviewed her twice—once before the war in Kosovo in the fall of 1996 and once after the visit of President and Mrs. Clinton to refugee camps in Macedonia in June of 1999. In between she has been a frequent guest at Howard University in the Women Ambassadors Program.

She greets you with a corporate winning smile and Macedonian warmth. Having spent many years in the United States, her accent is American with a dash of Macedonian.

MLS: Very often the Washington diplomatic corps has been described as a "men's club." What has been your experience as a woman ambassador in Washington, D.C.?

Ambassador Acevska: I certainly agree it is a men's club. Right now there are ten women ambassadors. So women are making a lot of strides. [In spite of the] progress . . . women have made, it's still a man's world. The higher up you go, the more it is of a men's club, a men's world. I am lucky in the sense that I have been well accepted, well received by my colleagues, by my male colleagues. But you know it takes them a few seconds of adjustment to realize that I too am the ambassador and not the spouse of the ambassador. So many times that mistake has been made where they think that I am the spouse of the ambassador.

MLS: What was the reaction to your appointment in your country?

Acevska: My situation is a bit unique because I have been representing Macedonia ever since our independence in September of 1991. I was appointed ambassador in October of 1995. Once we normalized diplomatic relations between the Republic of Macedonia and the United States, then my title changed from representative to ambassador. So when I officially became ambassador, the people in Macedonia were already familiar with me. I think there would have been less acceptance if all of a sudden I was appointed ambassador out of no where. Here they were familiar with me. But even still there was some questioning. The question was why her? The fact that I am a woman and relatively young to be in this position probably had something to do with it. The fact that I was doing this type of work for almost four years made it much easier to be accepted by the people in Macedonia. And the interesting thing is that I have the support of the president who is eighty years old and very traditional. Women's groups in Macedonia were absolutely ecstatic! I received a lot of congratulatory notes from them. They stated that it is a great step ahead for women. The younger women in particular were very pleased with my appointment.

MLS: I imagine that it must be quite challenging to be the ambassador of a country that is emerging. The country has to establish itself. You are pioneering all this effort. Can you describe some of these challenges?

Acevska: That is very true. The word challenging is still an understatement. We are doing everything from the very beginning. Being a newly independent country and building an embassy here in Washington takes a lot of work. You are trying to establish relations with the host country and on the other hand you have to build up an embassy here in Washington. It is hard work. You are starting from the very beginning. There is no precedence. You cannot go to the file cabinet and examine how your predecessor acted or find out what should be done. It has been very difficult. One of the things which I did when I started this job from the very beginning was to learn. I read a lot of books on diplomacy, on the tasks of an ambassador. When I was officially appointed ambassador I spoke to many of my colleagues and asked them for their opinion on aspects of their work. One of the interesting points in the discussion I had with one ambassador when I mentioned to him the difficulty with being the first ambassador to Washington was his reply that I should be grateful to have the opportunity to set the foundation. In that sense it is very positive. The job gives you the opportunity to take a lot of steps, set up a lot of initiatives you think will be useful in the future.

MLS: Do you see your role as a negotiator, the promoter of a new country, an interlocutor?

Acevska: Even though I did not present my credentials until February of 1995, I started this job officially in January of 1992. When I started, we did not even have relations with the United States. One of my major roles at that time was to establish diplomatic relations with the United States. In that sense, at that time I was a negotiator, trying to convince the United States to first of all recognize the Republic of Macedonia and then to establish relations with the Republic of Macedonia. That was one aspect. I also had to play the role of a promoter at the same time. Being a newly independent country, Macedonia was unknown to many people. Something else which works against us—we used to be one of the six republics that composed the Socialist Federal Republic of Yugoslavia. Whenever they would hear Macedonia, a lot of people would associate us with war-torn Bosnia and all the terrible things linked to war. The fact is that Macedonia is the only republic that declared independence from Yugoslavia peacefully. We are trying to relate that message, promote the country and inform, present the country—its politics, its culture, its economic situation. We made a lot of progress in the five years since I have been doing this job. Right now, to maintain the positive relations between the two countries and to continue promoting my country to official Washington and also to other cities are crucial. I give a lot of speeches at different universities and clubs. I travel across the United States. You have to promote your country! The more the United States hears about Macedonia, the more they will have a different perspective from the one or two lines they may read in the newspaper. That's an important role as an ambassador. I would like to go back to the fact I am the first ambassador of the Republic of Macedonia to the United States. If I had been ambassador to another country I would have been familiar with certain obstacles. . . . I did not know all the obstacles which I encountered. I felt they were just part of the job. So in a way it made it easier. But if you have served as ambassador in previous posts, then you know that this is not the way the ambassador should be treated. So that would have made it much harder.

MLS: Women in southeastern Europe and in the Mediterranean are usually viewed, and sometimes wrongly, as not having progressed a lot in terms of women's rights. What do you have to say in response to that generalization?

Acevska: Women in Macedonia have generally had a lot of opportunities. Even when we were part of former Yugoslavia, we were much more advanced than some of the other East European countries. There were a lot of opportunities for women in the medical field for example and in education. Women are [currently able to reach] high level positions. But certainly not as much progress was made before we became independent than since our independence. Macedonia is more of a patriarchal society where the men are dominant, where the decision makers are the men. But I don't know if I would say that women have been submissive. The women have not had as many opportunities in the past, but I think that right now women do have a lot of opportunities. We have a [woman] minister (one out of twenty-one) in our government. We have some members of parliament who are women. At the higher levels there are women. Women do not participate in the army. The army is strictly reserved to the males. But I think this is a good thing. If I may use myself as an example, being the ambassador to Washington is the most important diplomatic post. The fact that the government did agree to appoint me to the post shows that they are forward thinking.

MLS: Can you tell us about the inroads women have made in your country. To which extent have these accomplishments inspired you?

Acevska: We have two universities in Macedonia. The head of the largest university is a woman. The head of the privatization agency is a woman. This is a very important organization. Previously everything was state owned. Now we are going through a privatization process. The fact that now Macedonia is a true democracy brings more opportunities for women, for all the citizens of Macedonia. There is also the opportunity to travel abroad. Hopefully, only the good things are brought back over there.

MLS: What is the impact of your career on your private life? Did your ambassadorship prevent you from having a family life since you are single?

Acevska: Certainly, the fact that I became involved with this field has hindered my opportunity to have a family. This is certainly a twenty-four-hour job. Had I been appointed ambassador with everything already in place, it would have been much easier. The fact that I pretty much had to do everything from scratch, my whole focus, my entire time was devoted to my work (I would not necessarily say to my career), to this duty. I do not have any time for family. Right now I am becoming more conscious of that. I am trying to spend more time with my parents, with my brother and his family. I am also trying to spend more time with friends. It is also important to maintain a balance. The higher your position is, the more you end up sacrificing one or the other. It is great to have a balance at different times in your life. You have to put more focus on a different aspect. I chose this. I chose to focus on this career. I do hope to have a family, but with these past five years in diplomacy, it has just been impossible. Here, the difference between a man and a woman comes into play. It is so much easier for men to pursue their careers and to go up higher and higher. The same opportunity does not exist for women. As ambassador, I find out that a lot of the things I do would be dealt with by the spouse of a male ambassador. It is much easier for a man to be an ambassador because his wife plays a support role. A perfect example is entertaining. Traditionally women take care of that. I don't think the husbands of women ambassadors are willing to do a lot of the things that the wives of male ambassadors would traditionally have to undertake. So women ambassadors have to fulfill both roles.

MLS: Does your title intimidate men?

Acevska: Oh! Of course! I like to look at the person straight in the eyes when I say that I am the ambassador. All of a sudden the reaction tends to be different. Prior to that I was just a person. You put a title on the woman and, all of a sudden, men have a different reaction. I don't think it is fair because a person is a person regardless of what her title is. The reaction is different, not only from men, but also from women. I always like to treat people the same way, regardless of their title. I also say, "today you have this title, tomorrow you will not." Let's remember that. You have to have a down to earth approach to things. If you have an attitude because of your title of ambassador, it will not get you far.

MLS: What do you wish for women in your region and in your country in particular?

Acevska: My wish is more of a utopian nature that all of the people would have the same rights and opportunities regardless of whether they are men or women. That is my true wish. I don't think it can ever happen, neither in my country, my region or anywhere. Hopefully, people will become more accepting that there can be women ambassadors, prime ministers, presidents, leaders. To go forward from that and not to use these labels "men," "women," but rather to look at people in terms of their skills. A capable person is indispensable. That's what we have to work towards. The more strides women make, the easier it will be for them to be accepted. That's the other pressure on the woman. She is also going to be judged by her success or her failure. If [she fails], the first comment will be—"she is a woman." "We said that a woman could not do this job." There is an added pressure being a woman to do the job properly to be successful. You set the path for others to follow.

MLS: What is the biggest hurdle you had to overcome as a woman?

Acevska: The fact that I am a woman. As a woman you have to prove yourself over and over again. Show that yes you are capable of doing this job. My feeling is that if you are capable you can overcome all the obstacles that have been presented to you. You just have to work hard. You always have to convince other people that you are the ambassador. I get so much mail that is addressed to "Mr." or to "Ambassador and Mrs." It is a bit amusing, but after a while you just have to block it and not let that bother you. There are a lot of things women endure that men do not have to deal with.

MLS: Which one of your accomplishments are you the most proud of?

Acevska: The fact that I started the embassy from the very beginning—I do not mean to sound fastidious. I think that we have accomplished a lot since I started this work. I guess the accomplishment I am the most proud of is the fact that we have great diplomatic relations between the Republic of Macedonia and the United States. That we did not have when I started this job. People even questioned whether Macedonia could remain an independent country. The fact that this was achieved speaks for itself. Since I started this job, Macedonia has been accepted internationally. We are members of organizations such as the United Nations, the World Bank. Again the fact that there are good relations between the Republic of Macedonia and the United States is very important. Also the United States by sending the troops to Macedonia at a critical point showed support for my country. It viewed Macedonia as an important strategic country that needs to be kept peaceful.

MLS: Where do you see Macedonia five or ten years from now on the international diplomatic scene?

Acevska: My greatest wish is for Macedonia to remain peaceful. It is a great achievement that we obtained independence peacefully and have remained peaceful in the last five years despite the many obstacles that were presented to my country. The key is to remain peaceful, to continue the path to democracy, to continue the path to a market economy, to be viewed as an equal member of the international community—for Macedonia to be economically strong so that we are able to provide assistance to other countries. Certainly I also hope that good relations between Macedonia and the United States will continue, that the relations between the two countries will prosper. We are a small country but, nevertheless, we can make a contribution to the world. Being peaceful is a major contribution. If something were to happen to Macedonia a lot of different countries would have to get involved . . . to remain peaceful and democratic and to prosper economically, for people to know that yes this is the Republic of Macedonia, to be a major player in the Balkans as a democratic center. We are strategically located. We could be the center where a lot of activities can take place. A business center. That is what I am working towards. That is my wish.

MLS: Macedonia is located in a part of the world that is very volatile. What could be Macedonia's role in the area of preventive diplomacy? Also with Greece there was some controversy about the flag of Macedonia and even about the name of your country.

Acevska: That's a very good question. Not only do I see Macedonia as a negotiator but as an example. What Macedonia has achieved in the past five years is an example of preventive diplomacy for other countries to emulate. As you know we had a lot of problems with Greece. Many times these problems were very tense. But we did resolve our conflict peacefully. This is a great credit to the Republic of Macedonia and also to Greece. We chose to resolve our conflict via political dialogue rather than via arms. This is an example of how to resolve conflict. By sitting down and discussing the problems. Unfortunately, each country has to make a compromise. We made some major compromises on our part. We also realize that it was the necessary step. . . . Greece had to make some compromises [as well]. We can also play a role in helping other countries resolve their conflicts by being an example. To go back to your previous question this would be my wish for the future—that people view Macedonia as an example and for Macedonia to help other countries resolve their problems. The problems we had with Greece were very serious. It could have resulted in a conflict very easily. But another example is how the international community has reacted. The fact of sending the UN troops to Macedonia, especially the United States troops—other countries saw the potential for a conflict to rise in [our] country and they decided to take preventive steps. Of course our president had the foresight to request this assistance and these countries responded. This is the key to leadership. If you have good leadership it is much easier to resolve issues. We also have the experience of how to resolve these issues. We are never going to be a superpower like the United States. We will never have nuclear weapons. Well right now they are working to level nuclear weapons anyway. But we can play a key role in resolving conflicts.

MLS: You have had a lot of success in your career working tirelessly promoting Macedonia, being a negotiator. How do you transmit your knowledge to the next generation who is going to represent Macedonia in Washington or elsewhere in the world?

Acevska: Thank you very much. You are very kind. Can I have a copy of that tape [laughing]? I am not going to be ambassador forever. Whoever comes here hopefully will follow in the same footsteps. I send reports explaining the way I do things, of course with guidance from the Foreign Ministry and of course from the president. That actually is a very good question. What to do to ensure this?

MLS: After your post as an ambassador to Washington what do you intend to do? Are you going to continue working with the government? The next logical step would be Minister of Foreign Affairs.

Acevska: That is one of the hardest questions I am always asked. I really do not know what I am going to do next. One of the problems (not necessarily a problem), is that I have achieved this at a young age, so I still have a lot of time left to pursue a professional career. Being appointed ambassador to Washington is pretty much the top of a diplomatic career. Not only for Macedonia but for every country. For many ambassadors who are here from different countries this is their last post. After this they retire. In my case this my first diplomatic post. What I will do, I really don't know. First I will take a long vacation. [Laughter.] I would like to be in a job where I can contribute to world peace, something along those lines. Again, whether I will remain with the Macedonian Foreign Service or the government or pursue something else, I really don't know.

MLS: This is invariably the same answer I get from all of the women ambassadors I interviewed. They don't know and they take it in stride!

Acevska: The problem is that it is difficult to accept a lesser post. After this post there are only a few other posts that one can aspire to. Many have asked me, "What will you do next?" I love this job. It is a very demanding job. But, on the other hand, I know that I am not going to do this forever. But I would like to do something to contribute to peaceful coexistence between countries, people. There is so much chaos going on in the world. When you watch television and see what's going on in the world, especially in the Democratic Republic of Congo right now.

MLS: In certain circles in Washington whenever predictions are made about possible future Secretaries General of the UN your name comes up along with that of Hillary Clinton and that of some of the women ambassadors, particularly those posted in Washington or at the United Nations. How do you feel about that?

Acevska: My interest was always working for the UN. Unfortunately, the UN has come under a lot of criticism. Some of it is deserved. The UN has done a lot of good things. I have always been interested in the UN. I think it is a very necessary institution. They do make a difference. In Macedonia they have played a positive role. Unfortunately, you never hear about the good things. You always hear about the bad things.

MLS: What is your typical day like at the embassy?

Acevska: There are certain tasks which are typical. On certain days you pretty much have to go with the flow. Almost every day I speak with my president, also with the Foreign Ministry, just to get instructions, to clear up things. I try to speak every day with my contacts at the White House, at the State Department, at the Pentagon. There are U.S. troops in my region; therefore, the Pentagon is important at this moment. I try to stay in contact with Congress. I do a lot of reading, especially of newspapers. Information is extremely important. I am often involved in crisis management and prevention. Sometimes I would speak with the journalists. A typical day includes at least one reception.

MLS: What is the most challenging aspect of your job?

Acevska: I don't know whether I can answer that question. We have good relations [with the host country] right now. Certainly the most important part of my job is to maintain good relations with the United States. Since we already have good relations, to maintain and improve those relations is important. It is a challenge. But I would not say that it is an overwhelming challenge because there is this understanding between the two countries. Right now we are trying to improve business relations between the two countries, to increasingly promote Macedonia, to keep a smile on my face during the day.

MLS: How supportive was your family of your appointment?

Acevska: This is the type of work you cannot discuss, even with a spouse. What I do here does have an impact on the lives of the Macedonians. So having the support of my family in accepting this post was psychologically important to me. And my family has been very supportive. I have to honor the support and the trust I was given. That is why I try to be very conscious of what I say, of what I do, because otherwise I could start a war. I could ruin relations between the two countries. That is a lot of pressure. I also have the opportunity to improve their lives and that is very gratifying. That is why I devoted my life these past five years to this job. I also remember where I come from. I remember when we lived in Macedonia. We lived in a very small village. We were very poor. We had food to eat, but that was pretty much the extent of it. I have had a lot of opportunities. And that is why I am so committed right now so that the people of Macedonia have opportunities. Hopefully the same opportunities that I have had, but if not at least to have the opportunity to have a good life. That is what keeps me going every day. I hate this cliché, "It is lonely at the top," but it is. You can't really break away from this job. We are in a unique situation. Because we are a brand new country, a new embassy, new in every sense. In diplomacy you have to be very strong of mind, of body, of spirit. It is very important because there are a lot of pressures, certainly. There is no question about that.

MLS: Is diplomacy something that you had in mind already as a child or an adolescent?

Acevska: My family moved here when I was nine years old. The village I come from is a very small village where I still have relatives. We had food, but still that was pretty much it. When we came here it was very difficult. We did not know the language. We did not know the people. When I came here I did not speak a word of English. Nevertheless as I got older there were more opportunities for me. I always hoped that my relatives could also have an opportunity to do what they would like with their lives, to have the freedom to choose. I always wanted to be in a career where I could help people. I thought of being a doctor but I am afraid of blood. When I was in college I always had big ambitions and the goal to help people, although I could not forsee that I would get this position and at this early stage. This was an opportunity and I did seize it.

MLS: So you grew up in the United States from the age of nine until . . . ?

Acevska: [From age nine] I always lived in the United States. I went back to Macedonia only for visits. I would spend the summers there or just a few weeks.

MLS: At some point you did have American citizenship?

Acevska: Yes, I was a U.S. citizen, but I had to renounce the U.S. citizenship to be appointed an ambassador—U.S. law, not Macedonian law—U.S. law with which I agree. It was a difficult decision. I consulted with my parents and they were very supportive which kind of surprised me.

MLS: Could you have developed your career as a diplomat the other way around as a U.S. citizen?

Acevska: When I was in college my goal was to be in the U.S. diplomacy. I studied international affairs at Ohio State University. When I was in college I was always very ambitious but I always thought I would get involved with U.S. politics. That was my goal and my long term goal was to be Secretary of State. I will not be U.S. Secretary of State; that is for sure. I also had the goal to be ambassador. When I was a student at Ohio State University, I attended a conference where a U.S. ambassador came to address us. I went and listened to him. After that speech I thought, "Wow, that's what I want to be, an ambassador." Of course, a U.S. ambassador. . . . But again I never really envisioned myself working for Macedonia. But then that's how things evolve. When I was in college, I was very much looking into the United Nations. I always wanted to do something which would improve under-standing between people, between countries. . . . [M]y focus was East/West relations. The communist world versus the capitalist world. I always had that type of a goal. Do you want to know how I became involved with Macedonia?

MLS: Yes. From being a U.S. citizen to representing Macedonia in the United States.

Acevska: It is a typical assumption because how else can you be appointed to this post. After college I became involved in business. It was an oppor-tunity which arose. I thought I would do it for a while. . . . I was working then for an international trading company here. I thought I would start with business and eventually get involved in U.S. politics. But I was always interested in Macedonia—well at that time it was Yugoslavia Macedonia. In 1991, when all the changes were occurring in Eastern Europe and it was obvious that Yugoslavia was breaking apart, I met a Yugoslav diplomat here in Washington. He was originally Macedonian but he was in the Yugoslav diplomacy in February of 1991. When I met him, I recommended to him that Macedonia open an office in Washington and try to work on establish-ing relations with the United States. When he went back he told the pres-ident of Macedonia about me and about my idea that Macedonia should be represented in Washington. In August of 1991 I went to Macedonia. A meeting was arranged for me with the president of Macedonia. When I met with him again, I recommended that Macedonia open an office in Wash-ington. Basically they agreed to open an office and they asked me to rep-resent them. It was the first time I met the president. It was the first time I met any of the government officials. The only contacts I had with Mace-donia were my relatives. Again it was from that idea that there should be an office here that it all started. Of course I did not really realize what I was recommending!

MLS: And what you were getting into!

Acevska: That's true! Macedonia declared its independence in September. I was there on September 8th when we had the referendum for independence. I voted for that. I came back here and started to work on promoting Macedonia, to establish relations with the United States. That's how it started. This is something I always tell people—when you have an idea, pursue that idea. I never imagined myself in this position because I was a U.S. citizen; I did not even have political contacts or a base in Macedonia. It was an idea. I worked for it. They saw that I was doing a good job and that is how it all started.

MLS: Does your immediate family currently live in Macedonia?

Acevska: My immediate family (all U.S. citizens) lives in the United States in Ohio where they have lived ever since we moved here. I have aunts, uncles, my grandfather in Macedonia.

MLS: I know that they all must be extremely proud of you.

Acevska: They really are. When I went to present my credentials to President Clinton, my parents and my brother and sister-in-law were able to attend the ceremony. And this is something that is very memorable for them. It is a very memorable event as it is but especially for them. That is why I say that my situation is unique. I was not sent from there to be the ambassador. In essence, I created this post.

MLS: And in the process creating the idea of a country, then contributing to create the country itself!

Acevska: I was on special appointment to represent Macedonia in 1992 from January until September, I also covered the UN. I also did some of the European countries where we did not have representation. Right now we have very good relations with all the countries. Something that hindered our progress certainly was the problem we had with Greece and the influence they had on the international community. But we were able to overcome all of these problems. It is a great achievement what Macedonia has done thus far under difficult circumstances. [Greece had imposed embargoes on Macedonia.] There were the sanctions of Serbia which negatively affected trade. We were not yet internationally accepted. To achieve a peaceful independence under these circumstances is quite remarkable.

MLS: What do you think of the leadership style of some of the women in your region? I am thinking for example about women such as Tansu Schiller and trying to balance Western values with traditional Islamic ones.

Acevska: What is interesting is that there are women leaders in what you would think of as traditionally patriarchal societies. I have to have respect for women [from those societies] who achieve at that level. In her case she has been educated in the West and so was the former Prime Minister of Pakistan, Benazir Bhutto. You have to admire their courage. They have taken that route because they are strongly convinced of the contribution they can make. Although one is not necessarily always in a position to do everything one wants to do. But as long as you try. That is the important thing. Also for a woman it is important not to forget that she is a woman. If a woman in a position of power tries to be a man, that's not going to work.

MLS: Women seem to play an active role in the economy of your country.

Acevska: They do play an active role. There are not many women who are head of the largest companies. What is interesting, however, is that there are a lot of women who are forming their own companies, trading companies, computer companies, information companies. Because Macedonia is also an agricultural society, the women will also work in the fields. This may not be their primary jobs, but they also work there in order to provide food for their own consumption, but also produce for sale. They are making a contribution.

MLS: Do you still speak Macedonian after so many years spent in the United States?

Acevska: Oh yes, sure. The language I still maintained. Of course there are new words which I had to learn. Language is extremely important. It is a way of communicating. If you cannot communicate there are many obstacles. Regardless of the politics everybody wants to have good relations with the United States. This is something that every country strives for. This is something that I think is very important to maintain.

MLS: I hope that the following question will not offend you. Some women ambassadors have one advantage over some of their male counterparts in displaying and even exuding their culture. They can wear their national or traditional outfits. To which extent is appearance important for a woman in a post of ambassador?

Acevska: Very important. That is why I said earlier a woman must always remember she is a woman. To me appearance has always been very important. Even when I was very young, I always tried to be well dressed, well manicured. That has always been very important to me. Being a woman you are judged on every single detail. A man can go anyway he likes. No one would comment on his appearance.

MLS: Does a good appearance help or hinder?

Acevska: It is a combination. It is helpful in the sense that it is easier to get their attention. I can get the attention of any of them. At a reception it is always easier to get the attention of the men, but it is a hindrance because in a sense they just look at your appearance. You don't want them to look at your appearance if there is something substantial you need to discuss. There are also snide remarks that relate to my appearance. They think they are giving me a compliment, but it is not really professional. What makes a difference is also your age. If you are in your sixties and a woman ambassador, the fact that you are a woman is secondary. Usually people who know that I am a woman but who have not met me [on prior occasions] spontaneously tell me, "I expected you to be someone in her sixties." It is a stereotype. If you are a woman ambassador you ought to be in your sixties. That's why appearance is so important; you have to look the part. You have to look professional.

When a woman is attractive, there is always this question that lingers in people's mind, "How did she get to that post?" They don't realize the hard work that has gone into it. It is a question that people often ask me when I speak: "Is being an attractive young ambassador a hindrance?" I would say, "Yes, it is a hindrance because you have to work that much harder to prove yourself." Sometimes they look at you enchanted and they want to help. This is something I have discovered, especially with older men. I often work with older men. They want to help you along this path almost in a fatherly way. "Poor little kid," they think.

Since this interview, many things have happened, war in Kosovo, massive exodus of Kosovar Albanians to Macedonia, the visit of President and Mrs. Clinton to Macedonia. Ambassador Acevska's schedule has been more than hectic. Among her latest activities, organizing the visit of the American head of state on the Macedonian side. Regarding the visit of the Clintons to Macedonia she describes the people on the streets as "elated." This is what she had to say on the war in Kosovo, its effect in her country and her proposed solution to conflicts in the region.

Acevska: I am convinced that the answer or the model for good inter-ethnic relations, good neighborliness, peace and cooperation in the Balkans should be the Republic of Macedonia. Particularly aware of its influence and importance for the stability and prosperity of the state, the Republic of Macedonia devoted special attention to the advancement, protection and respect of human rights. Most importantly, emphasis was given to the protection and promotion of the rights of persons belonging to national minorities, which constitute one third (23 percent ethnic Albanians) of the overall population of the country.

Consequently, the protection of minority rights has been foreseen on a constitutional level and regulated by a clear and comprehensive legal framework which carefully corresponds to, and even surpasses the international standards.

Furthermore, the foreign policy of the Republic of Macedonia, based on the premises of good neighborliness, non-interference in the internal matters of neighboring states, regional and global cooperation and the integration in the Euro-Atlantic structures, also proved to be a generator of peace and stability in the region.

That is exactly the reason why I am confident that the states in the Balkans and the international community will recognize that the positive and constructive behavior of the only "success story" in the region on the domestic and international scene is the right and only path to peace and prosperity.

Extremely burdened by the effects of accommodating more than a quarter of a million refugees from Kosovo (which amounts to almost 13 percent of the population); by the complete cessation of trade with the biggest trade partner—Yugoslavia; by the cut-off of the only transport corridor to Western Europe; the cancellation of business contracts on behalf of Western partners (out of fear of instability in the region), and as a result of that a rise of the unemployment rate to almost 40 percent; the Republic of Macedonia is in danger of becoming the biggest innocent victim of this conflict.

And just as a reminder, the country proved to be an even bigger ally to NATO than some of its full-fledged members, allowing 30,000 NATO soldiers to be stationed on its territory which is twice the number of its own armed forces.

There should be no doubt in anybody's mind that the only solution to the problems of the Balkans is the inclusion of Macedonia in the European Union and in NATO. The immediate inclusion of the Republic of Macedonia and other countries in the region in these institutions will transform the Balkans from a source of tensions and conflicts to an integral part of democratic, united and prosperous Europe.

AMBASSADOR MALEEHA LODHI
OF THE ISLAMIC REPUBLIC OF
PAKISTAN

U.S. Senator Hank Brown said of her: "She is an absolute dyna-
mo. . . . They couldn't have picked anyone with more energy and
brighter mind. I am convinced much of the improvements between
the two countries, the United States and Pakistan, is because of her
incredible energy level." And in a 1994 article, *Time* magazine selected her as one of the world's 100 pacesetters. When she speaks on
American campuses, the former lecturer of political science of the
London School of Economics leaves crowds of students mesmerized
and wanting to change their major to international politics, but at a
reception in her embassy, she can easily be admonished by a 12-year-
old Pakistani for her workaholic habits. Among Pakistani American
students and young professionals Ambassador Maleeha Lodhi is both

an icon and an older sister figure who reinforces in them the importance of professionalism. Gracefully draped in her national shalwaar and kameez, the once shy student is today a dramatically powerful combination of brains and beauty.

Former Pakistani Prime Minister, Benazir Bhutto, whom she befriended a decade ago in London, appointed her ambassador of Pakistan to the United States at a critical point when relations between the United States and Pakistan were at an all time low. Maleeha Lodhi who is an independently minded journalist and was the confidant of former Prime Minister Bhutto, has also been one of her toughest critics.

Ambassador Lodhi's first career is journalism which she embraced by chance. She was invited to write an article on the political opposition to the military regime of General Zia ul Haq by a magazine and by the BBC. She soon became the much celebrated and outspoken journalist whose news analysis column was the most widely read in Islamabad among government officials and members of the diplomatic corps alike. Sharp, astute and erudite, her evaluations of Pakistani-U.S. relations and for that matter her analysis of world affairs always left food for thought. Frank and incisive, her outspoken comments on government mismanagement got her at times into trouble and demanded answers. She became the diva of investigative journalism.

When tapped for the post of ambassador to Washington, 40-year-old Maleeha Lodhi was fully prepared having extensively written about U.S.-Pakistani relations for over a decade. Having managed a staff of 150 for five years at Pakistan's English-language daily, *The News*, the thought of managing an embassy including 115 employees was not particularly daunting, even when that embassy happened to be located in Washington.

In Washington, she became more than a lobbyist. Between 1994 and 1997, she became a crusader with two hot issues to defend: the occupation of Kashmir which she perceived as an injury to Pakistan and to the Muslim world; and the Pressler amendment which she tirelessly denounced as unfairly treating Pakistan in the area of nuclear non-proliferation.

According to Dr. Lodhi, the Pressler amendment had singled out Pakistan in an attempt to eliminate the specter of nuclear proliferation in South Asia. Sanctions were implemented against Pakistan for having among other things acquired short range missiles from China.

Both China and Pakistan were sanctioned. While sanctions against China were lifted, those against Pakistan were maintained. From then on, Pakistan had to contend with the sanctions and with the conventional superiority of next door neighbor India armed with a highly mobile Prithvi missile, a possible threat to Pakistan. Echoing former Prime Minister Bhutto's message to President Clinton about the Pakistani embargoed F16 planes, "We want our money back," the Pakistani ambassador with the soft handshake and the firm, elegant approach championed the cause on Capitol Hill putting to the test her memorable sound bites and her astute strategies. She found this technique most effective when an elderly gentleman of the House fell asleep after five minutes of her presentation. Distraught and at a loss for words, Maleeha Lodhi and her aide were pondering over whether to let him continue his nap and surreptitiously leave his office or to wait a few more minutes, until he woke up. Upon awaking he reiterated her five minute speech indicating that it was forceful enough for him to remember even after a brief but sound nap.

The politically savvy Maleeha Lodhi had a formula that worked in Washington. Right-on-target Albrightesque sound bites, apropos punch lines and skillful strategizing became part of her rite of passage into the top diplomatic post. She set the stage for bilateral and multilateral talks. By the end of 1995 her efforts were rewarded and the Brown amendment counterbalanced the Pressler sanctions against her country. For the sake of evenhandedness, Washington had somewhat changed its position on the subject. Having contributed to mending the relations between the United States and Pakistan, Ambassador Lodhi earned the respect of government officials in both Washington and Islamabad.

Few women in Pakistan, and for that matter in Asia, have managed to break the social barriers and take a leap of faith into the political arena. Maleeha Lodhi is one of the exceptions. Traditionally, women in South Asia have been able to break the gender barrier by succeeding to their assassinated husbands or fathers. Maleeha Lodhi broke the barrier with her inner strength.

MLS: The *Washington Post* describes the diplomatic corps as a "men's club." What has been your experience as a woman ambassador in Washington?

Ambassador Lodhi: It is very much a men's club. Out of 172 ambassadors, there are only ten women. The statistics themselves speak volumes. I think that they are quite right in describing the diplomatic corps as a men's club. But I do not think it is restricted to representation of countries in Washington. You see this across the world where female envoys are regarded as some kind of novelty and as an unusual and extraordinary phenomenon rather than normal. I think that in turn reflects the fact that there are relatively few women [in this field]. It is encouraging to see that there is now a female Secretary of State in the United States. But the fact that it has taken a country like the United States so long to have a female Secretary of State itself is a statement.

There are still very few females working in areas of foreign policy and security policy representing their countries around the world. The foreign service or people representing their country and who happen to be female is still a rarity. Now, what impact does it have in operating in what is perceived to be a men's club? Most female professionals who have reached this position have done so on the basis of their very strong professional careers where gender has had nothing to do with the fact that they have achieved what they have achieved. It is very much a male prism that you are seen through and which makes your gender important.

In my profession, it is not relevant whether I am a woman and I think that most females who are operating in a male-dominated environment are going to feel that way. I cannot speak for them, but I can certainly speak for myself. It is others who make you feel unusual. We do not have a sense of ourselves as being terribly unique, although statistically we may be so. In terms of experience, often times I have been asked whether being female is an advantage. It has pluses and minuses. So in a sense it balances itself out. I do not think that we have extraordinary advantages as we start out. Certainly there is a tendency for people to remember us because we are regarded as unusual. By the same token when you deal with individuals outside of the administration, it takes awhile for them to understand that you are where you are despite your being a woman, not because of it. It takes perhaps awhile for them to evaluate that you are no different and that you should not be treated differently from your male colleagues.

MLS: What are the strong pluses and minuses?

Lodhi: The only plus that I see is that in a context where many countries are represented, the country with a female envoy is remembered because female envoys are the exception rather than the norm. But, over all in this context, gender is neither a handicap nor an advantage.

MLS: Are your duties as an ambassador in conflict with your personal life?

Lodhi: As a professional woman I have felt that. Not only as a diplomat. I have pursued careers which have been very demanding in terms of time and energy. Diplomacy like journalism is not a nine to five job. You are on call twenty-four hours. Yes, there is a great degree of personal sacrifice that goes with it. Whether you consciously make that sacrifice as you start is another question. It is very hard to combine the two roles. My experiences are the media and three years as ambassador to Washington. I have found it very difficult to balance that with my commitments to my family and to my son. Something does get sacrificed and in this case it was my family. I have a very acute consciousness of that. I often find myself rationalizing and saying that it is quality time that I give my family. But I know very well that it is a consolation. I am saying that to compensate myself as much as my family. I am not available, period. What this [post] demands of me is my entire self. And that is where gender comes into play. People's expectations of you when you are a female ambassador are that you have to play both roles: that of an ambassador and that of the spouse of an ambassador. And that is what makes it difficult. A male envoy would generally have a spouse. There are certain things that a male envoy would never be asked to do or to attend. With female envoys there is such an expectation.

Female envoys end up playing both "male" and "female" roles in terms of conventionally described roles. So you end up having to give more. Women still have a difficult time. Unless you are seen as superwoman by your colleagues and by those you deal with, you will never be accepted on an equal footing with men. So we still have to work twice as hard, put in twice as much energy, show everybody that we are way ahead of them. It is a cycle; we in turn have to work that much harder to show that we are ahead in order to just be where they are. For men certain things are presumed. We women have to keep proving ourselves. I do not think it ever ends. It has been my story. I spent six years in the academic world, nine years in journalism, three years in diplomacy. Perhaps the easiest time I had was in the academic world. It is pretty obvious why. As I entered journalism, which remains still male dominated, I found I had to do the same thing I do here, which is to prove myself every day, something our male colleagues do not need to do because the presumption is that they are good. With a female, the presumption is that we do not know whether she is good until she proves herself. So you keep proving yourself over and over again. That is something that the environment imposes upon you. You do it pretty subconsciously. It is not as if you wake up every morning and say, look I have to prove myself today. It is extremely tough being a female professional in any sphere, as much in this sphere as in other spheres. Perhaps the academic world is about the only world that is different in that regard. Certainly it has been my experience. There I did not feel that I wasn't taken seriously. People walking in my class did not look at me as odd or unusual. I was there by virtue of my credentials and was accepted as such. The problem is that in a male-dominated environment people view you as a total novelty which is something that does not sit comfortably with female professionals because we are not a novelty. We may be unusual statistically, but we are like everybody else, trying to do the same sort of things with the same sort of energy and the same sort of skills. . . .

MLS: Many of the women ambassadors are divorced. Is it linked to the pressure of the job?

Lodhi: I am divorced as well. And that in itself is a statement. I do not think it is a coincidence. That just shows the rigors of trying to combine professional life where you are committed and devoted to certain goals and trying to handle a family. Sometimes it is impossible to combine them and one thing has to go. My divorce took place before I became a diplomat, while I was in journalism.

It is hard for women to play the kind of conventional role that a lot of spouses do expect. It is very hard for male spouses to accept the great demands in schedule that women may have. Women are supposed to understand, but it never works the other way around.

MLS: What was the reaction in your country when your appointment as ambassador to Washington was announced?

Lodhi: In my case, one of my predecessors was a female. So I was not the first. It was not something unusual for Pakistan to appoint a woman to Washington. Even though there are very few women representing my country right now, the tradition of females representing Pakistan goes back to the 1950s and 1960s when the wife of our first prime minister, Begum Ranaliakatalekahn, represented the country. I think that there is a certain familiarity with the phenomenon and people do not regard it as exceptional. In later years there were very few women representatives, not even a handful; I would say one or two, but the fact that it was a known phenomenon, it was not regarded with any degree of amazement.

MLS: Has your son followed you to your post?

Lodhi: He is eighteen and attending university. He never really saw me as an ambassador because he lived in Pakistan while I came here. My family in fact [was initially] split by my decision to come here. It is only now that he has come here. He started university. Obviously I have not been able to give him the sort of time that I would have liked to give him. My family has been totally supportive of my career—even my son. I consulted him and asked him how he felt. He replied that I must go and that it was an enormous honor for me to represent my country in the most important capital in the world. He assured me that there should be no doubt in my mind about accepting the post, but at the same time he added very quickly that he was aware of the fact that he could not come with me because he had to complete his schooling in Pakistan. So I didn't impose a decision on him.

I felt he had made the correct choice. So obviously it was very hard on me. I missed these last three years of his development. That was a very painful decision, but I made it. Then he attended college and became all of a sudden an adult.

MLS: What was the reaction of your former husband to your appointment?

Lodhi: He was very supportive also. My entire family was very supportive and felt that I should go ahead and do this.

MLS: Is there any extra "baggage" in the fact that you are representing an Islamic country as a woman?

Lodhi: I do not have any problem in doing that. I believe very strongly in my Islamic identity. I do not have to adopt any behavior consciously. It comes very naturally to me because Islam is very much part of my faith, part of my tradition, of the way I dress. I do not see myself making any conscious effort to do that. Pakistan is an Islamic country, but it is a liberal democratic Islamic country. We respect other countries in the Islamic world and other conservative countries in the non-Islamic world also. So we respect them, but we do not have to change ourself in order to respect them. My identity is my own. My country's identity is my own. We respect those which may be different from ours. You adapt in terms of respecting, but you do not change. My country's identity is also very important. It's distinctive. It's different. No, I did not have to change myself in anyway.

MLS: What are your views on the condition of women in your country? Can you name some of its trailblazers besides the prime minister? To what degree have these figures inspired you?

Lodhi: My role models—I have not looked at in terms of gender. One of my role models is certainly the man who founded my country. If you ask about the condition of women in Pakistan, I will have to answer that obviously I cannot be satisfied with the condition of women in my country. I have problems with the condition of women elsewhere in the world also. Specifically in my country, the biggest problem is access to education. In Pakistan there is a very high level of female illiteracy. It is much higher among females than it is amongst men. But I think that it is a general problem because it is pretty high amongst men too. Pakistan needs to address that very fundamental issue because education is the key to everything. It is the key to a more enlightened point of view. It is the key to better health care for women, to population planning, all of it is tied to education. So if I had a single item on my agenda in terms of what anybody can do to change the status of women in Pakistan, it would be to make education accessible to the girl child and to ensure that there is family education available to girls as much as it is available to boys because both have that right. This is something I am very concerned about.

In terms of female role models, of course there are many inspiring figures in present-day Pakistan. Some of the most outstanding lawyers in Pakistan are women. Some of the most outstanding journalists in Pakistan are women. In terms of trailblazers, we have had female professionals breaking new ground in many of these fields. The academic and medical areas are the areas were it was traditionally considered respectable and safe for women to go. So there we have had a long history of women being in those fields. But in fields where women were not present conventionally, we have seen a change. There are now female lawyers, female architects, females entering foreign policy or security fields. These are important landmarks in women's desire to have an equality of opportunity. I do not believe in [a type of] affirmative action . . . where people are chosen simply because of their gender. I have a problem with that. I can see the rationality behind it. I think these policies have to be implemented very carefully because you could end up in the long run defeating your objective. You can end up with a separate but equal phenomenon. You do not want gender apartheid. We women want to be in the mainstream, because we are just as good as anybody else. What we are saying is: look at our professional credentials and determine what you have to on that basis. At times I think affirmative action is important. For example, in Pakistan, a certain number of seats always used to be reserved for women in the National Assembly. I think this is a very important thing to do because there was no other way for some time that female candidates could get elected on their own steam. I think that sort of symbolism and that sort of affirmative action are crucial. It is, however, important when you implement it not to carry it too far, and to implement it extremely carefully to see to it that people do not come to these positions simply because they are women. Otherwise, they can end up not being competent enough and, therefore, deprive all working women of a great reputation. It is this classic dilemma in the world.

MLS: What is the biggest hurdle you had to overcome as a woman in your career in Washington, D.C.?

Lodhi: I did not find many hurdles in Washington, D.C. I know it does not sound very interesting. Of course, one would have to define the word hurdle. The situations in which I found myself at times were humorous. Often, I would walk into congressional offices and people would presume that the male accompanying me was the envoy and I the secretary, the assistant or the aide.

There is an immediate presumption. Those situations I regard as rather humorous. They are not hurdles, unless of course you see that as a presumption again: How could it be a female! So for sometime, psychologically you try to break down that barrier that you feel must be on that person's mind, because why would he make that presumption in the first place?

I cannot think of any hurdle I confronted as a female. There were many hurdles I confronted but anybody would have confronted them, whether male or female. I think that the hurdles female professionals confront are usually at the very initial stages of their careers. That is when if you can achieve a breakthrough, I would not say you are home but at least you can move ahead. It is the initial acceptance that is crucial, the initial ability of men to accept you as a colleague.

MLS: Can you cite the accomplishments you are the most proud of in your career as ambassador?

Lodhi: There are three areas in which I have a sense of satisfaction. First, the very fact that I had the honor to serve my country in the most important capital in the world. That of course is not an accomplishment, but I can say that these three years have been rewarding for me personally as well as professionally.

Second, it was under my watch that the process of repairing the bilateral relationship began in a serious and substantive way. Of course, I myself played a very modest role in this, but the fact that it happened during my mandate also gives me a sense of satisfaction because when I first arrived here, relations between our two countries had essentially hit rock bottom. It became a question of trying to see how we could put relations back on a normal track. And I am happy to report that relations are back on a normal track. Of course they can never be what they were during the years of the cold war. But on our side also there has been a shift in paradigm in terms of how we see this relationship in the future. So having been involved in the process of redefining this relationship, I feel a sense of gratification for having been part of this process.

Thirdly, a more concrete progress: I chide words such as "achievement" and "accomplishment" because I feel that sometimes they may exaggerate our own significance in these processes that are very complex, which have many participants, which have many people playing a role. I step back and do not want to claim personal achievement. The best that I can say is that it happened under my watch. The third concrete progress that we have made in the last couple of years is the adoption of an amendment in the U.S. legislature. The amendment was to the Pressler amendment under which military and economic sanctions were imposed on Pakistan. The Brown amendment to the Pressler amendment at least addressed the issue of Pakistan's embargoed equipment that the United States has kept since 1990. Neither the equipment that had been embargoed nor the money that we had paid from our national funds was returned to us. The amendment, by addressing that problem, removed an important impediment in the conduct of our bilateral relationship. The issue is still to be entirely satisfactorily resolved, but to the extent that we found recognition in Congress and the administration on the principle of fairness and playing fair with nations, especially those that are called friends of the United States, the Brown amendment was an important gesture from our point of view. It also removed the ban that had been placed on non-military assistance to Pakistan. So, of course, this is something that is for us largely symbolic because we do not seek economic assistance from the United States. The days of economic assistance are gone. Nevertheless, this step was important. Movement in these spheres in the last three years, since I obviously had a little to do with these processes, has brought me some sense of gratification.

MLS: In your role as an ambassador you are a negotiator, an interlocutor, a mediator. Which role befits you the most?

Lodhi: The ambassador plays many roles. You are as you rightly said an interlocutor. You are a negotiator from your country with the government of your credited country. You are also an articulator, a defender of your country's interest. You are also a projector of what your country is all about in a more generalized sense, in terms of creating images. Obviously I have not been an envoy to any other country, so I would not be able to say what is required of an ambassador in other places—but here I have found that an envoy has to play multiple roles and address very different types of audiences. The envoy has to speak to the administration on behalf of his or her country. Envoys are representing their countries on Capitol Hill, again projecting their countries and making their cases before U.S. legislators. An aspect of the job that I have perhaps enjoyed the most is dealing with the legislative branch of the U.S. government. That, to me, has been the most enriching experience. The challenge is so formidable when you walk into the office of a member of Congress or a representative of the Senate, who has only so much time. You then have to somehow engage their attention and you have five minutes to do so. Either you succeed or you don't.

Dealing with the administration is somewhat different. Challenging it is also. There are people within the various agencies of the U.S. administration whose job it is to deal with countries like mine because they deal with regions where Pakistan is situated. So that requires a different type of skill and approach. Dealing with Congress is different. There, the audience may not know too much about your region. They certainly need to be briefed about the issues that are the issues of the day. Dealing with the press is also very important, not only in this country, but across the world in democracies, dealing with think tanks and dealing with places where policy is influenced, be they academic institutions or think tanks or be they the media. Again, you are saying the same thing of course, essentially, but you are addressing very different kinds of audiences. Multiple roles, never a dull moment, always on your feet. The sheer challenge of that, at a time when you find generally the United States, not necessarily turning inwards, but much consumed by domestic issues and problems. So the challenge is manifold then. Why should somebody in the United States really care about what happens in South Asia. In a very simple sort of way, one should address that question in as simple a fashion as possible. That is an enormous challenge. I end up playing multiple roles.

There is of course also here a large Pakistani American community residing in the United States. Another role that I have to play is to keep in touch with them, to service their needs, because they look to us as representatives of their country of birth or of origin. So we have to cater to the needs and demands of that very large community. There are so many different arenas, so many different audiences. Ultimately—and this I say because I have been here three years (I could not have said this in the first three months)—the ultimate judgment that you have to make is how much time to allocate to each area. And that in itself is a constant challenge. For example, here we are in the month of October and there are all these audiences that I have to keep in mind. How much of my time I devote to one particular audience or another is a crucial question.

MLS: You end up devoting more time to which aspect of your work?

Lodhi: Looking back, I think I have devoted the largest amount of time to trying to build relationships for Pakistan with centers of power and influence outside the executive, which is not to minimize my interaction with the executive. That remains important. However, I felt that Pakistani relations with those American centers had been unaddressed or inadequately dealt with in the past. And perhaps because I come from a background which is non-private sector, non-governmental, such a task came more easily to me. Perhaps bureaucrats, as much as I respect them for the insights they bring and experience that they have, do have a different approach.

MLS: Where do you see yourself in your career five or ten years from now?

Lodhi: I have been in professions that have put me in the center of a lot of action. [In Pakistan] I worked in the media where obviously you are at the center of everything that is going on in terms of political activity, developments and action. [As an ambassador I am posted in] the United States[, a country] that is very action oriented. I would like to step back now and reflect on some of these things and devote some time to writing news publications but also take a more reflective look at some of the issues I have dealth with both as a journalist and as a diplomat. In terms of a more academic exercise, a book or a monograph, I would like to do that. In terms of my career, I would like to return to the media. That's where I came from and that's where I would like to go. In terms of what I would really like to do next, it would be to look back at some of the things that I was so involved in and witnessed on a day to day basis, but did not have the time to explore at length and at leisure. I would like to take a step back and reflect. It is important and in the public interest to share some of this and make certain things publicly known, which is very rarely done in Pakistan. Usually people like me do not have an opportunity to serve in government. It is very unusual. Those who do, tend not to write their memoirs or record some of these things. Recording is extremely important. It enhances the public's understanding of the processes of policy making and conducting foreign relations. I would like to contribute to public knowledge in that fashion.

MLS: What is your typical day like at the embassy?

Lodhi: A typical day at the embassy varies from period to period. This is the leanest period of the year for everybody. Lean periods are rare. An average day during spring time starts with an internal meeting of the embassy where all the heads of division come together and we discuss what we need to do for the next few days, weeks. I am briefed about various activities in various departments. I try to provide some guidance. This is a large embassy. It has an information section, a defense wing. We have a military attaché, an air attaché and a naval attaché. We have a trade wing. We have an economic wing. We have an education wing, and we of course have a political wing. These wings comprise our foreign ministry people. It is a large embassy. The entire staff of this embassy is about 115. The early morning meeting is important for a coordinated approach. It includes eighteen heads of division. Then the day begins. I usually take trips to Capitol Hill to keep in touch with certain people. If we are in the midst of trying to get something going in Congress, then obviously more time is spent there. In such cases, there are times when I returned home after 7 P.M. in the evening having covered all my meetings. Those are [not] unusual days of course. These are days when Pakistan is being discussed in some Senate debate or an issue has arisen where there is a need to know what is going on in our region. So an average day would include time spent on Capitol Hill. If I have a meeting on that day with either the Pentagon or the State Department, I would spend some time there. There would be a considerable amount of time I would spend on the telephone talking to members of the Pakistani American community, returning their calls, listening to their concerns, catering to their needs. I can't think of a single day that I have spent in the United States where I have not spoken on the phone to a member of our community not residing in Washington (those residing in Washington can see me anytime), residing across the United States on some issue or the other. It could be passport renewal or information. I see to it that their needs are met. The only givens on an average day are morning meetings and the fact that a certain amount of time has to be devoted to Capitol Hill, to members of the media and members of think tanks who would like to discuss projects that they have been working on, or seek the views of the embassy. Washington is a very unusual city in the sense that there is very little interaction amongst diplomats. It is unquestionably a very bilateral town. All the diplomats are engaged in their own bilateral relations and very little interaction takes place.

MLS: Would you say that diplomats tend to interact within their own regions?

Lodhi [emphatically]: Yes! The only occasions when the entire diplomatic corps comes together is either when we are invited to the White House (obviously everybody gets asked, that's when we see each other) or on the occasion of the State of the Union Address: all the diplomats go and hear the State of the Union Address. Other than these two annual events, there are no other occasions when all the diplomats get together. You are right, they meet by region. All the Asian ambassadors would get together from time to time. Generally compared to other capitals such as Paris or London, this capital is very unusual in that sense.

MLS: To what do you attribute this lack of camaraderie among diplomats?

Lodhi: It is a function of the town we are operating in and also of the fact that there are so many countries represented here. Each is so involved in trying to pursue its own agenda and its own goals, there is very little time left. You may build your own personal relationships and friendships with people from the diplomatic community. But frankly, that has very little to do with your professional functioning. I think it is a function of Washington and the United States and not of the diplomatic corps. It is a very competitive environment. It is truly a bilateral town.

MLS: Which turn would you like to see the relations between Paskistan and the United States take in the next five or ten years after your tenure here?

Lodhi: I would like to see this relationship freed from the glue that it has been in for so many years now. I always say to my American friends and to my American interlocutors: the United States has treated Pakistan in a unique way. Countries like Pakistan that used to be called the third world do have a sense that certain standards are set and that all countries in the world have to comply by that set of standards. Sometimes it is said in my country that the United States wishes to remake the world in its own image. I think that this is a very simplistic statement, but it is a very popularly held view in countries like Pakistan. That is why we try very hard to persuade the United States that although many of the goals it seeks to promote globally are noble goals, good objectives, they must be tempered by understanding and respect for other cultures and other traditions. Certain universal goals are there, but in their expression in different cultures, in different worlds, they too take different forms and those should be respected. That is the only way that I can answer your question, the most diplomatic way.

MLS: Now a shallow question. All the women ambassadors look impeccable. In addition, they often wear garments or accessories that reflect their culture, a luxury that their male colleagues sometimes do not have. How much more important is appearance to female diplomats than it is to male diplomats? Is it an important part of their role?

Lodhi: When you represent your country, by your person you create images about your country. Working women in any case should neither look like Christmas cakes, overdone, nor should they particularly feel defensive about the fact that as working professional women they should be sedately or conservatively dressed. I think that the important thing is to really be yourself. In a representational job like this one, people do look at the country you represent, in a sense, through you. So your appearance does play a part. In Pakistan's case, we Pakistani women, dress in our own national dress. That's important. People remember us by our national dress. They identify us by our national dress. So in that sense one feels that one needs to devote some attention to that which perhaps otherwise one will not do. You know that other people are relating to you in that manner or viewing you in a particular way. So yes, appearance is important. Diplomat or no diplomat a working woman has to be somewhere in between overdone and too dowdy. When she is overdone that detracts. People are so distracted by an aura of glamour, which some women project. On the other hand being too dowdy also sends a negative image. Being too dowdy might mean not being meticulous about other things. That's the way I look at it. Of course I can't speak for all professional working women.

MLS: Any particular anecdote that you recall with amusement?

Lodhi: I do recall with some amusement the difficulty with which certain male colleagues have to adjust to a female boss and the awkwardness that some, not all, displayed. Many relate very easily. As I mentioned to you on the day we met, the more a woman asserts her gender, the more she is defining how others should react to her. In a sense, it is in her own hands. But despite all of that, there is so much she can control. I think of the awkwardness with which male colleagues react to female colleagues, not quite knowing what is correct and what is not correct, fumbling sometimes, saying the wrong things when they do not intend to. All of this is still a reflection of the sheer awkwardness of dealing with a female boss. And that is what I have confronted. When I was in a position in the media where I had a fairly large staff working under me, I noticed it there also. And I think the best one can do in these situations is pretending you have not noticed. Allow them to get over their own awkwardness. The more you notice it the more you are conscious of it, the more you make them conscious of it. And then they will never be able to adjust to you. Again, here we are, entering the twenty-first century still talking about the fact that female leadership is an unusual phenomenon, even though it is now of course much more widespread than before. Whether in the West or in countries like mine, it is still uncommon.

MLS: Was there anything in your childhood or your adolescence that predestined you for a diplomatic career?

Lodhi: Nothing whatsoever. Much of what has happened in terms of my career has been not by prior design or ambition, but by accident. Even my entry into journalism is not something that I thought about for years and years. For instance, I was teaching and was asked to write a piece for a newspaper as an academic. I enjoyed that process so much that I became a journalist. By accident, not by design. The same goes for this job here. I never thought about a career of any kind in the foreign service, but an offer was made to me. I thought about it. I thought despite the fact that I have no diplomatic experience, I like challenges, I would like very much to try this and give it my best shot. I do not know if the moral of that story is that the more you plan, the more things do not work out the way you want. Perhaps the moral is that you continue with whatever interests you and work hard at it. But at the same time do not always plan because things will come by. Opportunities will come by. It's really a judgment call at a certain point in time, that here is an opportunity that is presenting itself and I take a leap of faith and do it.

MLS: How were you brought up as a child?

Lodhi: I was brought up very much in a gender neutral sense. That had much to do with the drive I had. I come from a family where I am the only daughter with two male siblings. My parents saw me in a gender-neutral way. It would be incorrect to say that they saw me as one of the boys, however, the same rules and the same standards that applied to me applied to all the children in the family. Perhaps that made me very career oriented because I could think of nothing else than to be similar to the boys in the family. So in my childhood, now that I look back, that must have been a very significant factor. I have very supportive parents who felt that they had given me an education and that I had to go out there and achieve something with it. That was instilled in me at a very young age.

It's a question of opportunity. There are very few people in the world who are extraordinary individuals. Really. Most people who make it to important positions do so because certain opportunities have presented themselves and they have been able to utilize those opportunities. I do think that luck or the divine factor plays a big role. Otherwise why should these opportunities be available to some and not to others. There is something that is divinely ordained . . . luck . . . chance. The individual might not have planned it so. Something intervenes.

MLS: What is your family background?

Lodhi: I was born in Lahore, which is the capital of the largest province. I grew up in what became the capital, Islamabad. So I am very much a city person. My family is a very middle class family that puts a premium on education. I certainly don't come from a traditional background, in the sense of a rural landed feudal family, which of course all prominent urbanites inherited. Not at all. We are in my family very middle class, very self-made. But my father was exceedingly successful in what he did. He was an oil executive. He worked in the oil industry in Pakistan. My mother trained as a journalist, but then married my father and was not able to pursue her career. She was one of the very few Muslim women in prepartitioned India to study journalism. I never studied journalism. I became a journalist. That's the irony . . . My mother on the other hand actually studied journalism at Punjab University. She was awarded a scholarship to Columbia University to study journalism at that time when fate in terms of her marriage intervened and she was unable to pursue that. There must be elements in our upbringing and our background which have influences on us, but we are unaware of them.

MLS: Thank you, Ambassador Lodhi.

AMBASSADOR SONIA M. JOHNNY
OF SAINT LUCIA

In Washington these days people cannot help sitting up and taking notice of the island nation of Saint Lucia not only because it has had two Nobel Laureates (Derek Walcott for literature in 1992 and Sir Arthur Lewis for economics in 1979) and not only because Saint Lucia was recently voted top honeymoon destination in the Caribbean, but because its new ambassador, her Excellency Sonia Merlin Johnny, simply stands out.

For her, representation and the challenges that come with it all began at the tender age of ten, when she was elected to be the vice-captain of Saint Joseph's House (one of the competitive teams at the Catholic High School which she attended). She was the youngest student to be elected at the time. The captain because of illness was unable to lead the team at the annual physical training competition and as vice-captain, the duty fell on her. This competition entailed synchronized activities by 150 students (average age, thirteen) at the instruction of the captain. Because of her age and size, a number of people were skeptical about her ability, as to whether she could do it. Here was her challenge. On the day of the competition she marched out to the middle of the outdoor courts and proceeded to give instructions in such a loud and clear voice that the team was motivated to a flawless performance and the audience to a standing ovation. This had never happened before in the history of the school. Neither had the instructions to the team ever been delivered in such a loud strong tone. From then on, every captain proceeded to mimic her performance, which was discussed within and outside the school for years. "Challenges have always fascinated me," she says. And when she is challenged, she rises to the occasion and performs in her own style, mimicking no one.

Her voice, like her whole being, "boteroesque" in every sense of the word, resonates in universities, think tanks, the Congress and everywhere else in the United States. She dives into the ring welcoming the daunting task of talking about that crop that does not grow on American soil but is vital to the economy of her nation. At Howard University where I invited her and her colleagues to speak, the fire alarm malfunctioned and made a piercing sound—a true nightmare for me as the hostess. But undaunted, she continued her speech. The banana issue was too important to wait for a technician to fix the problem. She continued raising her voice a few decibels until it covered the sound of the alarm. She was more passionate than ever. The audience riveted, stayed in spite of the alarm, wanting to know more about Saint Lucia's trade issues. She has that ability to turn disengaged Americans whose interest in bananas does not extend beyond the breakfast table, into crusaders. On every panel in which she participates, she is usually the most solicited panelist in the discussion that ensues.

The ambassador has many reasons to be very passionate about bananas. Like many post slavery societies, the majority of Saint Lucia's population was for centuries barred from accumulating capital. The free labor of their forefathers, enslaved people of African origin, was the capital of their European masters. The colonial era that followed did not provide much more economically. Some of the indignities linked to servitude had subsided, but Saint Lucians were still by and large barred from economic participation. Since the 1950s this island nation, however, found a way for the first time to craft a modest and decent living cultivating bananas on small plots of land. Bananas quickly eclipsed sugarcane, the crop of choice of the British colonists. Bananas had many reasons to be favored by the Saint Lucians. The green crop is more adaptable to the small and steep hillside family farms of Saint Lucia. Its production is also far more intensive and generates income on a weekly basis. Approximately 10,000 families depend directly on the green crop for a living and many more thousands depend on it indirectly. But competition from a single United States company based in Central America with the ironic name of Chiquita can destroy all dreams of maintaining that modest but descent living and engender social upheaval. It might also affect Saint Lucia's plan of becoming a financial center.

The new international financial service sector is now banking on diversification. Attracting and retaining legitimate capital is its goal. In doing so one of the models for Saint Lucia is the Cayman Islands, now the fifth largest financial center in the world with 500 billion U.S. dollars in deposits. But for Saint Lucia, this is still a dream and its biggest challenge will be to find a niche. In an interview published in the July 31, 1998, Special International Report of the *Washington Times*, Dr. Kenny D. Anthony, prime minister of Saint Lucia, explains, "This niche must be based on an impeccable reputation. We are somewhat late in the game, and we have a great deal of ground to make up."

As Saint Lucia prepares for its launch as an international financial and world investment center one cannot help remember the late Sir Arthur Lewis (1915–91) who won the Nobel prize in economics in 1979 for pioneering research in economic development with special emphasis on issues facing developing countries. His comprehensive history of the world economy from 1870 until 1914 is a classic. At age seven his poor health prevented him from attending school. So his father, a teacher, taught him at home, covering in three months what the school taught in two years. But later the young student, armed with a burning passion for engineering and economics and supported by a local scholarship, was facing the brick wall of restrictions imposed by the British government on students of color from its former colonies. Studying engineering would have been a futile exercise anyway. At that time hardly any British firm would employ a black engineer regardless of his talent. Arthur Lewis settled for business administration and law where the quotas were less rigid because, in those fields, students from the colonies could make ends meet as clerks and retail assistants without government support. While attending the London School of Economics, which ironically did not offer many courses in economics at the time, Arthur Lewis never abandoned his two passions and continued to teach himself economics beyond the course curriculum. The rest is history—professorships at the Universities of Manchester and Princeton and the founding of the Caribbean Development Bank in Barbados in 1978.

Coincidentally sharing the same date of birth with Sir Arthur Lewis (January 23), Derek Walcott, the other Saint Lucian Nobel Laureate who won the much coveted prize in 1992 is in good company in the region. Next door in Martinique (home of the legendary writer Aimé Césaire, thinker of African independence) in the same year Patrick Chamoiseau won the French Prix Goncourt for his book *Texaco*. Further north in Guadeloupe, Maryse Condé's monumental work, *Ségou* is the kind of stuff around which entire Caribbean Studies departments spring up at universities in the United States. The Saint Lucian poet's work reflects unbridled imagination, multicultural foundation and an undeniable skill to mold the clay of language. In *Omeros*, a book-length poem on the fishermen in the Caribbean, his voice is as deep as his own character in real life is eccentric.

"The island of the poet" has quite a ring to it and is bound to attract honeymooners. Saint Lucia was voted number one honeymoon destination by U.K.-based *Caribbean World* magazine. On a vessel in Rodney Bay or on Pigeon Island, honeymooners keep flocking to Saint Lucia prompting the islanders to bank more on tourism and hotel chains and to double their facilities. Ambassador Sonia Johnny is proud of the island's progress in tourism. However, she deplores its forced 43 percent cut in banana production.

I visited her in her office on New Mexico Avenue in a fairly modern building, home to a cluster of Caribbean embassies. The simplicity of her office seems to underscore practicality over glamour. The TV where the small staff watches senate hearings is 1970s vintage with dial channel selection. She welcomes me with frank Caribbean camaraderie in her busy office. I can tell right away why her peers in the diplomatic corps respect and admire her so much. It's a vote of confidence she has earned. She started their embassy from scratch. In her case, however, her government preferred to send an older male specialized in agriculture as its first ambassador and to use her skills as a graduate of the Johns Hopkins School of Advanced International Studies to train him. But years later she is back and at the helm of the embassy—tireless, punch line eloquent, and a bundle of energy.

MLS: Bananas are the main crop and export of Saint Lucia. This is, however, an industry that is as volatile as it is under siege. It has known many hard times from hurricanes to falling prices. The crisis peaked in 1993 when several farmers were injured and two died in the aftermath of a strike. Today we even hear the term "banana war" between the United States and Europe. You have been, in Washington, a staunch advocate and savvy lobbyist for the banana industry of your country. Explain that position.

Ambassador Johnny: To some people, what has been termed "the banana war" or the dispute between the United States and the European Union (EU) over the latter's banana-import regime is merely a fight over the interpretation of new trade rules, but to us in the Caribbean, the "banana war" is a question of survival.

Banana exports are vital to our social, political and economic stability. The United States recognized this when it supported a unanimously endorsed 1994 GATT [General Agreement on Tariffs and Trade] waiver providing for continued access to the European banana market for the Caribbean countries. So you can imagine our surprise and disappointment when, in 1995, we witnessed a dramatic about face on the part of the United States as it decided to challenge the European banana regime at the World Trade Organization (WTO)—a regime which provided the very access that the United States had endorsed as a guaranteed right under the Lome Convention.

What was even more disappointing, to say the least, was the fact that the United States did so at the behest of one single United States owned multinational corporation, Chiquita Brands. Chiquita contends that the EU's banana import regime prevents it from increasing its 50 percent market share in the EU with its Latin American banana trade.

Collectively, Caribbean countries have only 9 percent of the European banana market. We believe that, unlike the Caribbean, Chiquita has the wherewithal to expand its already leading market share by targeting the 91 percent of the market to which the Caribbean does not have access. It would appear that Chiquita is of the opinion that it would be both easier and more effective to simply have the United States, via legal wranglings within the WTO, offer it the Caribbean 9 percent on a silver platter. This is what Caribbean ambassadors are faced with.

Financially, we do not possess the kind of money which Chiquita is willing to put forward to get its way. The Caribbean countries can only band themselves and, through numerous avenues, appeal repeatedly to United States policy makers to recognize not only the widespread instability and economic upheaval the elimination of the banana market would cause the Caribbean states, but also its crippling effect on the United States interests in the region. For me, it is an extremely difficult task, but the other Caribbean ambassadors have been extremely supportive and have demonstrated their confidence in me by electing me unanimously on two occasions as the Caribbean's coordinator on the banana issue.

MLS: What was the most challenging aspect of your role as an ambassador trying to convince American lawmakers who might have never set foot on a banana plantation of the merit of the banana case.

Johnny: For me the most challenging aspect of my role in trying to convince lawmakers of the merit of the banana case is getting them to visualize a one-crop economy and the debilitating effects the United States' challenges to the guaranteed market on that crop have had and continue to have on the economic, social and political life of the country. Getting lawmakers to visualize the hundreds of family banana farms that will be abandoned and, even as we speak, are being abandoned to be replaced by areas of illegal crop cultivation because of the United States' challenges is a formidable task. The task is even more formidable because we do not have the kind of financial resources that Chiquita has to smooth its path to the 9 percent of the Caribbean banana market share in Europe.

MLS: You undertake many cultural activities in Washington to promote tourism. For example, recently you brought to the Organization of American States an all-women steel band group. How rewarding are efforts to promote tourism? With new facilities such as those at Hewanorra airport, tourism is increasing in Saint Lucia. What is your outlook on the future of tourism in Saint Lucia and in the Caribbean in general?

Johnny: The tourism industry in Saint Lucia appears to be picking up. The government of Saint Lucia has increased its focus on the industry in the light of the banana crisis. Already, it has eclipsed banana production in contribution to the gross domestic product. That trend should continue.

In 1997 tourism grew by more than 5 percent and accounted for nearly 72 percent of the nation's export of goods and services. Cruise ship visits have increased by 59 percent and the number of stay-over visitors is up by 5.4 percent. The tourism sector is positioned for substantial growth, especially given the projected doubling of the number of hotel beds over the next five years. This certainly offers a significant investment opportunity to foreign investors.

MLS: Of all the roles an ambassador fulfills—that of a negotiator, a mediator, a promoter—which role do you enjoy the most and why?

Johnny: For me, the roles of promoter and negotiator go hand in hand. Promoting my country comes easy for me because of my commitment to contribute significantly to its development. However, I have increasingly found myself having to make the distinction between "promotion" and "sale" when dealing with potential investors. It is at this point that my negotiating skills come into play because in encouraging people to invest in my country, I have to set the terms and conditions under which this could be done. For us, investing in Saint Lucia means joint partnership with the country. The country, therefore, is not for sale as some investors seem to think when dealing with us.

MLS: The *Washington Post* describes the diplomatic corps in Washington as a "men's club." What has been your experience as a woman ambassador in Washington?

Johnny: The diplomatic corps in Washington may at this time, because of numbers, appear like a men's club, but it is not however a closed one as can be seen by the increasing number of female ambassadors being accredited to Washington. I must admit that, at first, I got a little flustered when attending a function with my husband and he would be addressed as "Ambassador." We, however, have learned to make light of it by my husband stating, "No, she is the ambassador; I am only the attaché." In general, as the Caribbean's only current female ambassador in Washington, I have been very well received. My Caribbean colleagues, who for the most part are extremely progressive in thinking and attitude, feel very comfortable in my presence (sometimes too comfortable!) and we have developed a camaraderie that is as natural as, for us, being Caribbean. Washington's female community, those members with whom I have dealt so far, have accepted with demonstrated pride, my position as my country's first female ambassador and the requests for speaking engagements have been overwhelming.

MLS: What was the reaction of your countrymen (and women) at the news of your appointment as ambassador to Washington?

Johnny: There was mixed reaction by my countrymen to my appointment. For the most part, the reaction was split along gender lines. The majority of women are ecstatic that a female was selected as ambassador; the minority who were not in favor based their disapproval on party lines. Some males, (clearly Johnnies come lately) questioned my ability to perform in what was regarded as strictly a male domain. Of course, they had forgotten that I was the first Saint Lucian female to be trained in the field of International Relations and that in 1984 I had been sent to establish the embassy of Saint Lucia in Washington and to teach the ropes to an older male who had been selected to be the ambassador—a male who had no knowledge of or experience in International Relations and who remained as ambassador to

Washington for fifteen years! They were quickly reminded of these facts in a national interview. I believe also that some of the male opposition was based on lack of knowledge of my ability, simply because I had been away from Saint Lucia for ten years. Those males who knew me and the work I did with the Foreign Ministry prior to my coming to Washington in 1984 stated to me and the government that it could not have selected a more deserving female.

MLS: Do you find that your duties as ambassador conflict with your other roles in your private life?

Johnny: There are certainly instances where I have found conflicts between my duties as ambassador and as a wife and mother. Balancing family life with frequent overseas travel, long office hours, and evening social obligations have enacted a toll. I am extremely fortunate, however, that I have a spouse who has been and continues to be extremely understanding, accommodating and supportive throughout my career. Most importantly, we see ourselves as partners who complement each other. Where in my present position as ambassador I have fallen short in my attempt to balance personal and professional life, he has been there to "pick up" for me. My 10-year-old son, however, is not that accommodating. A few months ago when he failed to say "goodnight" to me personally for five or six evenings because of my work schedule, he made me aware of this by pinning a note on my pillow which said, "Goodnight mom; when can I make an appointment to see you?" I vowed then to make weekends "quality time" with my son and, to date, it has worked extremely well.

MLS: Can you tell about the inroads that women in your country and in your part of the world have made in various fields?

Johnny: Before the first International Conference on Women held at Mexico City in 1975, little attention was paid to the general needs of women. Since the Fourth International Conference, significant inroads have been made in recognition of women, their work and their rights. In the Caribbean, politically, the stage has been set for women to forge ahead. In Saint Lucia, for example, for the first time in history, in May 1997 three young women contested probably the most rigorous election ever. This resulted in two women holding elected parliamentary posts, one of them the youngest member of Parliament in the region—a feat which she accomplished at the age of twenty-one. On September 1997, the Honorable Dr. Calliopa Pearlette Louisy was appointed Saint Lucia's first female Governor-General. Two months later, on November 17, 1997, I was appointed as Saint Lucia's first female ambassador to the United States and to the Organization of American States.

On the regional front, the Caribbean political arena has produced exemplary leaders in the persons of Dame Eugenia Charles, ex-Prime Minister of the Commonwealth of Dominica, and the Honorable Janet Jagan, President of Guyana. These achievements are highlighted amidst the stark reality of the social difficulties which confront the majority of women everyday of their lives and the fact that many women are still unappreciated for their contribution to the political process and their commitment to keeping the fabric of society together.

According to a 1995 study by the Caribbean Community (CARICOM) Secretariat throughout the Caribbean region, women in most countries constitute more than 50 percent of the population but fewer than 10 percent are at the highest levels of decision making. There have been some trends slowly creeping throughout the Caribbean as enlightened administrations respond to local, regional and international calls for women's increased participation in formal politics and recognition of their work. The resounding cry of "educate to empower" is reverberating throughout the region and women's groups are promoting this vigorously. What has been most inspiring for me is the sight of rural women taking up the mantle and moving forward in increasing numbers to educate themselves. Most importantly, using this education as a tool for empowerment.

MLS: What are the accomplishments you are the most proud of in your career?

Johnny: My proudest moment came when I was informed that I was selected to be Saint Lucia's ambassador to Washington and permanent representative to the OAS [Organization of American States]. To any diplomat, this is the highest point of her or his career. I had the confidence of the administrators of my country to make a difference overseas. To many, this was long in coming, given my career path and my unique experiences.

MLS: Do you believe that women's approach to diplomacy is different from that of men?

Johnny: I believe that in any field, a woman normally has an approach that is different from that of her male counterpart. Usually, the woman's path to reach her male counterpart's level is not similar to his; she therefore makes use of her experiences in her approach to any task. In the area of international affairs, women have to go that extra mile: they have to acquire international experience and language skills early on in their careers. They also have to learn how to exceed performance expectations, take risks and develop transferable skills. So when a woman reaches the top of her international affairs career, she is bringing to that position diverse skills, new perspectives, much needed expertise, effective management styles and a strong desire to prove doubters wrong. This translates into efficiency, hard work, a desire to resolve issues by consensus and a collaborative style, rather than one of instruction.

MLS: What do you want your legacy to be once you leave this post?

Johnny: I was sent here to reorganize the embassy and to have it structured in a manner which can more efficiently and expeditiously achieve the foreign policy goals of Saint Lucia. I therefore hope that by the end of my tenure, I would have created such an office. I would also hope that my tenacity and professionalism would inspire other female foreign service officers and that they would see in me a success story of one who has weathered many storms and setbacks, and encountered numerous obstacles and was able to toss these aside in the name of commitment. I also hope that I have emblazoned the way for female foreign service officers so that their paths to the top would not be as arduous as mine.

MLS: You are one of Washington's youngest ambassadors. You have landed the most prestigious post. What's next career-wise?

Johnny: Having reached the pinnacle of the diplomatic career, a number of people anticipate that I will enter the political field. I have not given too much attention to that direction. However, I do have a second career in the legal field and I had been preparing for the attainment of the pinnacle of that career—judgeship—when I was called to be Saint Lucia's ambassador. For me, there are many options and I will focus on one closer to the end of my tenure as ambassador.

At the conclusion of the interview her 10-year-old son appears, having discreetly knocked on the door. This time I am the one who feels guilty having perhaps stolen a bit of the quality time she was talking about earlier. I had the opportunity to meet with Ambassador Johnny on numerous other occasions. At the OAS she fills the stage at an event organized for the benefit of battered women in Saint Lucia. For the occasion she flew in an all-female steel band from Saint Lucia. The buffet is a treat complete with Saint Lucian delicacies and Barbay rum. While her guests are clearly having a ball, she confesses to me she is worried about every single detail and does it all with a large welcoming smile.

Wondering what's next for her after this post, some fancy her heading an organization like WTO. For the ambassador from an island with Nobel Laureates in poetry and economics, that would be poetic justice.

AMBASSADOR CHAN HENG CHEE
OF SINGAPORE

Tucked between the southern tip of Malaysia and the northern coast of Indonesia, Singapore belonged to the trading empire of Sumatra in the thirteenth century. In the fourteenth century the Javanese coveted it and marched on it. By 1819 Singapore, the Lion City, had awakened the colonial appetite of Britain for far away places prompting Sir Stamford Raffles to lease it from the Sultan of Johore. This group of sixty scarcely inhabited islands, three and one-half the size of Washington, D.C., became a British colony in 1824. Throughout the nineteenth century Singapore's population steadily increased with an influx of immigrants from China, India, the Malay peninsula and the Indonesian islands. Immigration was at its peak after the opening of the Suez Canal in 1869. Occupied by the Japanese during the Second World War, Singapore was governed by the British once again—shortly after the war until 1959 when it became self-governing. Belonging briefly to Malaysia in 1963, Singapore became a full-fledged independent nation on August 9, 1965.

With hardly any resources other than its people, Singapore has become one of the greatest success stories in the world. Today this densely populated metropolis, reminiscent of Manhattan, exports electrical and electronic equipment, office machinery and transport equipment, petroleum, and petroleum products, and chemicals and can boast of a per capita income of $28,255. One of the architects of the success of this well-organized and highly disciplined society is Lee Kuan Yew, premier from 1959 until 1990 and one of the founders of the People's Action Party. Capable of weathering even the toughest Asian financial crisis of the late 1990s, Singapore enjoys an excellent communications network and a formidable pool of financial capital. After Tienanmen Square, western economic relations with China declined and were quickly replaced by investments from Chinese communities from Hong Kong, Taiwan, Singapore and Macao. China having the land, resources and inexpensive labor—the partnerships are ideal. So ideal that the Chinese populations of southeast Asia occasionally have to reassure their compatriots from other ethnic groups that their loyalty is to their countries of birth and not that of their ancestors. With a population that is 77 percent Chinese, 14 percent Malay and 7.6 percent Indian and Pakistani, the Lion City has inherited at least one characteristic of Imperial China; it perceives itself as the guardian of the people's interest. In the late 1980s the country grappled with the issue of becoming a modern society without becoming Western. In 1989 President Wee Kim Wee responded to his compatriots' concerns by defining the Shared Values of Singaporeans as follows:

Nation before community and society above self;

Family as the basic unit of society;

Community support and respect for the individual;

Consensus instead of contention; and

Racial and religious harmony.

If the world stage were a classroom, Singapore would be among its best students, particularly in the economics department. It is certainly first in competitiveness, first in discipline, first in efficiency, and first in equal distribution of wealth. To represent this model student, Prime Minister Goh Chok Tong decided to send one of Asia's best professors to the capital of the sole world superpower. Educated at the University of Singapore and Cornell University, Chan Heng Chee is one of Asia's most high profile women. A recipient of the much-coveted Inaugural International Woman of the Year Award presented by the Organization of Chinese American Women (OCAW) and of Singapore's first "Woman of the Year" award, Chan Heng Chee is celebrated on her continent for her activism, her prolific writing on matters of Asian politics and her in-depth analysis as an independent thinker. Winner of a number of book awards, including, the 1991 National Book Award for *A Sensation of Independence*, Chan Heng Chee received honorary degrees of Doctor of Letters in 1994 from the University of Newcastle, Australia and the University of Buckingham, United Kingdom in 1998. The very cerebral Chan Heng Chee is also a doer. Inspired by the United States Peace Corps, the Singaporean professor of Political Science created her own version—the Singapore International Foundation, sending an average of eight volunteers to selected Asian and African countries. Her career as a diplomat began in 1989 when she was appointed Singapore's permanent representative to the United Nations and concurrently high commissioner to Canada and ambassador to Mexico. She was appointed ambassador to the United States in July of 1996 and is currently on sabbatical from her post as a professor in the Department of Political Science at the National University of Singapore. I caught up with her at the Embassy of Singapore one morning in September of 1996.

The marble-floored embassy has wood paneling adorned by the works of commissioned Singaporean artists Han Sai Pori, Chen Wen Hsi and Pan Shou, among others. Its clean cut industrial design, work of architect Rodman Henderer, reflects Singapore's efficiency, financial success and its gaze at the future. After waiting a few minutes in the vestibule sipping Asian tea and browsing through coffee table books on the Malay, Chinese and Indian cultures of Singapore, I am ushered into her office. She appears steel orchid with a firm handshake. She embodies her country—a small place that enjoys being big in many ways. For the media savvy diplomat she is, this interview is a break from a grueling schedule. She does not pay attention to the tape recorder I place on the coffee table. Interviewing her in this pristine off-white office bathed with sunlight, one gets the feeling she never left the classroom.

MLS: Is the diplomatic corps a "men's club"? What has been your experience as a woman ambassador in Washington?

Ambassador Chan: Certainly there are far more men than women in the diplomatic corps. In bilateral diplomacy, ambassadors work with the host nation, primarily. And you don't really need a club to help you as such. So I am much less aware of Washington being a men's club than I was when I was at the United Nations, where it is multilateral diplomacy and you have to work with ambassadors. Here it is one-on-one. The ambassador with the host agency, the Hill. In that sense you do not rely on the other ambassadors as much. If the male ambassadors have a special advantage that women do not have, since I do not know it, I do not miss it! I suspect that it is easier to bond or get to a closer relationship when a male ambassador meets a congressman or a male senator. I think that with women, it may take a little longer and it's a different relationship.

This question appeared to evoke some irritation from the Ambassador. On subsequent occasions, I was to learn that this apparent irritation was a reflection of her belief that diplomatic performance should be evaluated upon its own merits and not in gender-coded terms.

MLS: In the Western world, women in Asia are still perceived as rather submissive. What are your views on the perception and condition of women in your country and on the continent-at-large?

Chan: It depends on who you are talking about. Women in the developing countries and in Asia have to be viewed as different groups. [A distinction has to be made as to] whether you are talking of working class women, middle class women or women who are educated and are now part of the strategic elite—those are the movers and shakers of the nation. I think for those in the working class, a lot of women in Asia need change and development. That's where the problems occur. It also depends on what sort of country you are in. Is it a more socially conservative country? Religion also dictates certain behaviors. But once you become a professional woman, in developing countries where manpower is scarce, women do get a lot of opportunities. In my country, in Singapore, I never found it too problematic to be a woman, to do what I want. I never questioned whether people were listening to me, whether they took me seriously. I always felt they took me seriously and I assumed they would take me seriously. I think a lot of women have that attitude too and they are successful women doctors, lawyers, judges, managers, bankers in Singapore and in southeast Asian countries such as the Philippines, Thailand, Indonesia, Malaysia. My sense is once you break through and become educated you are bound to succeed. The society can't afford to discriminate in countries where expertise is scarce. Your expertise is welcome irrespective of gender.

MLS: Can you tell me about your appointment as ambassador to Washington and how it was received in your country?

Chan: My appointment came very simply because I had been an ambassador before, permanent representative to the United Nations from 1989 to 1991. I think the first breakthrough was when I was appointed the permanent representative to the United Nations because I was the first woman to be appointed an ambassador in my country. Until I was appointed, no woman had become an ambassador. In fact, I never thought of being an ambassador. It was not within my realm of thinking or ambition. Being appointed ambassador to the United Nations came as a big surprise. Women welcomed it. It was a surprise and yet not a surprise. It was a surprise because it was the first time a woman was appointed. But when I was appointed, the knowledgeable, what I consider the political public, were not surprised it was I. This was because I have been active as a political commentator. I am a political scientist. I write columns in the papers. So people have associated me with politics. In a sense, they were surprised that the government appointed a woman. They were not surprised I was appointed. I gather they felt if it was a woman, I was the most obvious choice or appropriate choice. With regard to my coming to Washington, again, they were pleased. The women were very pleased that a woman got the Washington job, but by then they were no longer surprised; many had said "She is an obvious choice to be ambassador to Washington." I am the only woman from the Asia Pacific countries, that is from Japan to Myanmar, to have been appointed ambassador to the United Nations and also the only woman from that region to be appointed ambassador to Washington. India and Pakistan, the subcontinent, have had female envoys, not the Asia Pacific countries.

MLS: Could you comment on the inroads that women in Asia have made in politics. The obvious names that come to mind are Benazir Bhutto and her struggle to remain in power, Aung San Suu Kyi under house arrest, Megawatti.

Chan: Let me put it this way. If you look at all the figures of women who have become heads of state, all of them inherited a husband's mantle or a father's mantle: Benazir Bhutto; Indira Gandhi; Bandaranike, even Aung San Suu Kyi wears the mantle of her father; Cory Aquino wore the mantle of her husband. I think the family connection propelled them and turned them into figure heads and symbols which meant election or promotion to leadership positions much faster and easier. It has been surprising to many that in the most conservative societies, such as the Indian subcontinent, women have taken over in so many instances. I have said to the *New York Times* that Indira Gandhi is an interesting person. She was chosen by the Congress party bosses to be the successor because she was a compromise candidate. After Nehru died, they could not decide who should be the leader. They thought if they got Indira Gandhi they could manipulate her. But she turned out to be a woman in her own right. She was a strong leader. In fact, in India they called her the iron lady. She cut an image for herself and she succeeded in many ways. Benazir Bhutto has not had such an easy time. She had one spell. Now the second spell. She seems to have been pushed up. The reports and analysis suggest that she has not always been on top in managing the economy. Corruption has become a problem and so have law and order. Cory Aquino did something. She did not do what everybody thought she would complete. I think she did help restore credibility to the political institutions in the Philippines. Aung San Suu Kyi is fighting a steady fight in her country.

MLS: How do you reconcile work and private life in a twenty-four-hour job?

Chan: I am divorced. I brought up two step-sons who came to me as teenagers. Well, let me put it this way—when I was ambassador at the United Nations, I went alone. I didn't go with my family. I went to New York and my husband did not come along. I think it affected my marriage. I divorced. Now I come to Washington without a family. As I was working in my career, before becoming an ambassador, I had a very active career. I was speaking in all kinds of forums, attending international conferences, writing. I won two book awards. I published "umpteen articles." I was very active. I was married. I had a household to run. Somehow I managed, especially when I was younger. I used to write from about 10 P.M. to 2 A.M. I had about five hours of sleep, six hours at the most. In the past when I was younger, I could do with three or four hours of sleep and no one could tell the difference. I would function just as well. Now I need more sleep.

MLS: Can you pinpoint some of your best accomplishments as ambassador to the United Nations?

Chan: There were two very clear ones. I went to the United Nations in 1989. My main task in the United Nations at that time was to work with the Association of South East Asian Nations (ASEAN) countries to maintain the vote to push through a resolution on Cambodia and to hold the vote in support of a comprehensive political settlement for Cambodia. In 1989 when I went to the United Nations, Vietnam announced a unilateral withdrawal of its forces. Everybody told me, "You will not get support anymore." But Vietnam did not agree to a comprehensive political settlement supervised by the UN. So it was neither here nor there. The question was whether I could hold the vote. People were asking why keep bashing Vietnam and why pass this resolution because they have announced a withdrawal of their forces? So let's close the issue. My job was to keep the vote for our resolution. It was considered tough in light of the changing circumstances and also because many of the Western countries who supported this resolution were always a bit uncomfortable with the fact that Cambodia was under Pol Pot. I held the vote. I increased the vote. I increased the sponsorship to the surprise of everyone. I ran far more sponsors for our resolution and brought in two or three extra votes, which was beyond everybody's expectations. So I was very pleased with that.

The second achievement was that a few months later I had one candidate, Ambassador Tommy Koh, successfully elected as the chairman of the preparatory committee for the UN Conference for Environmental Development at Rio. I ran our candidate against Sweden, which is associated with environment [issues], and my candidate won. My colleagues told me that they took note of that. You have to be active. You have to speak out.

MLS: To what do you attribute your success in negotiation?

Chan: I had a good team with me, the mission, my headquarters, persistence. Persistence, but also you have to persuade. You have to persuade people to be on your side.

MLS: Could you talk about some of your accomplishments prior to your diplomatic career?

Chan: I won two national book awards. Before this I would say that in the region of southeast Asia, I believe I was taken as a serious scholar, a good scholar. I was respected as a scholar and that is very important to me. I was perceived to be somebody who could give a clear analysis and this I am proud of. If you want someone to talk about theory and to think in the abstract and not just collecting empirical data, I was identified to be that. I was seen as someone who could give a good overview, a broad picture and who could theorize.

Given the reams of data that exist on her academic accomplishments Chan is quite modest in her response.

MLS: You put together an organization that is similar to the Peace Corps. Could you talk about that? What is its role in Asia?

Chan: It is a very modest effort. When I returned from the UN, my government said it would give me a one-time endowment grant and a very powerful board to raise money. I went to Washington to the Peace Corps to see what the Peace Corps did and then set up its equivalent in Singapore. Then I visited New Zealand which has a Volunteer Service Abroad, [similar to the U.S.] Peace Corps organization. I thought of New Zealand because it is roughly our size, with our level of resources and three million people. I thought that this might be nearer our experience. So I took from both organizations and came up with something of our own for Singapore. I am proud of that. I am pleased to do it. I don't see it as my own achievement because I worked with a team of young people. I think the achievement is shared. I was the leader. I was the director and it worked. I am proud because it has been a channel for altruism in Singapore. It gives idealism room. In Singapore, at the time we created it, it was thought that there were not that many such channels. We could do the charity bit, we would visit old folks homes and so on. However, we did not have an organization like the Peace Corps or Vista, and this was it. The Singapore Volunteers Overseas now serves in Ghana, Botswana, Sri Lanka, Nepal, Indonesia and Vietnam. At the time I left we had been to the Philippines too. We were looking to place volunteers in Cambodia, Laos and Myanmar. But we do not have hundreds of volunteers. We have about eight volunteers in each country. My colleagues who worked for me said that I created a very special organization, that they felt they could channel idealism in the spirit of that organization. The organization is called the Singapore International Foundation. The SVO is one component of SIF. I was the oldest one. None of my colleagues were above forty. In fact, most of them were under thirty-five. It is a very young and lively organization.

MLS: What is the biggest hurdle you had to overcome in your career as a woman in general?

Chan: I never thought I had any problem as a woman in my career. Gender did not come to mind. First as a student, I got my scholarship. I topped the class and that's how it started. I was an honor student in political science. I was the top female graduate of my faculty when I graduated. I got a scholarship to go to Cornell. I came out of Cornell, went back to Singapore to teach. I was the first Singaporean to join the political science faculty. I thought everybody was very helpful. So there were no obstacles. I felt that when I had an obstacle, I was not sure whether it was my gender or my politics. I thought it was my politics actually because I was fairly anti-establishment in those days. So I thought it was my anti-establishment politics. I never thought gender was a major problem. I never wanted to be the head of anything, to be the head of a department for example. I just wanted to be a good scholar. That was the most important thing to me. I wanted peer group recognition. I wanted other scholars to view me as a good scholar. I wanted to be a good teacher. I believe I was a good teacher. To this day students still write to me, connect with me.

MLS: You did have a lot of success among our students at Howard University! You are an academic at heart!

Chan: I like young people and I deal with them well. That was the most important thing to me. You can be successful. . . . I never sought the headship of the department. Because I had published so much and was very serious and committed as an academic, it was very apparent I should be the deputy head and eventually the head of my department. My promotion to professorship at my own university was very slow. I have no doubts that had I been a man I would have been promoted much faster. But it never bothered me because it did not take away my international recognition. I could get entry into the best universities as a visiting professor. I attended the conferences. They see the papers you write and know about the lectures you deliver. So even there I did not feel it very much. I never agitated or pushed or banged the table demanding a promotion. I just did not get caught in that. The fact that my peer group gave me recognition was enough. And that's probably why I feel they did not trample on my rights as a woman. I would have been just as happy staying at the university. Then the ambassadorship was offered to me. I was asked many times whether I wanted to go into politics. I did not want to go into politics. I think because I did not really shoot for the positions, the rank as such, I did not feel the frustrations of pushing. Had I wanted that, I would have felt frustrated. I think that was what happened. And then I found I was appointed to "umpteen" things. Later, what happened, Marilyn, is that it was the era of the woman. It was important to appoint women to things in the nineties. Then I began to realize that there were advantages to being an articulate woman. Many told me, however, "We did not put you there because you are a woman, but because you are a good political scientist." The absence of frustrations has to do with the fact that I did not aspire to these ranks. I used to write a great deal. I was quite productive as a writer. So I derived a lot of satisfaction from that.

MLS: What would you like to write about in the future?

Chan: I have a wish and ambition to do a novel. I would like to write a novel. I don't know if I will manage it. I think when I wrote a biography I was already reaching out beyond social sciences for something else.

MLS: What would you like the theme of that novel to be?

Chan: If I write a novel, it obviously is going to include politics in the background, a work . . . that gives you a feel of the times.

MLS: A few years from now, where do you see your position in politics in your country?

Chan: If I said this to you, you would not believe it, but this is true. I never planned a career in diplomacy. I think I have been very lucky in that whatever I do I enjoy doing it. If you ask me what I am going to do when I go back to Singapore, I have not even thought of it, but I know something will crop up. We are a young country. We are short of talent and of trained people. If I can be useful, let's see what is offered. As I said, I have never done anything I did not like. Instinctively I know that if I do not like something, I won't accept it. So I have not thought clearly about it. I could teach. I could do something else. You see Singapore is a very small country. Three million people—and the educated still do not constitute a very thick layer of the population. I saw the country coming to independence in 1965. I belong to that generation that feels a sense of responsibility and duty to help, to support this experiment of nation building. Singapore is very precious because it is a city state. It is an island city state. It has no resources. I am part of the generation that is very aware of it. I feel I can and I have to help strengthen it. So whatever there is for me to do, I will do.

MLS: Tell us about the inroads that women have made in your country in various fields and the extent to which these accomplishments have inspired you.

Chan: The level of achievement of women in Singapore is roughly parallel to that of Britain. It is not as good as that of Canada and the United States or the Nordic countries. It is about the level of Britain. It's much better than Switzerland's. It's better than Korea's and Japan's. In terms of the southeast Asian countries, it's not bad at all. We don't do so well in politics because women don't want to go into politics. In the United States, if you go into politics, that's one career and you are a full-time member of Congress or senator. In Singapore if you are member of parliament, you still have to carry your regular job. So you do two jobs. And women, I guess, don't want to do three jobs. They have opportunities to have a fulfilling career. So they engage in their career and their housework. There are not as many women in politics as there should be. Women have done very well in terms of education. It is 60 to 40 percent enrollment. Women are being educated and they are getting the jobs. But women always feel there is a glass ceiling. At the top slots, they still see men there, but I think there are enough moving into the next ranks. In the public service it seems a bit slower. Women in the private sector do very well in Singapore. In the public service, if you are in the professional service, it's fine. It's when you become permanent secretary, which is a top civilian post, that the gender makeup is noticeably different. They are all men! Not a woman yet.

Was I inspired by the inroads of women in my country? I am part of that generation of women in Singapore who are pushing. There were not that many women before us who achieved. We had some fighters, but they took a more political activist line. I did have role models, but my role models had nothing to do with the public life I embraced. My intellectual mentor at Cornell, Ruth McVeigh who lives in Italy now, an American scholar of southeast Asian politics, was my role model. She is very serious. She is a very fine scholar. She taught me quality. I have a great deal of respect for her. She has a special place in my life. She is now retired. I think I had that other quality of being a public speaker as well and having this activist nature which I did not recognize initially. It took me into public life and public policy.

MLS: When did your public life start?

Chan: My public life started almost as I entered the university. I seem to attract controversy. When I was an undergraduate in the first year I wrote a poem. There was so much brouhaha over the poem! People said I was writing political poetry. I just wrote a poem. It was published and they started analyzing it. My poem said it is easier to be a painter than a writer because when you paint, nobody knows what you paint, but a writer cannot hide that much behind words. When I came back from my master's program at Cornell I was a Singapore political scientist. There are so few of us around. I felt a sense of duty to comment on politics. I wanted to do that as a citizen. I participated in forums. I did a lot. I was pushed into this public role. I enjoyed speaking. I was not afraid to do so. So I have that public dimension although I was a teacher and a scholar. In my country there were very few people who wanted to comment on politics. And I did. And I was quite critical of government, which is very unusual. I think that's how I got to be noticed internationally. But when I did it, I did not do it for notice. I did it because I felt I should do it as a citizen. And I did not know where it was going to lead. I was never a politician. I never joined a group. . . . I was always very clear in defining a role for myself as a public clutch with no ambitions. I do not belong to any party. I never formed a political organization. I wanted to be this neutral objective observer passing judgment, and I defined that role for myself. I was successful because I defined this neutral place for myself. I felt there was a role for scholars to play. They could be commentators. Academics are society's expensive pets. The least they can do is to have a comment. They are paid to have a point of view.

MLS: What do you wish the most for women in your country?

Chan: I wish that they be comfortable with their choices first of all. If they want to fulfill their careers that they be allowed to do so and they should have the opportunity to do so. If they want to choose a home career, they should not feel that this is a weak choice. And I would like to see more women in politics in my country and in other countries in southeast Asia. Women bear the burden of poverty and suffering. Education, tools of development, should reach them soon.

MLS: I have asked you what you wish for women in your country and on the Asian continent. Now what do you wish for yourself?

Chan: In my country it is not so much the underdevelopment that is at issue because we are rather developed. In my country I wish that women be comfortable with their choices and that more women opt to attend college. More women should have good careers. I haven't thought about what I wish for myself.

MLS: Do you believe that women have a slightly different approach than men as far as politics are concerned?

Chan: Probably. I think to be a good politician you have to have certain qualities, whether you are a man or a woman. Some men or women may not be made of that stuff. They have to adopt those qualities. Because of the socialization of women, women have an extra hurdle. They have to overcome the socialization.

MLS: Where do you see Asia five or ten years from now and where do you see women in Asia five or ten years from now?

Chan: I have predicted that Asia will become more affluent. It will be on an economic track and you are going to see a belt of industrializing and industrialized countries emerging from Japan to Myanmar, and I think India too. I think women will be very much part of this development process because women will be mobilized into the work force. Women will be given more opportunities for education. It might not be one-on-one, but I think you will see this social revolution taking place.

MLS: In a recent lecture at Johns Hopkins University, you mentioned that you wish that in your country and in Asia in general there was more room for creativity and less order. Where do you see the creativity coming from?

Chan: Creativity cannot be structured. You can create conditions that allow creativity to flow. But I don't think you can teach creativity. You can learn some things. I suspect that stimuli is creative. Change happens quickly; you become quite creative because you are reacting to that change. I tend to think that pain, chaos, not that I wish it, disjunctures tend to make people more creative. Being among creative people helps one become more creative. So it's a slow learning exercise. A lot of countries in Asia are concerned that by emphasizing eccentricities, you become excessive. It's hard to find a balance. It is something we just have to feel our way through. Lack of creativity has not stopped any country from being rich. I would say that Japan, for example, is getting more creative. [Creativity] comes with time and change. . . . It has to do with how one recognizes creativity also. It is whether our definition of creativity now is far too narrow. Japan is very creative with group organization and productivity. It is a form of creativity. Creativity . . . that's a big question!

MLS: Which publication of yours are you the most proud of?

Chan: Gee! I have to say that every time after I write something I get tired of it. I don't have one publication I am particularly proud of. I won two book awards, but now if you ask me about it I would say that's passé. I liked the biography I wrote on a Jewish politician in Singapore.

MLS: Thank you Ambassador Chan.

AMBASSADOR SHEILA SISULU
OF SOUTH AFRICA

Ambassador Sheila Sisulu arrived in Washington bearing a family name that was anointed in the trenches of the war against apartheid. Walter Sisulu, her father-in-law, was President Nelson Mandela's closest friend in their four-decade struggle against apartheid. The son of an African domestic worker and a wealthy European-descended magistrate of the court who never acknowledged him but paid for his education, Sisulu, a prominent businessman and local leader, met President Nelson Mandela in the 1940s. Nelson Mandela was a law student at that time. In his book, *The Long Walk to Freedom*, Mandela describes Sisulu as someone who "despite his youth seemed an experienced man of the world." Mandela quickly relied on the experience of the young businessman and sought his advice and recommendation on his first job as a law clerk working for Lazar Sidelsky. Nelson Mandela, accused number one and Walter Sisulu, accused number two of the Rivonia trials, have a history of loyalty and solidarity unmatched in mankind's history of liberation struggles.

Together and with unparalleled dignity they confronted the notorious cruelty of the Kleynhans brothers, three warders in Robben Island prison whose pastime was reading books about torture. Indignities on Robben Island, particularly in the 1960s, included prisoners being forced to work under the scorching sun; prisoners splitting rocks with hammers until exhaustion; simulation of live burials for those who passed out, in an effort to break the spirit of other prisoners; beatings until loss of consciousness; allowing prisoners showers only twice a week; overt censorship of letters written to family and friends; plus other methods of torture and insults.

The two men endured together in perfect tandem. It was Sisulu who was by Mandela's side when Winnie Mandela received a banning order while visiting her husband in jail. It was Walter Sisulu who was by his side when Nelson Mandela was informed about the passing away of his mother. When Thembi, Mandela's oldest son died in a car accident, Sisulu was with his friend grieving in silence. In both cases, Mandela's requests for permission to bury his family members were rejected. The outrage and the pain were expressed in silence by the two friends.

But outside the prison the words, "We the ANC are sure of victory" were carved in cement on Robben Island harbor. By the end of the 1960s Mandela and Sisulu emerged as leaders in the infamous prison. There, they created their own war room against apartheid. Mandela, Sisulu and their friends worked to create a "community in prison." They discouraged hostility towards the warders and advocated among the inmates a courteous and dignified attitude. Using, among other tactics, painters as informants and kitchen staff to smuggle messages, the two leaders created sophisticated networks within the cells to keep prisoners informed of the struggle waged beyond the prison walls and educate them. Mandela and Sisulu were adamant, emphasis had to be placed on education. Mandela told prisoners that they had to educate themselves in order to govern in the future. Even under the watchful eye of Colonel Badenhorst, the commander of Robben Island's prison, the two managed to impart some pearls of wisdom to the inmates and to teach. Walter Sisulu taught them political history.

Outside Robben Island's prison walls a young woman named Sheila Violet Makate, soon to marry Sisulu's son, was also waging a war—one against the miseducation of black children. Very active in the field of education, she graduated from the universities of Botswana Lesotho and Swaziland (UBLS) and Witwatersrand and held various senior positions in the 1970s in the South African Committee for Higher Education. In the late 1980s and early 1990s, as Education Coordinator of the African Bursary Fund of the South African Council of Churches (SACC), she canvassed member churches and organizations of the SACC to develop a critical understanding of issues and debates in education. Today, she reminds young audiences that not so long ago, in 1976 young black children were massacred while peacefully demonstrating for the right to learn.

The war against apartheid caught the attention of the international community through that very struggle for a better education for black children. In Soweto, the tomb of young Hector Peterson and the mural dedicated to the young victims of the June 16, 1976, massacre are somber reminders of that struggle.

To future generations of South-Africans—as it is now for younger African Americans with regard to segegation—it may be difficult to realize how pervasive apartheid was. The Native Land Act of 1913 established the principle of segregated areas, confining the 67 percent black majority population to only 13 percent of the country's rural land. The architect of apartheid, Hendrik Frensch Verwoerd, forced black South Africans to carry a passbook and made the right of residence in the cities contingent upon an employment contract. The Marriage and Immorality Act banned marriages and sexual relations between whites and non-whites. Furthermore, the law did not recognize trade unions. In 1983 revamping a constitution condemned by the international community meant calling an all-White referendum and creating separate chambers for whites, coloreds and Asians, leaving out the black majority, and giving more executive power to the president. In the late 1980s Pieter Willem Botha was replaced by Frederik Willem de Klerk who began to negotiate with the African National Congress (ANC) leaders while the international community kept pressure on the apartheid regime through sanctions.

The release of Nelson Mandela from prison in 1990 ranks among the most important events in human history. The presidency of the charismatic Mandela sparked hope in the hearts of South Africans, of Africans all over the globe in general. At the close of the millennium when the newly-wed Nelson Mandela retires from political life and passes the baton to President Thabo Mbeki, he does it with full confidence in the future of his country.

South Africa is a middle income country with an abundant supply of resources; an excellent communication network and well-developed financial, legal and transportation sectors. Economic growth has been positive since the election of President Mandela. Nevertheless, the charge of President Mbeki is daunting. In a country of gold and diamonds and where the standard of living is superior to that of much of Africa, there are pockets of ragged squatter camps headed by impoverished kings and unemployment remains high.

Ambassador Sisulu arrived in Washington at the juncture between the Mandela presidency and the post-Mandela era at a time when the world was riveted by the tragedy that unfolded in Kosovo which is the size of a small fraction of one of South Africa's provinces. In her inaugural speech, Ambassador Sisulu is adamant that her beautiful country of spectacular beaches, breathtaking wildlife, and colorful intricate Ndebele architecture is a beacon of hope for the continent and will succeed. Joining the Ambassador in a toast to South Africa's success (in the embassy dining room beautifully paneled with the rare South African "stinkhout" wood and enlivened by an abundant selection of vibrant works of the country's contemporary artists) were Professor Ronald Walters, the political scientist, and Johnnie Cochran, the lawyer, along with U.S. State Department officials and members of non-governmental organizations (NGOs) among others.

The reality is awsome—South Africa's ambassador to the United States, a black African woman named Sisulu! This outcome was almost inconceivable in the early 1980s when one recalls being among the handful of outraged people of conscience who demonstrated against apartheid daily outside of the South African Embassy.

I met with Sheila Sisulu two months after her inaugural address as ambassador to the United States.

MLS: The era of Mandela brought a lot of hope not only to South Africa but to Africa and the developing countries in general. However from an economic standpoint South Africa quickly found itself competing with countries from the former Soviet block. After the demise of communism it seems that a higher level of attention has been paid to saving the East [eastern Europe] than to strengthening a post-apartheid South Africa that could lead the way for an entire continent. What is your reaction to that situation?

Ambassador Sisulu: Speaking of South Africa specifically, we have a bi-national commission (BNC) with the United States. South Africa is one of less than a handful of countries that have a BNC with the United States. The BNC forms the basis for a sound and positive relationship between the United States and South Africa.

In general, yes, there has been more attention paid to the reconstruction of eastern Europe than to economic relations with Africa. Having said that, President Clinton began to break out of that mold through his trip to Africa which helped to focus on Africa from an economic and trade standpoint. Subsequently we have had the Africa United States ministerial held here in the capital. There is a shift. But it does not match, by any means, the attention that eastern Europe is getting. That needs to be underscored! But there has been a shift. Initially there was no interest or rather no apparent interest in having meaningful economic relations with the continent and greater emphasis was given to the former Soviet republics, but that seems to be changing.

MLS: What should the post-Mandela era emphasize on the international scene in order to gain more of that attention and to involve the international community more in the reconstruction of the post-apartheid South Africa?

Sisulu: I think what the President elect of South Africa is going to do is to strengthen and try to accelerate the vision that he has articulated along with other African leaders about the renaissance of Africa. One of the elements of that renaissance will be economic integration through regional structures such as the SADC [Southern African Development Community], the Economic and Social Council (ECOSOC). Through those structures Africa can in a more meaningful way engage in the global economy.

MLS: There are quite a few obvious similarities between the history of the United States and the history of South Africa. What do you estimate that the economic toll of the apartheid regime has been as far as the black population in South Africa is concerned.

Sisulu: To say it is immeasurable is to understate the case. Not only was the disadvantage economic, the black population was disadvantaged in every possible way. You name it: housing, education, health, social security and welfare or safety and security, and employment. The economic aspect was only one aspect. In that regard, cognizance has to be taken of the impact of apartheid on the economy of the region, particularly those countries that were seen as supporters of the liberation struggle: Lesotho, Botswana, Zimbabwe, Zambia, Angola, Mozambique and Tanzania. These countries were targeted specifically to be destabilized economically. Many of them are still recovering from the devastation caused by apartheid.

MLS: In organizations such as the World Bank and the IMF, are the damages done by the apartheid regime taken enough into consideration in relation to the economic development of South Africa and of the southern Africa region in general?

Sisulu: These organizations, unfortunately, even during the time of apartheid, could have definitely done more. Because they did not do as much as they should have, a backlog has been created. I do not know whether it was due to insufficient appreciation of the impact of apartheid or whether it was because the organizations were simply sticking within their own guidelines to economic development in those areas. Whatever the reasons, the outcome is the same—major underdevelopment. Have they doubled the efforts? There are commendable efforts, but they are not anywhere near the levels required to remedy the situation which is why there has been this call for the restructuring of these organizations so that they can be much more responsive to the needs of developing countries.

MLS: South Africa is often perceived as the next possible giant in Africa. Is it an overstatement? What would need to be done in order to place South Africa in a position of leadership for the entire continent of Africa?

Sisulu: It depends on what standard one is using when one uses the term giant.

MLS: An economic giant that would inspire and lift other countries in Africa.

Sisulu: South Africa has a good economic infrastructure. There is no denying that. But so does Botswana. Botswana actually surpasses us if you use the currency as a standard: their currency is stronger than ours. Their economy has been growing steadily for several years. We do, however, have a role to play because of the resources we have. But our role will be more that of working in a partnership with other countries. We would go rather for a partnership role where another country has the strength and capacity that we can match or complement. We have a lot to offer but we offer it in partnership and in recognition that other countries in the region also have a lot to offer.

MLS: What is needed to foster a more intense regional cooperation? What is the role of intraregional trade in it?

Sisulu: I think intraregional trade is critical. It is important to begin to trade as equal partners. Our growth is integrally tied to the growth and economic development of the region. Otherwise our economic development is unsustainable. In the global economy single countries with the exception, of course, of the United States cannot survive on their own. We need to strengthen the integration of the region. Part of integration means intra-regional trade and economic relations of the regions to make them viable economic entities. The fact that we have 40 million people in South Africa as opposed to 200 million in the southern African region immediately tells you as a region we are in a different ball game.

MLS: There is still a huge disparity between the economic situation of blacks and whites in South Africa. The figures glaringly reflect that disparity. For example there is a 40 percent unemployment rate among blacks as opposed to a 4 percent rate among whites.

Sisulu: Our President elect raised this issue in a statement he made before Parliament. He wanted to put the debate on the table. South Africa does have two nations. One has it all and the other has very little. It does, as a legacy of apartheid, translate into the nation that has it all being predominantly white and the nation that has very little being predominantly black.

MLS: How well is this message understood by the white minority?

Sisulu: Well, it is a debate that he raised. It created a lot of interest both in Parliament and in the media. It is an ongoing conversation in the nation. He has indicated in his victory speech recently that his government will have to accelerate the delivery for the majority of people who have given the ANC a resounding mandate to accelerate the delivery of services to people. How are we going to do that? We have decided we will do it within the framework of our macroeconomic policy—that is, through economic growth. We need the economy to grow as quickly to enable us to do this. Therefore, we will do everything we can to ensure that it is through the economy that we deliver to our people. How else do we do it? Do we say the economy is not moving as fast as we wish, therefore, our people cannot get water, cannot get housing? We cannot do that. The challenge is going to be how we as South Africans step up to the plate, especially those of us who have jobs and resources. It will also mean that we make sacrifices. The interesting thing is that while this divide is largely racial, it is not entirely racial because during this short time span of the last five years the black owned companies on the Trans-South African stock exchange form 18 percent of that stock exchange from zero. There were none in 1994. 18 percent are now black owned. So, there is movement. It will take all of us black and white who fall into the category of those that have now to step up to the plate. We hope that it will cease quickly from being purely a black and white issue.

MLS: Is there any evidence that whites in South Africa have understood this message? In this country that has also gone through apartheid, decades later there are many debates but for a long period of time few and far between were the serious debates that tied the issue of race relations to that of economic empowerment. Is it going to be otherwise in South Africa by virtue of the fact that the victims are in the majority?

Sisulu: We are trying to do both. To make sure that post-apartheid means a better quality of life for all our people and that includes, therefore, a closing of the economic gap between those that have and those that have little. The issue of the attitudes of some white people and I want to underline some is one that we are looking to address. Not all white people have fully comprehended that we will all sleep easy if this gap is closed, that it will bring job creation, therefore greater stability, and reduce crime. Ultimately, the responsibility falls on those that have. If the economic cake does not grow, we have to share whatever cake that there is. It is not about redistribution. It is about the fact that those of us who have jobs should do their jobs efficiently and effectively. It could be about trimming down the size of the public sector. That may well be the case. The racial composition of the public service is changing very fast. So in that situation, it will not be black versus white; it will be everyone. Attitudes take a long time to change. They are not changed by debates or even by sustained debates. As you well know, in this country President Clinton had to institute a commission on race after how many years of the civil rights movement, after how many years after the abolition of slavery? We have had only five years. I would like to think that we will do it differently. And we will probably do it even more differently under President Mbeki. The issue will be on the table. It might be uncomfortable. It might be uneasy. It might create a situation where people feel that they are being singled out. But, together we shall find a solution or together we shall perish for failing to find a solution. It cannot be carried out by one group alone. The burden of reconciliation—politically, economically—with our history cannot be the function and the responsibility of black people alone. History has disadvantaged black people. All of us must come to the table and work for reconciliation.

MLS: Which brings me to the following question about the Truth and Reconciliation Commission (TRC). The TRC has been perceived by some in the world, according to various reports in the international press, as not having exactly brought justice. Some people have suffered and others have come forward, admitted guilt in some cases, then walked away in all impunity.

Sisulu: Again, it is that definition. It is that standard. How do you define justice? We have opted for justice that is compassionate in as far as the victims are concerned and also the perpetrators. Justice, nonetheless, that is based on compassion informed by truth and reparation. This is the formula and for us, it seems to be working. It has not been perfect. Nothing ever is. But other alternatives would have meant that we would not be having this interview. The very fact that we started to negotiate a peaceful settlement meant that we were seeking a solution. We would have been negotiating in bad faith if all along when we were negotiating with the apartheid regime we were intending to indict them, to throw them into the sea, or into prison. Having arrived at a peaceful settlement we almost immediately defined a process of achieving justice for the wrongs of the past through a different mechanism that would not begin in the courts. A very important difference also is that prior to the TRC, there were a number of court cases that failed. The information, the institutional memory and records of what happened were in the hands of the previous regime, through the security forces, through the courts, through the police. In fact a moratorium had to be put into place to stop them from shredding evidentiary information. Going the TRC route meant that much of the truth has come out which otherwise would not have come out.

Let me take a case in point—Steve Biko. Almost three inquests and court cases did not reveal a fraction of the truth that was later revealed as to exactly what happened through the Truth and Reconciliation Commission. Yet even that was not the complete story. The generals and the police who came to ask for amnesty were not granted amnesty because the TRC decided that the generals had not met the condition of full disclosure. If they were to be indicted, the evidence gathered is much more substantial now than it had been prior to the Truth Commission process. So, yes, it is an imperfect process but in the same way as President Mandela comes out of prison after twenty-seven years and says "it is important this country finds peace, more important than how I feel." For the good of my country we have to go on this path to forgive so that we can move forward as soon as possible. It is easier for people who sit outside to say we should have done this way or that way. We would have been on the front page of your newspapers today had we done it otherwise. We would have still been fighting.

MLS: Do you see South Africa as a trailblazer for the world as far as reconciliation of a nation in concerned. How do you look at the events unfolding in Kosovo in relation to the Truth and Reconciliation Commission?

Sisulu: It is very difficult to prescribe to others because we were not prescribed to. The concept of a Truth and Reconciliation Commission is a model that was tried out by South Africans in South Africa and so far has worked. In Kosovo the context is different. Ours will be to say whatever solution the people of Kosovo find, it has to be a solution from the people of Kosovo themselves supported by the international community. We would be happy to share our experience. But they would have to take from that what best works for them. That's the essence of what we see as our success in this process. We took from the world. We did not just dream this up because we are super brilliant. We took pieces from a lot of experiences and worked a model that we thought would best serve our society and came out with that unique recipe. We will share it. We will respect the people of Kosovo when they choose whatever is in the TRC process that works for them.

MLS: In 1985 I used to demonstrate in front of this embassy. Today I am happy to see a black person heading it and a woman at that. As you know there are so few women in the diplomatic corps that the *Washington Post* describes the diplomatic corps as a men's club. Do you agree with this assessment?

Sisulu: Simple arithmetic. There are approximately 180 ambassadors here. Typically there are eleven women ambassadors. May I hasten to say that five of them are from Africa. I find that generally there is very little interaction between ambassadors. We tend to meet at the regional level. In our case we meet through SADC. I chair the SADC Forum because South Africa is president of SADC. Within SADC there are two other women out of fourteen. I have not found being disadvantaged in that group and in the African group in general for being a woman. There is an effort among women ambassadors to network more closely. It is usually the general public that assumes that I am the ambassador's wife and makes that kind of "faux pas" over and over again. I certainly have not yet experienced any condescension or a different treatment among my colleagues.

MLS: What was the reaction of your countrymen at the news of your appointment as ambassador to Washington?

Sisulu: Previously, as consul general to New York there was no difference in the level of congratulations either by men or women. None made reference to my gender. I am not unique. The ambassadors to Germany, Italy, Austria, Switzerland, EU Brussels, France and Malaysia are women. Several South African women were appointed ambassadors after 1994. Under apartheid there were hardly any women in such posts.

MLS: Do you find that your duties as ambassador conflict with other roles in your private life?

Sisulu: There are many challenges but because of the support system one gets as an ambassador; the household demands are less. Pressures as mother continue. We have two grown-up children and a 13-year-old. Our youngest goes to Edmund Brook School in D.C. She loves the idea of being here, but misses her friends. She has adjusted well. My husband is not around long enough to do the social functions.

MLS: Can you tell us about the inroads that women in your country and in your region have made in various fields?

Sisulu: In the political arena we have made major strides, sixteen to eighteen ambassadors and in the last Parliament 25 percent of the members were women. The Speaker of the House is a woman; [so is] the deputy head of the equivalent of the Senate. There are several women ministers: housing, health, welfare. Five women are deputy ministers. In the last five years major strides were made. The first governor/premier in one of our provinces, the Free state, is a woman. On the education front, three presidents of universities out of approximately twenty-two are women. Each one was a first appointment.

MLS: Who is the woman who most inspired you?

Sisulu: There are two women, my mother and my mother-in-law.

MLS: Could you talk about the role and the saga of the Sisulu family in the struggle against apartheid?

Sisulu: The role of the Sisulu family in the struggle against apartheid started a long time ago. My father-in-law, Walter Sisulu, became very conscious early on of the injustices of the apartheid system. He was in the African National Congress even before the apartheid government came into being. He was already a member of a political organization as early as 1943 when he met his wife, my mother-in-law Albertina. At their wedding in 1944, one of the speakers is supposed to have told my mother-in-law that, having married Walter Sisulu she had married a man who was married to the struggle for freedom and she would have to share him with that struggle. That was very true. She joined him in the struggle. And the rest is history. He went to prison having instilled in his children the need to fight for democracy and justice. Subsequently all became involved in the struggle at different levels and to varying degrees. He recruited President Mandela into the African National Congress. In his book, *The Long Walk to Freedom*, President Nelson Mandela says he was a willing recruit against the advice of the law firm to which he was retained. They both ended up in prison. The rest is history.

MLS: What is the biggest diplomatic challenge in representing South Africa in the United States?

Sisulu: The issues change from day to day. It is difficult to [single out] a specific issue. It is a question of getting and keeping the attention of policy makers, to influence them in favor of one's own country's national interest. This is a particular challenge in the United States because the country is very big. Although the power base is the capital, Washington, D.C., the states are important and as diplomacy increasingly has to do with issues of trade and as many of the states are independently developing trade relations with other countries, covering the entire country is a daunting task. There is not only one sphere of influence in D.C. or in the states. There are layers and a variety of networks that determine and inform policy. To know and to connect to all of them is quite a challenge. Being a medium size country we face a new challenge we did not have before. We had President Mandela and had become used to his name almost magically giving us access when normally other countries of our size would not have access. It will be a challenge to maintain that access once we become an ordinary middle-size country or a small country, if you look at our economy.

MLS: Of all the roles an ambassador fulfills, that of a negotiator, a mediator, a promoter, which role do you fulfill the most and which one do you enjoy the most and why?

Sisulu: They all come together on any issue that we deal with. I do not think you can separate them. Personally I prefer to engage people in closer contact, therefore small gatherings work for me better than big public platforms.

MLS: Could you summarize Winnie Mandela's place on the South African political landscape?

Sisulu: Winnie is held in high esteem by the masses of our people and holds a place in their hearts. She is in the present government. Democracy is served, she has a role to play. She is a member of Parliament. Proportional representation on the basis of party rather than individual is part of our system. She was popularly elected for the next five years.

MLS: What are the accomplishments you are the most proud of in your career?

Sisulu: My career has been very brief to be able to talk about achievements at a point when one is still learning. I would like to fulfill the mandate that I have been given, which is to contribute to strengthening economic, political and social relations between South Africa and the United States.

MLS: What do you wish for your compatriots?

Sisulu: A better life. The major challenge we face is unemployment. We need to address the issue especially among the youth and women. Jobs and more jobs.

MLS: Thank you Ambassador Sisulu.

AMBASSADOR
CORINNE AVERILLE McKNIGHT
OF TRINIDAD AND TOBAGO

In the dark room of a strip joint, the only glowing spot is the cage-like structure where a statuesque woman is contorting her naked body in an unconvincing routine, her face expressionless. It is very hard in such a place to find anyone in charge amidst the crowd of overly excited middle-age men. Someone assuming that I am next in line for the afternoon performance kindly points me in the direction of the dressing room. "You can use Candy's make-up," he shouts in a hurry competing with the loud music. Finally the bartender helps me. Hunched over the invitation card sent by the embassy of Trinidad and Tobago with his flash light we discover the mix-up in address. On the way to the ambassadorial reception in the semi-dark taxi, the elaborate calligraphy of the embassy had been misread.

A few minutes later and six blocks away I attend the farewell reception for Ambassador McKnight; in the dignified gathering of State Department officials, Organization of American States (OAS) representatives and Trinidadian notables, praises for the departing ambassador abound. U.S. Ambassador Babbitt thinks the world of her colleague. Other officials punctuate their speech with superlatives when referring to the Trinidadian ambassador. There is nothing of a conformist routine in their farewell speech. Ambassador McKnight is indeed one of most respected ambassadors in Washington. It has as much to do with being the voice of wisdom of the OAS as with her commanding presence. She is known for measuring her words; true diplomat in the traditional sense. In public appearances her speech combines a deep voice, slow rhythm, slightly longer than usual pauses followed by incisive punch lines that delight her audience. In a crowd of students she is a natural motivational speaker. They all flock to the former graduate of the University College of the West Indies (now University of the West Indies) and of the London School of Economics for advice. She exhorts them to maintain a good balance in life. "I had accomplished a lot in my career, but I was an emotional dwarf. So at age 54, I got reckless and got married," she tells students at Howard University. You can pretty much imagine her in her student days, perfect posture, diligent student, avid sportswoman, always eager to discuss issues and generally too busy to notice the men in the library.

At the other farewell party, the one hosted by the Caribbean community and held at the Islander restaurant, the mood is more relaxed, the praises also point to her wisdom and her foresight. At the Islander she is not only the diplomat from Trinidad and Tobago but also a Caribbean central figure, the matriarch. Those who came to bid her farewell come from virtually all the Caribbean states. Over curried chicken, cod fish fritters and a guava accented rum punch the animated crowd already evokes her legacy. It includes working diligently to allow her country to contribute personnel to the multinational force bringing stability to Haiti. In addition to her active involvement in the Association of Caribbean States, part of her legacy is also her contribution to the signing of two bilateral treaties between the United States and Trinidad and Tobago, the Intellectual Property Rights Agreement and the Bilateral Investment Treaty. On the surface her country seems easy to represent in Washington. It has always enjoyed good relations with the host country. Thanks to oil reserves and natural gas Trinidad and Tobago, the most industrialized country of the anglophone Caribbean, does not depend on the benevolence of the northern giant to survive. Trinidad is even one of the oldest oil producing countries in the world. Its first well was drilled in 1867, only eight years after the first American well. Not involved in any international dispute, the Republic of Trinidad and Tobago tends to promote the cohesion of its region by playing a leading role in the Caribbean Community and Common Market (CARICOM). Its parliamentary democracy modeled after that of the United Kingdom is stable. Its external image is shaped in the mold of carnival. During the several day parade of floats, extraordinary costumes, glitter, steel band, calypso music and dancing until dropping, Trinidad and Tobago becomes paradise island.

Ambassador McKnight's delicate task is to remind the United States that even in a post cold war context where much remains undefined, the Republic of Trinidad and Tobago has an important role in the Caribbean region. The other aspect of her task is to keep the American business community engaged and interested in investing in her nation to help decrease the 16 percent unemployment rate. Already fifty of America's largest corporations have commercial interests in Trinidad and Tobago, a beneficiary of the Caribbean Basin Initiative. Although the Caribbean nation trades with France, Colombia, the United Kingdom, Brazil, Germany and CARICOM nations, 50 percent of its exports, mostly oil, gas, steel and petroleum products are sent to the United States. By diversifying and emphasizing other sectors such as tourism the Trinidadian government is attempting to render the country less dependent on oil in order to avoid the rollercoaster effect of the falling oil prices of the early 1980s.

Of the two islands the more developed is Trinidad. Tobago has had a slightly more tumultuous history. Between the Spanish, the Dutch, the French and the British the island changed hands a record twenty-two times. Today attracted by its natural beauty many German tourists have settled there buying the island house by house, "a dangerous phenomenon" warns Prime Minister Basdeo Panday in a press interview at the National Press Club in Washington.

Another task on the plate of the ambassador: the celebration of ethnic harmony. The population of 1.28 million includes:

African descent	40 percent
East Indian descent	42 percent

Mixed heritage	15 percent
Chinese	1 percent
European	2 percent

After the abolition of slavery in 1833, the Europeans brought East Indians to the island as indentured labor. Later East Indians from the business community migrated to the Caribbean island. In the recent past politics were very predictable. It was organized along ethnic lines, with Trinidadians of all persuasions supporting the People's National Movement (PNM) and the East Indians supporting the United National Congress (UNC). In 1986 politics became less predictable when the National Alliance for Reconstruction ended the rule of the PNM and broke the ethnic barrier.

Far less predictable was the 1990 attempted coup by the Muslim group, Jamaat al Muslimeen. Holding the Prime Minister and members of Parliament hostage, the action of the group triggered five days of riots in the capital Port of Spain, their grievance, land claims. The Republic of Trinidad and Tobago has since recovered from this odd episode. When Ambassador McKnight meets with prospective investors the emphasis is on other matters. The ambassador's pitch contains the natural resources of the island, its high literacy rate of 97 percent, its decent per capita income of $4,300, the ingenuity of a people capable of performing an entire opera on one single instrument, the steel band.

I met the ambassador in the Fall of 1996.

MLS: Ambassador McKnight, can the diplomatic corps in Washington be described as a "men's club"? What has been your experience here so far?

Ambassador McKnight: That's a difficult one. It is predominantly a men's club. When I came here in 1992, there were three of us. Two of us presented credentials on the same day. By and large over the course of my career I have been accustomed to the fact that women were in the minority. It has not in any way affected the fashion in which I have operated. What has been most important for me is winning the respect of my colleagues.

MLS: What would you say to those who stereotype women in the Caribbean as rather submissive. What are your views on the status of women in your country in particular and in the Caribbean in general?

McKnight: Oh! I don't think that any one can really view Caribbean women as submissive. To my mind, throughout the Caribbean, one would find that we have a very matriarchal society. The woman is the strong figure who keeps the household together, the one who assumes the responsibility for the home, the children. I would think that in the majority of the homes, it's what the mother says that goes. Women in the Caribbean tend to be expected to be strong and to take the lead in some respects.

MLS: Can you tell about the inroads that women have made in various fields in your country? How have these accomplishments inspired you?

McKnight: There have been, through the years, many strong female figures in the society, in Trinidad and Tobago. This may have been encouraged by equal access to educational opportunity and the legal requirement to educate all children (we have compulsory education from age six to age fourteen). Indeed, I would say that although my generation is probably the first generation that saw women graduating from university in numbers, entering into professional fields and accepting equal responsibility with men has always been there. I cannot think of a time in my life when I was not aware of outstanding women in Trinidad and in the Caribbean. Most of them were involved in volunteer social work and the arts but there were also professionals, enough to demonstrate that there was a role for women in national life and . . . possibilities . . . outside of volunteer work. We were propelled and encouraged to seek higher education and go out and become productive citizens and leaders.

MLS: Could you mention some of the pioneer women in your country?

McKnight: There was Audrey Jeffers who founded the Coterie of Social Workers, working mainly with underprivileged children; Dr. Stella Abidh a medical doctor, great humanitarian and social worker; in the arts and dance Beryl McBurnie and Sybil Atteck; in politics Dr. Adah Date Camps, also a medical doctor; and Mrs. Marguerite Wyke. They have inspired me in every way because these were Trinidadian and Caribbean women of every ethnic representation whose approach said "The world is open, go for it." That was their message, so my generation of women did not have any inhibitions or second thoughts about undertaking a profession and pursuing our dreams to the furthest limits.

MLS: In Trinidad and Tobago right now there is a lot of talk about unifying all the ethnic groups. I believe "unification" is the term used often by Prime Minister Basdeo Panday.

McKnight: It is indeed the right term. This is a concept that has been enunciated not only by Prime Minister Panday but as far back as our first Prime Minister Dr. Eric Williams and often repeated through the years. I think it is an appropriate concept because the growing segmentation is an unnatural and highly unnecessary phenomenon. It is something that is being engineered. It replicates the days of slavery where those in power contrived to divide in order to rule. They literally set the slaves against each other; the house slaves against the field slaves; the lighter colored ones against the darker colored ones. It is something that our culture has chosen not to recognize and deal with, perhaps because it first has to be dealt with internally and by each one of us. This is a matter that requires a concerted effort to make our people realize the power that we give others over us when we allow them to divide us. There is a program that goes on in this country. It is called the sisterhood program. It brings Japanese women and American women across the spectrum together. The whole idea behind it is to bring the women of the East and the West together and through them truly heal the subconscious hurt and mistrust from World War II. The basis of this program is a strong belief that women can be the catalyst to bring real healing between these two societies. Each time I have participated in it I could only keep thinking, my God, if only something like this could happen in Trinidad and Tobago. As a people we need to realize that we are one. We do hurt each other, that is inevitable, but we ought to be able to talk it out, to live through it, to grow through it and emerge a stronger family for the experience.

MLS: Do you think that women are better equipped to be mediators?

McKnight: It is second nature to us. There are few women, I dare say, whose daily existence does not require this skill.

MLS: Have women of African descent achieved more in Trinidadian society than women of Indian descent, the Indian society being somewhat more traditional?

McKnight: No. Success among women in Trinidad is not based on ethnicity. Among the outstanding female contributors of Indian descent to our country I can immediately think of Mrs. Ruth Seukeran and her daughters Diane Seukeran and Rhadica Saith, Anna Mahase, Dorinda Sampath and Sahedan. There is also a significant number of women of Indian descent who have attained the highest levels in their chosen careers—law, medicine, civil service, and so forth.

MLS: In the Caribbean in general, among the leaders for example, we can cite Prime Minister Eugenia Charles. Do you think that her becoming Prime Minister held a lot of promise for women in politics in the Caribbean in general?

McKnight: I think that Dame Eugenia did a fantastic job. She did prove that a woman at the helm in the Caribbean could do an exceptional job. To what extent she inspired others to follow her example. . . . However, I think there is something in most women that says we don't want to expose our families, in particular, to the depths of the political campaigns. Equivalent and superior psychic reward can be gained from service in other areas. Material reward definitely is not to be sought there.

MLS: Do your duties as an ambassador conflict with your role as a wife?

McKnight: Yes. Perhaps this is all mental with me. Early in my career I decided that the foreign service was not the type of career that mixed well with marriage and childrearing. It's a most demanding job. It has me for twenty-four hours a day. Since I got married very late in my career, in fact just before coming to Washington, I guess perhaps I have not been able to change my orientation and thought processes of a lifetime. I keep saying to myself—it's only for a few more years. It's difficult. It's very difficult on the family. Fortunately, or perhaps, unfortunately, I do not have children, as I am sure I would have incorporated the quality time needed to give them at least what I got from my mother. Given the fact that one's time is not one's own. I don't know whether every service runs like mine, but very often I just have to pack up and go at a moment's notice even though everyone has known that the particular meeting would be happening for months. I think that governments are not perhaps the most caring, thoughtful institutions in the world. I've got to admit that I have the greatest admiration for my colleagues who do the juggling trick successfully. It can be the source of great tensions! [Laughter.]

MLS: What is the biggest hurdle you had to overcome as a woman in your career?

McKnight: My own character. I have this quaint habit of describing things as I see them. Add to that the fact that for most of my political career I have been operating in a multilateral situation where when you speak, you are conscious of the fact that whatever you say has to be interpreted into various languages, albeit by professionals who are competent but usually not native speakers of English. So I developed the habit of trying to deliver my message as clearly as possible. For a very long time that meant being as precise and clear as possible. Because of that, many of my superiors have had doubts as to my capacity for being tactful and diplomatic.

MLS: You are in a way reinventing diplomacy and creating a diplomacy that does not have to be tactful.

McKnight: Well, yes and no. I have discovered over the years that you can be direct without being assertive, because assertive is not acceptable in females. That is always seen and interpreted as adversarial. Add to that the fact that my voice is in fact two registers deeper than I think it is. I have learned to be careful with the manner in which I deliver my messages. I tend to work with humor rather than coloring or diluting the message. And it works for me. Very often I find out that it takes awhile for the message to sink in. It is the difference between giving a hundred percent clarity to whatever I'm saying and doing enough to achieve the immediate goal. Whereas the latter suffices most of the time, there is usually something else that has to be done at a later stage to achieve what could have been achieved by delivering an absolutely unambiguous message. This way I have to commit to longer hours on one project but the end justifies the waste.

MLS: How important is the role of women in the economies of the Caribbean. How would you describe that role in Trinidad and Tobago?

McKnight: We Caribbean women are working side by side with our men in forging the development of our region. Women are completely integrated into the economic fabric of the countries, but yet their full potential remains unleashed. Caribbean societies still lack the social infrastructure that would allow every woman who needs or wishes to make the full contribution that she can. I am fully aware that what I am trying to describe is the perfect society, utopia, that does not exist. Even though women are to be found involved at all levels in the economies of the Caribbean, they are still expected to shoulder the major responsibility for the home and the children and be the volunteer army to monitor and bridge the gaps in social services. The regional cultural baggage seems to demand that we maintain our traditional roles even when we successfully execute a substantial share of those tasks traditionally assigned to men and the colonial masters in the pre-independence era.

MLS: How do you see the role of men in that? There is still a lot of stigma about male chauvinism among men in the Caribbean. Is it diminishing?

McKnight: Male chauvinism is alive and thriving in the Caribbean. That won't change because the women encourage it and promote it. Many mothers still do not expect their male children and men to perform household chores or to be self-sufficient as their daughters are self-sufficient. And until men are totally humanized and society understands that they have equal responsibilities within the home, within the family for child supervision and education, for supervising children's leisure time, we will not have a totally functional society. It takes two people to produce that child, but society continues to ignore that it takes two people to rear a functional human being. In the Caribbean it has been demonstrated that one parent (sometimes this is a male parent) brings up a perfectly functional human being, but when that child, product of a one parent family, becomes an adult, at some stage that person looks inward and understands that there are areas within its soul, areas of need, areas where he or she now has to go and find the supplements needed to become a whole human being. Now, when I was growing up as a child there were grandparents around who filled some of these role model needs. There were always uncles, aunts nearby, so that even though there might have been a mother or a father who was in charge of the home, there was the presence and the involvement of all of the complementary role models that a child needs. That extended family has broken up with the resulting effect on the whole society.

MLS: You grew up in a family environment that fostered intellectual growth. To what do you attribute that?

McKnight: My parents both believed strongly in education. My mother believed that every member of the household had a job. Hers was to be there for us, to nurture us, and ours was to absorb our education. She always told us education was our work and that we had to do it properly. She did not understand failure or excuses. She would chastise us if the work was not properly done. It was that simple.

MLS: What do you wish for women, not only in your country, but in the entire Caribbean region?

McKnight: What I wish for women everywhere—reverence. A willingness to celebrate of the intrinsic value of each sister. The opportunity to live a full life, to be able, each one of us, to realize our full potential be it as a professional, a homemaker, an artist, in voluntary service. I believe that each of us is here to make a unique contribution. We are also in duty bound to support and assist each other en route to fulfilling our own dreams. And most of all, I wish that we individually and collectively, enjoy the journey.

MLS: Do you see the economic independence of the woman as a way to accomplish what you just described? Independence from the income of the spouse?

McKnight: It should not be necessary. I think if two people pledge to each other and their decision is to have a family together, the major decision should then be the division of labor and rewards. Whichever one is the primary breadwinner is not important. If the woman opts to assume the major responsibility for the day to day care of the children, this must not prevent her from having the time, opportunity and resources to pursue whatever constitutes a full life for her while she devotes the time to her home and her children. I am sure there are men who wish society allowed them to stay home, look after the children and work from home, but society says that the man must go out to work. This will probably change as jobs outside of the home get scarcer. However, that said, I am a pragmatic person and in today's world I would definitely encourage every woman to develop a viable independent revenue stream since good men tend to die young, often before they have made their fortunes! We also have to start letting people know that it is possible and acceptable to earn money legitimately without leaving home.

MLS: When you were appointed ambassador of Trinidad and Tobago to the United States, what was the reaction of your countrymen and women to your appointment?

McKnight: It was amazing. There were people who said Corinne who? Most people who knew me thought that the recognition was long in coming and I thanked them. I think nothing happens before it's time. The timing was perfect, I was ready for it. For a long time I was capable and I would have done the job, but inside of me there would have been a little rebellion because I always understood that an ambassadorial appointment meant giving up some of my precious freedom. Now I think it's a good thing that I had this in the back of my mind because I still did not realize the extent to which being an ambassador was a twenty-four hour job. As I said, the time was right. Now I can do it, enjoy it and look forward to retirement.

MLS: Which role would you like your country to play in its region in the future?

McKnight: I see Trinidad and Tobago working closely, first with the rest of the Caribbean and within Latin America to propel the region into the twenty-first century. In the Caribbean region we have the intellectual resources and Trinidad certainly has material resources that can be harnessed to this end. This would require a degree of commitment which must be preceded by a massive area-wide education campaign which would allow every citizen to embrace the dream. Without a shared vision, an agreed strategy and a realistic division and acceptance of responsibility within the region, our best hope would be a tidal wave. I would like to see my country take the lead in revitalizing the Caribbean.

MLS: What is or was the biggest diplomatic challenge in representing Trinidad and Tobago in the United States?

McKnight: Dividing my time and energy equitably between the bilateral matters and the Organization of American States. On the bilateral side, attracting and holding the interest of Congress in a country that was not a problem (and therefore off their radar screen) but had a serious ambition of joining NAFTA was the greatest challenge. I got lucky and the NAFTA dream got derailed by an election and change of government. On the OAS side, the ever reforming mountain of words and shifting political realignments provided a constant and awesome but totally enjoyable challenge.

MLS: Of all the roles an ambassador fulfills, that of a negotiator, a mediator, a promoter, which role do you fulfill the most and which one do you enjoy the most and why?

McKnight: In the role of ambassador to the United States, while there was ample opportunity for negotiation particularly with respect to Agreements, I spent most of my time and energy in promoting Trinidad and Tobago, always with a view to attracting some favorable outcome. I particularly enjoyed this aspect of the job since it gave me access to a wide cross section of people, agencies, non-governmental organizations, and so forth. It allowed me to hone my public speaking talents and kept me totally abreast of what was going on at home. I like to think that my mediation skills were at work in my OAS existence [says she, tongue firmly in cheek].

MLS: Do you believe that women's approach to diplomacy is different from that of men?

McKnight: Not really. The job that must be done requires of all its practitioners regardless of sex the same personal qualities of integrity, intelligence, persuasiveness, tact, assertiveness, humor, resilience, self-confidence for success. While female diplomats may have the added advantage of being able to distract some of their colleagues, I doubt very much that the effect is lasting. I should add, however, that my experience, particularly in multilateral forums, has been that female diplomats generally arrive at meetings better prepared than their male colleagues.

MLS: What are the accomplishments you are the most proud of in your career and what do you want your legacy to be after you have left this post?

McKnight: I have helped to make the Diplomatic Service a traditional career choice for females in my country. Throughout my career I have always earned and maintained the respect of all of my colleagues. I would be completely satisfied if I have raised the bar for the quality of representation that is expected of Trinidad and Tobago.

MLS: You landed one of the most prestigious posts in diplomacy. What's next careerwise?

McKnight: My next career will be in motivational speaking and personal coaching, aimed mainly at young girls and women. I feel a need to help in creating my successors and encouraging women to push the ceiling ever higher!

MLS: I thank you for this interview, Ambassador McKnight.

AMBASSADOR EDITH SSEMPALA
OF UGANDA

He was a ruthless and whimsical ruler. Some of his eccentricities included having European expatriates carry him on their backs or suddenly expelling Asians from his country. According to him, the idea of the expulsion was revealed to him by God in a dream. Idi Amin Dada was Africa's worst nightmare, Europe's poster boy for cowardly justifying colonialism and neocolonialism.

Today, Uganda's image shines through the brilliant and highly educated woman with top notch diplomatic skills who serves as its envoy to the United States. Ambassador Edith Ssempala belongs among the crème de la crème on the world diplomatic stage. A couple of decades ago another woman was already making headlines in the American press representing Uganda. Elizabeth Bagaya Nyabongo, a true princess, gracious and graceful, was already beginning to change the image of her country. But the new and fresh face in Ugandan diplomacy today is not only mending the image of a country nearly destroyed by the Dictator Idi Amin, but she is also focusing on making a difference in matters of investment and trade.

While trouble culminated with Idi Amin, it did not start with him. In 1870, shortly after the opening of the Suez Canal, King Kabalega of Uganda constantly had to fight the British and the Egyptians who expected total submission of his Kingdom and the end of his rule. The King prevailed. The British and the Egyptians retreated, only to come back two decades later splitting Uganda in two. King Kabalega had converted to Christianity and King Mwanga to Islam. Mwanga killed many Christians while Kabalega executed Muslims. In the 1890s scramble for Africa, the Germans sent Carl Peters; the British, Frederick Dealtry Lugard; and the French, the Catholic White Fathers led by Père Lourdel. All were poised to collect the "Pearl of Africa." Taking advantage of the religious division, the British took over, sent the two kings to exile in the Seychelles and picked their own king. The Baganda oligarchy, with its façade of traditional government, was indirectly ruled by Britain. Inevitably riots broke out in 1945 and 1949 against the oligarchy, against the Europeans and the Asians who had a monopoly on the crop trade.

At independence on October 9, 1962, Uganda was different from other British colonies. It had a high percentage of Western-educated people. Most of them alumni from the local Makere University. It was endowed with one of the most modern hospitals, Mulago Hospital. Sir Frederick Mutessa, one of the founders of the nation, had many issues on his plate. Keeping the country unified, eliminating the kingdoms and nationalizing British assets were among the most daunting. Nine years later, on January 25, 1971, while Premier Milton Obote was attending the Commonwealth Prime Ministers' Conference in Singapore, he was ousted by Idi Amin. The reign of terror had begun. It lasted eight years and culminated in the dictator's folly to invade Tanzania. Both Ugandans in exile and Tanzanians stopped the plan.

Today somewhere in Saudi Arabia behind a wrought iron gate one may be able to catch a glimpse of an aged colossal figure. The military uniform of the former general has been traded for the long caftan of the exiled. He holds his prayer beads. One can't help wondering what Idi Amin thinks about his past rule. The ruthless dictator Idi Amin was replaced by a returning dictator, Milton Obote. After five years of liberation struggle President Yoweri Museveni seized power in

1986. His record, however is dramatically different. Wherever he travels in the world, President Museveni is generally praised for improving the lot of his country of 22 million inhabitants. Uganda previously ranked fourteenth in the world poverty index. Today, it ranks seventeenth among the poorest nations according to the United Nations Development Program (UNDP). This progress is due largely to charismatic leadership, to a strong program of investment in rehabilitating the country's infrastructure, providing incentives for production and export, and the return of exiled Indian Ugandan entrepreneurs. From 1990 to 1997, economic growth was a record 5 percent on the average and exports of coffee, gold, cotton, tea, corn and fish to Europe increased, particularly to Spain, France and Germany. Meanwhile President Museveni "went legit." He held elections in 1996 and won, hence strengthening his position on the world stage. After all, at the Organization of African Unity (OAU) summit in Algiers in July 1999, it was proclaimed that "any regime that mounted a coup d'etat will not be allowed to join the OAU, will be diplomatically isolated and will not be welcomed at the OAU summit." Quite an irony since more than half of the leaders present mounted coups to attain power.

President Yoweri Museveni, however, is eager to prove to the world that democracy, like a diamond in the rough, can emerge out of the murky waters of a struggle if the leader is the right one. To the several opposition groups who have mounted a guerrilla campaign killing at least a dozen people in bomb attacks, he has extended an olive branch. He has other equally pressing concerns. Deforestation, the draining of wetlands, overgrazing, soil erosion, the killing of cattle by hyenas and poaching are among his agricultural concerns. Improving the standard of living of Ugandans and providing for refugees from Sudan, Rwanda and Congo are among his social concerns. On the international scene the question of the role of his country in the Congo conflict inevitably surfaces. In addition, there is a need to boost tourism which has enormous economic potential. The National Museum in Kampala has an exquisite exhibit of rare musical instruments. The spectacle of the "imbalu" dancers at the mass initiation ceremony of the "Bagisu" boys is unforgettable. Listening to the stories of elderly Chwezi people, one always returns home with some pearls of wisdom. For some, the highlight of a visit to Uganda is mountain climbing, tracking the fabled Bwindi gorillas stopping only to enjoy the "mulamba" local beer. U.S. ambassador Nancy Powell did just that in March of 1999.

Meanwhile in Washington Nancy Powell's counterpart, Ugandan

Ambassador Edith Ssempala, is walking the corridors of power. At the World Bank she discusses investments, loans. With American environmental institutions she tackles the topic of the $12 million U.S. loan for the preservation of wildlife. Meeting with members of Congress she addresses the Africa trade bill, trade with Africa, health issues, the AIDS epidemic on her continent. She seems to be everywhere her country or her region are discussed. If one were to draw a list of the ten most active ambassadors in Washington, Ambassador Edith Ssempala would certainly be included. A fine strategist, she is always keen on drawing her cards at the right moment. When meeting with tourism investors, the Ugandan's relatively high literacy rate is skillfully plugged in as an asset. When meeting with women's groups, she emphasizes the need for improving the education of girls and points out Uganda's 50.2 percent literacy among women. Ambassador Ssempala earned her degree in Civil Engineering at the Lumumba University in Moscow in 1979. She began her diplomatic career as Ambassador to the Nordic countries of Europe. Today she is recognized in the world as a leader in the democratic development of Central African States. Her writings highlight the evolution of democracy in Uganda.

I met with her in the winter of 1996 in the Embassy of Uganda, an unpretentious brick home located on 16th Street in Northwest Washington. We also met in the spring of 1999. The following is a combination of these two interviews.

MLS: How do you perceive the condition of women in your country?

Ambassador Ssempala: The situation is not bad, but we still have a long way to go. For example, some traditions ought to change. Those aspects of culture that are repressive or that demand that women be less should be changed as provided for by Uganda's 1995 Constitution. We women should retain only the positive aspects of cultures and traditions. Sometimes we have to contend with the diminished expectations of women by women who are content with just a little, with being good housewives and embracing only the traditional careers such as nursing and teaching. When I was growing up I was not looking at these traditional roles. I was very gifted in mathematics and mostly considered technical fields. I always found myself competing with men. I was comfortable in the company of boys and even enjoyed fighting with them. I never really saw myself as a woman. In fact it used to annoy me tremendously when people looked at me first and foremost as a woman, as a girl. Now, I have matured. I have outgrown that. I think basically I wanted people to see me as a human being and see what I could achieve as a human being and not as a woman. Of course, I want my husband to see me as a woman! [Laughter.] But the rest of society should see me as a human being.

MLS: The *Washington Post* describes the diplomatic corps as a "men's club." What has been your experience as a woman ambassador here?

Ssempala: My experience in Washington is very short. I have just arrived here. I have been an ambassador to Nordic countries for the past ten years. So I have more experience in the Nordic countries as an ambassador. Yes, it is a profession dominated by men. There is no doubt about that. But many other professions are no different. In this profession, you deal with all the biases and the stereotypes women are confronted with. People see you first and foremost as a woman. What I have observed in the Nordic countries is that women have made a lot of progress in politics, although they do not have too many women in diplomacy either and also lack women in the corporate sector. But in politics and in the administration there are many women. In Washington I haven't had much experience yet. However, as a woman ambassador here as everywhere else people are very keen to find out whether you are the wife of the ambassador. That's the natural thing to be, I guess. On the phone, I am often asked rather impatiently "I want to speak to the ambassador, can you put him on, please." I then have to explain "The ambassador is not a he; the ambassador is a she and I am the one." I take it with humor normally. I take my job very seriously and people realize it. They realize that I am the ambassador and not the wife of the ambassador.

MLS: What has been the biggest hurdle you had to overcome as a woman in your career?

Ssempala: The biggest challenge as I see it is being a mother and being full time in my career. This is definitely a big challenge because I have a great passion for being a mother and being able to deliver as far as my kids are concerned. I also have a great commitment to my job. Yet I have only twenty-four hours in a day and I find that time is insufficient. Very often I feel it is my children that are sacrificed. I do not feel good about this. But I think, if we have to make any headway, we have to be able to balance our roles as mothers and even as wives with the roles of professionals. We have to advance in our professions and that requires hard work and a lot of time, which is taken from the time devoted to the kids. In order for us to succeed we have to make sure that our male colleagues also participate and play their roles as fathers and as husbands. They have to share in raising the family. My husband is very supportive. He is very close to the children which is not typical for an African man and I appreciate that very much. And so do the children.

MLS: You have three daughters. Is any of them following in your footsteps?

Ssempala: My first daughter, Patricia, and my third daughter, Felicia, have some of my traits of character. My middle daughter, Priscilla, is a quiet intellectual.

MLS: Is the Western stereotype of a rather submissive African woman merely a stereotype? What are your own views on the status of women in your country and on the continent at large?

Ssempala: It is true that largely African women are submissive. I think we have accepted the theory that we came from the man's rib. Somehow, we have been really submissive. That is a fact. We have also socialized our girl children to be submissive. In our culture we send our daughters to the kitchen and our sons to the sitting room. So they grow up knowing that the place of a woman is in the kitchen and the place of a man in the sitting room. This is where we have to begin changing our attitudes toward gender. But also women have not been too clear on this. Unless we encourage women to take up gainful paying jobs, we cannot move forward. I also think that we need to find a balance between advancing our careers and taking care of our families. This is not easy. It does not behoove us alone. It behooves our male partners as well. They have to learn to appreciate us, to share and to also play a supportive role, a partner's role so that we are able to manage. I think it's important we make men feel comfortable, not feel that we are replacing them. Our aim as women is not to replace men. Our aim is to have a role to play. And this I think must be explained sufficiently so that we do not have unnecessary antagonism between men and women, which definitely would not be healthy for society as a whole.

MLS: Recently Mrs. Ruth Sando Perry was appointed President of Liberia by all warring factions. What do you think of her appointment and of the promise that it holds for women in politics in Africa?

Ssempala: It is good, especially if she succeeds. Then it will go a [long] way in demonstrating that women have these abilities in mediation and conflict resolution. I think it is not the monopoly of women. But I also believe that our nature as women is that of mediation. We are mediating all the time. African women are mediators in their homes and in the communities. So men having realized that they haven't succeeded and recognizing that a woman can do well is positive. I think it is very positive that the different factions have confidence in her ability to reconcile them. When I met President Perry I told her how excited I was that she had been identified as the person who could lead her country towards peace. My worry with the whole process is the speed with which they want to move. Peace and reconciliation are processes that take a long time, a lot of patience and a lot of hard work. She mentioned that their aim is to have elections next year. To me it is rather too ambitious. I wish they could take as long as necessary to succeed. They should not push themselves. It is important that they establish a trend that would lead to sustainable peace.

MLS: Can you tell us about the inroads that women have made in various fields in your country?

Ssempala: Women have made a lot of progress in politics. As a matter of fact, we now have a woman vice-president, Dr. Specioza Kazibwe. She is a surgeon. I think Uganda is lucky to have leadership which has recognized the importance of women's participation. President Museveni believes that women's participation is not only good for politics and human rights but it is also good economics. Uganda has made economic progress recently and women have contributed to it. We have also made progress in the commercial sector. We have many women entrepreneurs now and we have women in all fields. When our vice-president was here recently, she emphasized the need to target the rural poor. And the rural poor are first and foremost the women. When we target the woman, we are targeting the family, we are targeting the community. Every cent a woman has goes to educating the children and improving health and nutrition. Targeting the woman, therefore, is the key to progress and to development.

MLS: What do you wish for women in your country and on the continent of Africa?

Ssempala: I would like to see women become full participants. Not only for my country, not only for Africa, but for all women all over the world. I want to see women become more aggressive, not in a negative sense, but aggressive as in terms of not being passive. Women should be active in everything—in politics, in economics, in all endeavors in life. I think the world would be a much better place if women fully participated.

MLS: Is being a professional woman with a good appearance a hurdle, an asset or none of the above for you?

Ssempala: That is a very difficult question. I have never thought about that. I have never seen myself as an attractive woman. As I mentioned earlier, compliments used to annoy me a lot. I thought people were looking down on me as a woman. I had that kind of complex. Now I take it easy. If someone compliments me, I take it positively, as goodwill, not bad will. But I never really think about that question. So I don't know how it has affected me.

MLS: You are the second woman ambassador of Uganda to Washington. Is it going to be a tradition in your country to send female envoys or are we far from that?

Ssempala: My country is open to women. Not only in terms of diplomacy but in all other fields as well. In fact, our constitution demands that women be given equal opportunity to participate. The constitution recognizes that women in the past have been disadvantaged and marginalized, and that there should be affirmative action as a corrective measure. Women are not appointed for the sake of it, but they are given possibilities also. On the other hand, I would hope that my appointment was not just part of a tradition but based on my record as ambassador to the Nordic countries that I was called upon to represent my country here. I believe I did a good job in Copenhagen. Since Uganda considers the United States a very important post in diplomacy, my government saw my appointment as fitting. So to answer your question, I believe there will be both female and male ambassadors to this country in the future.

MLS: Have you met your male counterparts here? How do they react to women ambassadors?

Ssempala: I have not met too many. When I came here, it was a very busy time. I have not had any problems with the ones that I met. I am used to being around male decision makers. In Copenhagen the majority of my colleagues were men and I think intelligent men would look at a professional woman for what she really is. If a woman has a complex, lacks self-esteem, they will probably act on that. I see male colleagues as colleagues and I expect them to do the same.

MLS: What is the most challenging aspect of your diplomatic career?

Ssempala: Of course, being a woman in any profession you have to work about three times more in order to achieve the same recognition as a man. I know that if I succeed, I will succeed as Edith, as myself. But if I fail, I would be failing because I am a woman. I am always conscious of this fact and I do not want to disgrace myself, but I especially do not want to disgrace my womenfolk. I would also like my success to be seen as the success of women. My success should demonstrate that women can do as well as men. We need role models of successful women so as to demonstrate that point and inspire young girls. Women who have the opportunity should try their best. As a woman, I am still a full-time mother, a full-time wife. My husband still expects me to serve him a cup of tea. [Laughter.] And by the way, I enjoy all those roles, except that I do not have enough time. I find that we sacrifice a lot in order to be able to do what we are doing. We don't want to give less to our kids either. We don't want to give less to our families. We find ourselves working almost twenty-four hours.

MLS: Thank you, Ambassador Ssempala.

EPILOGUE:
MRS. ALICE PICKERING
ON LIFE AT THE AMBASSADORIAL
RESIDENCE

The function of representation as part of a mission has two aspects. One of them is the work of the ambassador which includes establishing good bilateral relations through negotiation, promotion and mediation, all of which might sometimes lead to the signing of major agreements among nations. The other aspect is to represent one's country in the host country. The residence of the ambassador must reflect the art, culture, food and other traditions of the country in the best way possible, that is it must portray the country represented. The ambassador and the spouse of the ambassador are the president's personal representatives in the eyes of the people residing in the host nation. One of the best opportunities for portraying a country outside of the official duties is through functions at the ambassador's resi-

dence which provide a venue for people of the host country and the
ambassador's country to get to know each other, eat together, enjoy
culture and the arts of the nations together and to establish rapport.
This type of personal contact among people is a critical element of
diplomatic life.

Regardless of their marital status, a common theme existed among
these women ambassadors. Each wishes she had a "wife." In other
words, each needs the same level of support from a spouse or another
person as their male counterparts traditionally receive from female
spouses. In trying to understand this phenomenon I decided to pay
a visit to the woman whom many around the world refer to as one
of the most accomplished of diplomatic wives, Mrs. Alice Pickering.
Mrs. Pickering, who holds a Master's degree from the Fletcher School
of Law and Diplomacy and a Master's in Library Science, has accompanied her husband for the past forty years to ten posts including
Switzerland, Zanzibar, Tanzania, Jordan, Nigeria, El Salvador, Israel,
the United Nations in New York, India and Russia. In her quiet
Virginia home surrounded by her books she explains,

While the ambassador knows more about the political intricacies and economic issues and reports on them, the spouse is more in touch with the
educational and cultural spheres of the country. The spouse, therefore, is
able to understand the people a great deal more and is able to respond to
what they are saying in a way that is less confrontational. The spouse has
room to show concern and to foster relationships between the two countries. The wife is usually the one who learns the most about the local culture.
The ambassador usually goes from the residence to his office. He may [mas-
ter] a local language, but he is using it only in an official capacity whereas
the wife and the children are the ones who are interacting every day and in
every way with local people, transportation, local markets and local work-
men. The family and the spouse are the ones who have the real experience
of living in another country and learning its culture.

From that vantage point, a spouse can indeed add a lot to the ambassador's role in trying to understand the host country. So far some
diplomatic wives have made a dramatic difference in the life of the
residence. Their involvement usually includes supervision of the
household staff, setting the tone for the visit of an official or the hair-
raising experience of a presidential visit. Diplomatic wives sometimes
work in concert with the ambassador's secretary or with the person
in charge of protocol although they do not always have such a luxury.

The administrative aspect of representation entails keeping inventory of materials. Although the ambassador's wife is not in charge of procurement she is often closely involved in it.

The household staff which is not actually part of the embassy staff is the responsibility of the ambassador but the ambassador already has his or her hands full heading the embassy staff. Inevitably the spouse of the ambassador becomes a labor negotiator, making sure that the hiring of local household staff complies with the local laws. In many posts there is no embassy officer for that, so the duty falls on the spouse of the ambassador who takes on a role that is similar to that of a hotel manager. "I insisted that the residence staff get health exams every year and be checked for TB. When we got flu shots, I had to fight with our embassy to get the household staff flu shots," Mrs. Pickering continues. For all these duties that include supervision of staff, procurement, organization of events and public relations, the wife of an ambassador receives no salary.

According to Mrs. Pickering:

It is no longer obligatory for us spouses to perform these functions. But if a wife chooses to accompany her husband on these postings, she may have to perform these functions. Many senior wives still feel a responsibility to represent their country, to assist their husband in that role and to find personal satisfaction in doing what I have always considered as professional a job in that representational area as they possibly can, and that includes learning languages, running a smooth household and establishing contacts outside of the official contacts that their husband may have.

People who are more policy oriented would deny the importance of those unofficial contacts, but Mrs. Pickering who has lived forty years in many countries in the world knows that sometaimes, not absolutely always, a personal relationship with a head of state, a foreign minister, a head of a university often leads to a more successful outcome of negotiation.

However, all these activities performed by the wives often go unnoticed, unacknowledged and certainly unpaid. Governments simply do not pay diplomatic wives a salary. The ambassador is the one in the spotlight. The wife is the woman behind the man. The compensation for the wives is a rich and rewarding experience. In the case of Mrs. Pickering, a former USIS officer and a professional librarian, she was able to expand the world of art and culture in many ways. Among her many activities, she took her husband to excavating archeological sites in the Middle East and organized in Moscow an exhibit in conjunction with the Moscow Art Studio bringing together American and Russian artists.

Women ambassadors in many cases have to fulfill both roles of an ambassador and of the wife of an ambassador. Organizing an embassy dinner for a visiting official is one of these "wife" duties that the single women ambassadors have to undertake. While a woman ambassador has total control over the event, the wife's task is more delicate. She has to help as much as possible, organizing and strategizing, while not preempting the role of those in charge of social affairs. It is a delicate situation.

In the case of American diplomatic wives, it is difficult to make the State Department and the White House understand that they are the guests and not the host and appeal to them to refrain from doing things their way. The embassy is invariably caught in the middle trying to work with the people in the country, work with the president's people and explain what is feasible in the host country. For a diplomatic wife, it means a stressful process because women are traditionally viewed as hostesses and, in this case, the outcome of an official lunch is a reflection on the wife. Despite reams of papers, endless correspondence and scenarios, things change at the last minute.

When the White House insisted on using a rectangular table and consecutive interpretation for a lunch hosted in Moscow in honor of Mrs. Clinton, Mrs. Pickering cringed. The rationale was that the rectangular table would facilitate dialogue. With knowledge of the local customs Mrs. Pickering knew that this would not work. Mrs. Clinton wanted a dialogue American style. "Russians are not that far along in their political process to know what political dialogue means," Mrs. Pickering says. The women present were representatives of the Duma and of other political structures. Questions and answers style with three minutes talking time was the format requested by the White House. The Russians are not known for being succinct in speeches. Before even beginning to answer the questions, the Russian women spoke at length about their institutions and their program. One of the women in a "democratic" move took the microphone to criticize President Yeltsin. Meanwhile, requests from the White House to serve lunch within a certain time frame dictated speed and sent a frantic staff waltzing plates. From a logistical point of view, the lunch was a searing experience.

Invitations are also a delicate issue at an embassy. The guest list is important. The wife works in tandem with the protocol officer and the social secretary of the ambassador. Keeping track of the guest list is meticulous. One has to keep all the information on file—who was invited, who came, who did not show up after five invitations, and so forth. All the information is computerized and forms an important database. In the pre-computer days, the amount of work was night-marish particularly at large embassies. In concert with the ambassador, the spouse usually checks the list because the spouse is the one who knows more about the local people. Who is seated next to whom is a very delicate decision. She recalls the time when "Mayor Lushkov of Moscow in response to an invitation from the American embassy, inquired whether another person had also been invited. When he was told that the other person had been invited, his next request was to disinvite the person. The protocol person explained to him that this could not be done. So he did not come."

Representation has its glamour but in a cold war situation, it can simply mean the cold shoulder. Mrs. Pickering recalls those days of the cold war in Zanzibar when people would simply not come to the Consul's residence for political reasons or because their government would not allow them to accept an invitation. In these cases again the wife of the Consul had to find a way through non-governmental women's organizations to establish contact.

I was less of a target in a cold war context, although the contact established had to be fairly circumspect. No one would play with my son; the Revo-lutionary Council was in control of the country. The only way I could have any contact with any local people at all was through a woman's group in-herited from the British days, like the Women's Guild. They wanted me to teach these women how to knit. First of all, I did not know why they would knit in Africa, but I found out that the cool season to people there was cold and they liked to have wool booties and hats for their babies. And I could not knit. My mother sent me some basic knitting books. For about a year-and-a-half I would meet with these ladies and we would knit. In the country we had a difficult time, but it had to do with politics, not with us personally. It was a very good learning experience for me. Upon my departure at the airport, all the women from the knitting group came to say goodbye and gave me presents. It was the nicest thing that ever happened to me!

As Mrs. Pickering details her "wifely" duties, one is struck by the volume of work of the woman behind the man. One cannot help reflecting on the changing role of the spouses of diplomats as more women ambassadors enter the diplomatic scene. The term "wives of diplomats" which conjures up images of tea parties and delicate china, increasingly will be replaced by the term "spouses of diplomats."

Associations of wives of diplomats abound in Washington. The latest group is that of the Association of Wives of Arab Diplomats. It is interesting to note that even the groups that formed recently still bear the word "wives" as opposed to "spouses."

Male spouses of diplomats are redefining not only the terms but also the roles and the duties that go with the terms. While most of them are very supportive of their wives, their support does not, by any stretch of the imagination, compare to that of a Mrs. Pickering!

Many women ambassadors who are married rely more on their staff or on extra hired hands to organize the social life of the residence. What makes things easier is that social activities of embassies are becoming less and less formal; probably adapting to the social changes of the diplomatic corps and in anticipation of a time when "women will make up 50 percent of Embassy Row."

SELECTED BIBLIOGRAPHY

Bhutto, Benazir. *Daughter of Destiny: An Autobiography.* New York: Simon and Schuster, 1989.

Bingham, Clara. *Women on the Hill. Challenging the Culture of Congress.* New York: Random House, 1997.

Blackman, Ann. *Seasons of Her Life: A Biography of Madeleine Korbel Albright.* New York: A Lisa Dew Book/Scribner, 1998.

Blackman, Francis. *Dame Nita: Caribbean Woman, World Citizen.* Kingston, Jamaica: Randle, 1995.

Crapol, Edward P., ed. *Women and American Foreign Policy: Lobbyists, Critics, and Insiders.* Westport, CT: Greenwood Press, 1987.

Faludi, Susan. *Backlash.* New York: Anchor Books, 1992.

Felder, Deborah G. *The 100 Most Influential Women of All Time.* New York: Citadel Press Book, 1996.

Fisher, Helen E. *The First Sex: The Natural Talents of Women and How They Are Changing the World.* New York: Ballantine Books, 1999.

Friedan, Betty. *The Feminine Mystique.* New York: Dell, 1983.

Griffiths, Sian, ed. *Beyond the Glass Ceiling.* Manchester: Manchester University Press, 1996.

Joekes, Susan P. *Women in the World Economy.* INSTRAW (United Nations International Research and Training Institute for the Advancement of Women). Oxford: Oxford University Press, 1987.

Mernissi, Fatima. *The Forgotten Queens of Islam.* Minneapolis: University of Minnesota Press, 1997.

Miller Morin, Ann. *Her Excellency: An Oral History of American Women Ambassadors.* New York: Twayne Publishers, 1995.

Nyabongo, Elizabeth. *Elizabeth of Toro: The Odyssey of an African Princess.* New York: Simon & Schuster/Touchstone, 1989.

Sheed, Wilfred. *Clare Boothe Luce.* New York: E. P. Dutton, 1982.

Sheehy, Gail. *Hillary's Choice.* New York: Random House, 1999.

Walton, Hanes, Jr. *Black Women at the United Nations: The Politics, a The-oretical Model, and the Documents.* San Bernardino, CA: Regin-ald/Borgo Press, 1995.

Weiers, Margaret K. *Envoys Extraordinary: Women of the Canadian Foreign Service.* Toronto: Dundurn Press, 1995.

Williams, Leaford C. *Journey into Diplomacy: A Black Man's Shocking Dis-covery.* Washington, DC: NorthEast Publishing House, 1999.

Woods, Harriett. *Stepping Up to Power: The Political Journey of American Women.* Boulder, CO: Westview Press, 2000.

INDEX

About the Author

MARILYN SÉPHOCLE is Associate Professor of German at Howard University. Professor Séphocle has served with the United Nations and worked as a business consultant in the field of cross-cultural human resource management. She has published articles on cultural and social contributions of people of African descent in Europe, particularly in Germany. She is also author of *Die Rezeption der Négritude in Deutschland*, written in German, focused on the German critique of major African and Caribbean writers.